WHAT PRICE PERJURY

I would rather that India perished than that she won freedom at the sacrifice of truth.

MAHATMA GANDHI

Normally persons cannot be brought before a tribunal and questioned, save in Civil or Criminal Proceedings. There are, however, exceptional cases in which such procedure must be used to preserve the purity and integrity of our public life, without which a successful democracy is impossible. It is essential that on the very rare occasions when crises of public confidence occur evil if it exists shall be exposed so that it may be rooted out, or if it does not exist, the public will be satisfied that in reality there is no substance in the prevalent rumours and suspicions by which they have been disturbed.

JUSTICE SHAH quoting Lord Justice Salmon

What Price Perjury

Facts of the Shah Commission

JAGGA KAPUR

ARNOLD-HEINEMANN

Published by Gulab Vazirani for Arnold-Heinemann Publishers (India)
Private Limited, AB/9 Safdarjang Enclave, New Delhi 110016
and printed at Kay Kay Printers, 150 D Kamla Nagar, Delhi 110007.

*To Those Who Suffered
And Made This Possible*

Contents

NOTIFICATION

New Delhi, the 28th May 1977

S.O. 374(E).—Whereas there is a widespread demand from different sections of the public for an inquiry into several aspects of allegations of abuse of authority, excesses and malpractices committed and action taken or purported to be taken in the wake of the emergency proclaimed on the 25th June, 1975 under Article 352 of the Constitution;

And whereas the Central Government is of the opinion that it is necessary to appoint a Commission of Inquiry for the purpose of making inquiry into a definite matter of public importance, that is, excesses, malpractices and misdeeds during the emergency or in the days immediately preceding the said proclamation, by the political authorities, public servants, their friends and/or relatives and in particular allegations of gross misuse of powers of arrest or detention, maltreatment of and atrocities on detenus and other prisoners arrested under DISIR, compulsion and use of force in the implementation of the family planning programme and indiscriminate and high-handed demolition of houses, huts, shops, buildings, structures and destruction of property in the name of slum clearance or enforcement of town planning or land use schemes in the cities and towns resulting, *inter-alia*, in large number of people becoming homeless or having to move far away from the places of their vocation.

Now, therefore, in exercise of the powers conferred by Section 3 of the Commissions of Inquiry Act, 1952 (60 of 1952), the Central Government hereby appoints a Commission of Inquiry consisting of the following, namely,

Chairman—Shri J.C. Shah, Retired Chief Justice of the Supreme Court of India.

2. The terms of reference of the Commission shall be as follows :—

   (a) to inquire into the facts and circumstances relating to specific instances of—

   (i) subversion of lawful processes and well-established conventions, administrative procedures and practices, abuse of authority, misuse of powers, excesses and/or malpractices committed during the period when the Proclamation of Emergency made on 25th June, 1975 under Article 352 of the Constitution was in force or in days immediately preceding the said Proclamation,

   (ii) misuse of powers of arrests or issue of detention orders where such arrests or orders are alleged to have been made on considerations not germane to the purposes of the relevant Acts during the aforesaid period,

(iii) specific instances of maltreatment of and/or atrocities on persons arrested under DISIR or detained and their relatives and close associates during the aforesaid period,

(iv) specific instances of compulsion and use of force in the implementation of the family planning programme during the aforesaid period,

(v) indiscriminate, high-handed or un-authorised demolition of houses, huts, shops, buildings, structures and destruction of property in the name of slum clearance or enforcement of Town Planning or land use schemes, during the aforesaid period,

provided that the inquiry shall be in regard to acts of such abuse of authority, misuse of powers, excesses, malpractices etc. alleged to have been committed by public servants, and

provided further that the inquiry shall also cover the conduct of other individuals who may have directed, instigated or sided or abetted or otherwise associated themselves with the commission of such acts by public servants;

(b) to consider such other matters which, in the opinion of the Commission, have any relevance to the aforesaid allegations; and

(c) to recommend measures which may be adopted for preventing the recurrence of such abuse of authority, misuse of powers, excesses and malpractices.

2. The inquiry by the Commission shall be in regard to —

(i) complaints or allegations aforesaid that may be made before the Commission by any individual or association in such form and accompanied by such affidavits as may be prescribed by the Commission, and

(ii) such instances relatable to paragraph 2(a) (i) to (v) as may be brought to its notice by the Central Government or a State Government or an Union Territory for inquiry.

4. The Commission shall make interim reports to the Central Government on the conclusion of inquiry into any particular allegation or series of allegations and will be expected to complete its inquiry and submit its final report to the Central Government on or before 31st December, 1977.

5. The Central Government is of opinion that having regard to the nature of the inquiry to be made and other circumstances of the case, all the provisions of sub-section (2), sub-section (3), sub-section (4) and sub-section (5) of Section 5 of the Commissions of Inquiry Act, 1952 (60 of 1952), should be made applicable to the said Commission and the Central Government hereby directs under sub-section (1) of the said Section 5 that all the provisions aforesaid shall apply to the said Commission.

[No. II/16011/32/77-S&P (D.II)]
T.C.A. SRINIVASAVARADAN, Secy.

In Gratitude

One evening in late June, 1975 I found myself in a heated discussion on the need to do something. Then someone queried, "What are you willing to do." Well frankly, I did not like the idea of confessing to him that in fact my soul was being needlessly tortured. It was not unlike those days before India's independence when I was much younger, but then poignant memories fade out slowly but painfully.

I tried to look back to the days of Bhagat Singh and who did what he felt was right. I am told he was defended by a dear uncle who is no more, and this was arranged by my grandfather who although a poor sweet and provision seller's son became an eminent authority on law. Not surprisingly his father wanted him to help him in the business, but this young man was determined to study even if it meant being beaten up and having his arm broken. This still did not stop him from spending his nights studying under one of Lahore's few street lamps, that were not put off in those cold winter nights.

When Singapore fell to the Japanese in 1942, my father chose to be taken prisoner of war, and not a single Indian jawan under his care did anything other than follow him. It is difficult to imagine the suffering man is willing to undergo for his beliefs, except there aren't too many of us who would care to live for four years with one pair of trousers, four shaving blades, seven ounces of milk, three ounces of sugar and nine thousand ounces of rice served with wild foliage grown with their own faeces.

My mother's suffering was of a somewhat different kind like so many women in her predicament. She not only had to do without her man and financial security, but was also caught between love, want and need. She survived it because of her compelling desire to believe in her own truth, which was that there is something infinitely beautiful in suffering.

And now those who resolutely stood up for what they believed in and suffered during the dark days of our recent history. Many of them have had an opportunity to describe their beliefs and their sordid tales of woe. Countless others have not been so lucky, but their faith and suffering is no less, and in their hearts lie a great tale of fortitude.

I said to myself how pleased Gandhiji would have been today to be told of the Indian's discovery of the truth of their government of the past. There must be something terribly beautiful about India for which so many have given their lives. . . and surely this MOTHER INDIA deserves something better. . . .

I look back at all those feats of human endurance, and now at the dedication of the Investigating officers of the Shah Commission of Inquiry in their efforts to unravel the truth. It only proves that though Mahatma Gandhi died 30 years back this day, the Indian continues to believe in "Truth is God."

I am especially grateful to J. C. Chawla and others at the Press Information Bureau for their assistance.

My thanks to my numerous friends in the "gallery", who unfortunately for reasons of space must go unnamed for patiently watching with me the unfolding of a true human tragedy, and then having to face up to their own trials and tribulations.

Last, but not the least my special thanks to my publishers for their kindness and understanding.

Finally, many many thanks to my brother for his love and patience and for many, many things without which this book would not have been possible.

New Delhi   JAGGA KAPUR
January 30, 1978.

Introduction

In exercise of the powers conferred by Section 3 of the Commissions of Inquiry Act, 1952 the Government of India appointed the Shah Commission on May 28, 1977 to inquire into:

> Subversion of lawful processes and well-established conventions, administrative procedures and practices, abuse of authority, misuse of powers, excesses and/or malpractices committed during the period when the Proclamation of Emergency made on June 25, 1975, under Article 352 of the Constitution was in force or (and these are important words) in days immediately preceding the said Proclamation.

When a public inquiry is instituted by government and headed by a distinguished judge, to look into any accident or incident of great public importance, it brings out the facts of the tragedy. The people have the right to know what truly transpired in an accident and the results of the various Commissions appointed in the past are an adequate testimonial to its efficaciousness. This is different, as for the first time anywhere in the world a series of public Commissions under law have been appointed to inquire into the workings of people in power, and to bring out in the open in the public interest, the true facts that have remained buried in the debris of secrecy and self-serving standards for so long.

There is a crisis of public confidence in government today and though the procedure out of necessity has to be Inquisitorial, it is the only way known to man in which true facts can be brought out in the open. The deliberations of such a Commission may make or break, and even vindicate the reputation of many a person, but the evils, if any of a society must be exposed so that we learn something from it.

The Shah Commission of Inquiry is however, only limited to inquire into the misuse of authority, excesses and malpractices committed during a limited period, and is not directed at any individuals. The trouble is that the true facts being revealed by this Commission are so unbelievable, that they make even Indira Gandhi feel a little remorseful. She does not consider herself responsible for all of them as because of their enormity, a number of other persons have to be involved.

What this Commission is faced with is having to bring out right in the open, the double standard, the immorality and the hypocrisy that may have existed in our country for so many years. The revelations in the honourable Commission's findings point out that there is something terribly wanting in all our institutions, and to name a few, the Civil service, the Police service and even the Press. The business community one can understand, as one witness put it succinctly:

> We only know how to make money
> and are willing to salute whoever
> is in power . . .

When the emergency was imposed were these institutions or their members willing to fight for what they believed to be right. Could the emergency have been imposed if they had functioned properly and would people have been appointed to high office in public corporations for reasons of personal gain. Would people have been deprived of their lifetime's savings, their jobs, their property, have their houses raided, even be put behind bars for months endlessly, have their women raped and even be shot to death. In fact did any rule of law prevail. . .?

Some members of the Press and Indira Gandhi's Cabinet have testified that they were shamed in agony but could not help anyone. The sonorous line "I wish I had spoken" is common with all of them, but none of them resigned in disgust or wrote anything about it. Instead they continued to chug along huffing and puffing, but none refused to print their newspaper for a change.

Why did the Press and the Public servant fail? Was it dereliction of duty or the new-found art in the politics of promotion or even survival. Was it a plain but well planned consipiracy, or is it a national malady? Are we a nation of people with no sense of purpose or shame?

The Shah Commission has been sitting since September 29, 1977 and has received over 50,000 complaints. To put it in the words of Justice Shah:

> A number of persons have been examined, a number of transactions have also been looked into. In those cases where I, prima facie, thought that even though there might be grounds for suspicion but no case prima facie of the commission of an excess was made out, I have ruled out the presentation of such cases before the Commission. Where, however, there appeared to be prima facie evidence of the commission of an excess, the cases were presented before the Commission with a view to ascertain whether there had been commission of an excess and, obviously, the commission of an excess necessitates inquiry into the involvement of some person or persons into the commission of acts or transactions, which may amount to excesses.

> For that purpose, an open inquiry, which under the terms of section 8 I was entitled to make, has been made. It may be that at this stage some persons may feel that they have something to say or without representation on their part, their reputation may be affected. I have, therefore, given them ample opportunity to come before me and explain their conduct, which may prima facie amount to an excess, but for which there is ample explanation forthcoming.

> Some persons have come; many have come; some have kept themselves out of the Commission; some have come on some occasions and declined to come on other occasions. (referring to the non-appearance of former Ministers V.C. Shukla and Pranab Mukherjee). But that again, as I said, is a matter of no concern to me. If once I come to a conclusion that there is a prima facie evidence in regard to the commission of an excess examined through in the light of the refusal without adequate reason to appear before the Commission and explain their conduct, the second part of the inquiry will be held and according to Rule 5 and Section 8B, and the fullest opportunity will be given to all concerned to explain their conduct.

Meanwhile, the Commission is startled by the shocking revelations of (to borrow Justice Shah's phrase): "Man's inhumanity to man", during the earlier regime. One witness Piare Lal said :

I pleaded to the Officers not to demolish my own house built with the life-savings of three generations. He coldly pointed out the bizarre Notice on the bulldozer as it mercilessly crushed everything that came its way. 'I am blind from my eyes, deaf from my ears and I am also dumb'—I hope God will let this Officer's wish come true.

"These chaps were drunk with lust for power", said witness Yadav.

"May be you can give Jagmohan a hut in Turkman Gate and then give him to me... I will then ask him what this was all about," mourned another witness.

Another said, "Rukhsana Sultana visited us accompanied by Navin Chawla and we offered her water. She spitted it out and this is the water we have been drinking for months."

One did not read of these activities as the news media was censored but this did not prevent a handful of journalists to continue thinking, though what they thought was also censored. One of them related what were obviously good and funny pieces of caricature but the censors had no sense of humour. One cartoon mentioned by him showed Indira Gandhi and Sanjay in conversation. In one corner stood Swaran Singh pointing out: "Here is a national debate on the Constitution amendments."

In his reply to a reader's question "who is Indira", he said:

She is Motilal Nehru's grand-daughter, Jawaharlal Nehru's daughter and Sanjay's mother.

Another witness described her regime more directly:

Born in lies, nurtured in lies and flourished by lies.

We did not know if one would be hanging upside down

in Connaught Circus for even publishing lines from the
Gita.

"The word Gandhi should be taken away from Sanjay and
let him die with Nehru's name", said another witness in tears.

"Your Honour, I want you to enquire into what has happened to us in India since the Bangladesh War", pleaded former
Cabinet Minister Raj Bahadur.

Her own Cabinet Minister T.A. Pai belatedly confessed:

Power in this country had been used to create tears
in the people's eyes instead of wiping them. The Secretary to the Government of India was in Moscow on an
official visit and his wife was being detained in Delhi.
If that is Indira Gandhi's concept of honesty, then I
am glad I am dishonest!

A corruption of a whole system was being unfolded which
reminded one of the dark days of feudalism. The Justice
conceded in a tone of anguish :

There was no safety of person. People were whisked
away to Jail, they were forced to suffer indignities and
their properties searched.

In fact, tyranny was glorified in the name of liberty.

Justice Shah was shocked at the sordid events narrated to
him in some detail under oath by witnesses. Senior I.C.S.,
I.A.S. and I.P.S. Officers were responsible for carrying out so
many of these heinous acts. Were they being ambitious, over-
zealous, too smart or too dumb? Were they covert acts and
were these public servants put into play as a result of
the brutalization of public life? Some of these questions will
have to be answered one day by the Commission whether some
individuals choose to assist it or not.

For the present, the honourable Judge was unable to res-
train himself from commenting:

All this should have happened in a civilised nation!

Soon after, another senior Public Servant's testimony intri-
gued the former Supreme Court Chief Justice :

Question by Justice Shah	:	What offence did he commit?
Answer	:	None to my knowledge.
Question	:	Under what authority of Law did you ban his music records, tapes and even his films?
Answer	:	The Secretary's Order.
Question	:	This was a high-handed action when a Rule of Law prevails.
Answer	:	Since the Government gave publicity. . .they expected obedience.
Question	:	I thought there was no slavery in the country.
Answer	:	Sir. . .there was Government pressure.
Question	:	Who is Government?. . .Government is not just someone.
Answer	:	It was in the PUBLIC INTEREST.
Justice Shah	:	Even in the Emergency there was no slavery in the country. . .there is no constitutional law which says if I don't want to see a Government Officer, a crime is committed. . .this is what has damaged the fabric of Society. . .

A whole new morality play was now being enacted except it formed no part of the theatre of the Absurd, it was a real life drama. There were days when everyone in the Commission's hall, even the stern Chief Justice known for his scrupulous regard for decorum, had tear filled eyes listening to the woeful tales of human suffering and degradation.

"Thank God. . . Someone is willing to listen today. . . in those days they were Gods and we were dogs", lamented yet another witness.

Indira Gandhi was summoned on December 20, 1977 to appear on January 9, 1978 to answer the following 11 points on which the Commission has sought her version:

1. Reversion of Justice R. N. Aggarwal, High Court, Delhi.

2. Reappointment of Justice U.R. Lalit, an Additional Judge of the Bombay High Court.

3. Institution of CBI cases against R. Krishnaswamy, Deputy Secretary, Heavy Industry, A.S. Rajan, Development Officer, DGTD, L.R. Cavle, Chief Marketing Manager, STC and P. S. Bhatnagar, Deputy Chief Marketing Manager STC.

4. Appointment of T.R. Tuli as Chairman and Managing Director of Punjab National Bank.

5. Appointment of K.R. Puri as Governor, Reserve Bank of India.

6. Deviation from the established procedure and irregularities in the reconstitution of Air India and Indian Airlines Corporations.

7. Detention of inspectors of Textile Committee/inspectors of Customs under MISA in June 1976.

8. Detention of B. Sen Sachar and seven others under MISA.

9. Requisitioning of the Vishwa Yuvak Kendra, Chanakya Puri, New Delhi.

10. Alleged improprieties committed in regard to Mangal Bihari, IAS of the Rajasthan cadre, and termination of the services of Mrs Chandrawati Sharma, an assistant teacher.

11. (A) Events between June 12-22 1975.
   (B) Events between June 23-25 1975 and
   (C) MISA detentions and other arrests on the night of June 25-26, 1975 and thereafter.

Earlier Indira Gandhi had refused to respond to the various invitations extended to her to come and assist the Commission of Inquiry and which made Justice Shah point out :

Let an impression not be created that by refusing to remain present before the Commission they would be entitled to avoid an inquiry into their involvement. It is open to a person to say that he will not come before the Commission at the stage of determining whether an excess has been committed. It is his privilege to do so. But it will be open to the Commission, once it is established on the evidence led before the Commission and in the light of the refusal of persons concerned to remain present and drawing such inference as is permissible from that fact that there is prima facie evidence of the commission of an excess and his involvement in it, it will be open to the Commission to call upon him by a proper summons or appropriate procedure to remain present and to examine him.

His Lordship was justly perturbed with the considerable expenditure that necessarily has to be incurred by the State for her security every time Indira Gandhi is expected to turn

up for a hearing. Having noticed this frequent non-appearance
he quipped:

> In our poor country all avoidable expense should be
> saved so that the benefit of that money may be avai-
> lable to the uprivileged members of our community.

In the meantime the legal wranglings are going on at
Indira Gandhi's residence with her lawyers burning the mid-
night oil, and each justifying his existence. But presumably she
realises that she had no choice but to come as refusal to make
an appearance on a summons under law would make her liable
for arrest and then be brought to the Commission of Inquiry,
a wholly unsavoury thought, to say the least.

Is Indira Gandhi frightened of telling the truth or of the
more painful task of having to face herself. The Shah Commission quite unknowingly is doing just that and she is resolutely
resisting it all the same, even though when she is there making
her forced appearance, she is cold, tense, and fidgety and her
face shows pain and anguish.

Once she was dressed up in a yellow and white Sanghaneri
print saree with a contrasting short-sleeved pullover and
freshly coiffed up. This may make a grand Ballroom entry
resulting in a stunning effect on spectators. After all, it is
Patiala House and coincidentally the Grand Ballroom too,
where under the chandeliers so many indescribable things
may have happened many years back, but this honourable
Commission is limited to inquiring into her conduct in
regard to 11 cases of possible misuse of authority.

What one notices is her discomfiture at not finding the
razzle and dazzle, the glittering gowns, the not-so-covered
breasts, the Hapsburg Princess looks, the beauty, charm,
elegance and especially the attention she received when she
entered one of those International Film Festivals. Instead,
besides the 20 odd A.P. Sharmas and the likes of him, there
are only plain, common Indians amazed at her continuing
propensity for receiving attention.

She appeared accompanied by her family and her retinue of 20
"Admirers". Her leading Counsel, Frank Anthony, argued for
three long hours and Justice Shah heard him patiently expound-
ing his theories of the possible meaning of an "excess". The

Commission Counsel, Khandalawala climaxed his detailed reply to the points raised by expressing surprise over Anthony's poser on what was the definition of an "excess".

Defining an "excess" Khandalawala said, "If innocent persons are prosecuted for personal reasons, it is an excess. If you suppress an entire nation by irregularities and malpractices, it is an excess."

Pran Nath Lekhi, Government Counsel, rebutting Frank Anthony's arguments said one thousand five hundred pages of typed material on the 11 cases on which she had been asked to file a statement had been sent to her. What more natural justice and opportunity did she want, he asked. Indira Gandhi looked visibly agitated, when Lekhi spoke of the "missing files" and asked her counsel to counter his insinuation. "There was no natural justice given in 19 months of the emergency," Lekhi observed.

Frank Anthony continues to plead with the words, "With great respect". Justice Shah finds them annoying and quips "Cut that out".

On the issue of Anthony's repeated stress on his client's "reputation" being affected, Justice J.C. Shah observed, "I regard the reputation of any person as of equal significance, be he poor or rich, be he occupying a humble or a high position. That is immaterial to me." He also added that a humble person may tell the truth while a person in a high position may not do so, depending on the circumstances.

275 minutes have gone by when Justice Shah dictated an order indicating that she is under an obligation to give her version of the facts under oath.

Frank Anthony then asks for an adjournment to consider the matter and Justice Shah reluctantly agrees adding, "Asking for an adjournment has become a second fundamental right. No wonder we are in the kind of mess in terms of justice."

Indira Gandhi appeared the next day and this time also accompanied by Sanjay carrying a good few heavy law books. She was dressed in a pink silk saree and a red pullover, frequently resting her hand on her chin, when she is not playing with her black rimmed glasses. Thereafter, arguments pursued ending with the exchange of supposedly witty remarks against one another.

After this yet undecided one hour battle of legal vituperation was over, Indira Gandhi chose to make a "submission". Justice Shah did not welcome the idea but as the Commission's learned Counsel aptly put it,

It is difficult to put in a word to an angry lady!

That was that and this took another 30 minutes of invective which only showed her contempt for the "honourable" Judges and utter disdain for everything else.

She unwittingly was also telling us that in this land there have always been two classes of citizens—the extraordinary and the ordinary, the privileged and the unprivileged, the special and the not-so-special, the VIP and the commoner. And now to infuse the word morality into a whole gamut of continuing inequitable human relationships, simply because she is no longer in power is an "excess" in itself—only this time it most definitely is being inflicted on her. Justice Shah was again disturbed by the fact that she deliberately forced the poor Indian tax-payer to incur considerable expense in getting a large number of witnesses from all parts of the country, and even one from the United States. All this could have been avoided if she was not willing to assist the Commission, except on her conditions. Obviously, he felt he had heard enough for the day and asked her if she was willing to be examined under oath and this invitation she quite happily declined. But she did not let it rest there and ended up in not only not taking the stand, but also adding that anything she uttered in that not too comfortable a witness chair will be in violation of her oath of secrecy, which she took when she was Prime Minister some years back.

A legal opinion was sought by the Commission from the Law Ministry and which was concurred by Law Minister Shanti Bhushan. This opinion does not help her and she is bound to say that he was not of much help to her, when he was a simple lawyer either! In fact he was a major cause for her political ruination, though all he did was to bring out in court the perfidious nature of her character as a politician.

Justice Shah ordered that in his view, prima facie, an offence under section 179 of the Indian Penal Code has been committed and directed that the case be forwarded to a Magistrate.

Eight days later, she is summoned to appear again. Her retinue is smaller and she is a little more subdued. Sanjay is with her but more nervous, biting his lips and when not, he is at his finger-nails. This time the "submissions" took only 30 minutes of mundane matters which irritated Justice Shah a little, and then he enquired again if Indira Gandhi had filed a statement as required of her. The explanation in the form of another "submission" took another 40 minutes explaining the word "bias" and a lot more, followed by the usual brief replies by the other Counsels.

As Justice Shah began dictating the Order, Indira Gandhi got up from her seat with a sheet of paper and moved up to the nearest microphone and started to read from the paper :

Excuse me Sir . . .

Justice Shah : Sit down, I am busy dictating an order.
(She moves away but returns again. . .)
Indira Gandhi : Excuse me Sir.
Justice Shah : (coldly) Sit down.

Frank Anthony reluctantly rose again but it was too late; he is admonished sternly:

You are not accustomed to Courts in which judgements are delivered in the Court itself. The proper thing to do is to rise after the judgement is delivered and have your say.

All this did not have much effect on Frank Anthony or on Indira Gandhi, for that matter. Justice Shah in his ruling mentioned the impropriety of the unfortunate suggestion of "bias" in the Commission, and Frank Anthony continued to insist that there are facets of bias and to explain what he meant by something being "beautifully vague". Here Justice Shah was neither vague nor biased, when he said, "there are no facets of bias."

Thereafter the harangue followed and this time it was not against the "Judges" but the Commission. It was in stages of dramatic movement, with Justice Shah repeatedly asking her if she was willing to come to the witness chair, to say why she did not want to say anything under oath. She walked up and down between her chair and Anthony's desk in stage fright, followed by a microphone repeating the stagy line, "I am not legally and constitutionally bound to make a statement before you."

As a result, this time for refusing to answer any questions she was charged with having committed two offences under the Indian Penal Code, instead of the previous one. The added charge was for refusing to take an ordinary oath to say, "I swear, I will speak the truth, and nothing but the truth.

Government's counsel Lekhi in an outburst of presumably juridical humour stood up and remarked, "She has been taunting the law. She has been flouting the law . . . If the Law cannot reach her then the law would be having something like two standards." For once, he was right—the double standard, and we may have had this in us for a long, long time.

For the first time in history a former Prime Minister will appear in a Magistrate's Court on a complaint lodged by a former Supreme Court Chief Justice. She is charged with having committed two offences under section 179 and one under section 178 of the Indian Penal Code for refusing to answer questions and taking an oath.

But why the double standard. Is it that we are so concerned with ourselves and our own selfish ends that the profound question of what is moral and immoral, ethical and proper, honest and dishonest has for us now become a needless, time-consuming and painful exercise in self-examination? Have we convinced ourselves that everything we do has to be fair, because we are no longer capable of doing any wrong. . .?

Is loyalty so important as former Cabinet Minister Subramaniam described when asked why he did not resign, when his advice against the appointment of K.R. Puri as Governor of the Reserve Bank was flouted by Indira Gandhi :

I could have done so. . .but my personal loyalty
to Indira Gandhi stood in the way. . .

In the way of principle and self-respect one may venture to ask—may be we are unable to face the truth about ourselves.

For the first time this Public Commission will have to tell what is wrong with people in public life and public servants who willingly carried out orders of even "a small fry" like R.K. Dhawan, as he prefers to describe himself these days. Not a terribly immodest act since he was only her Private Secretary in the first place. Small fry or not, even the President of India was more than willing to meet with this odd looking "small fry" at odd hours of the night. He unfortunately is dead, and some say happily, but there are many others who are helping the Commission in establishing whether the rumorous whispers that were heard are false. If there is nothing in them, then there should be nothing to answer for anyone.

Police Chief Bhinder, civil servants Krishan Chand, Navin Chawla, Jagmohan, N.K. Singh, P.N. Behl, CBI Chief D. Sen and Income Tax head S.R. Mehta may be just a few, who by their invidious actions have already reached the gates of perdition. The question is how did the whole system of a Government of laws fall apart—why did we make a mess of our system. Only the Shah Commission can tell, and it is for once no *Tamasha* or an Indian spectacle for one's entertainment, loud, ritualistic and mixed with a certain kind of depravity. The impelling question is whether "Where we have come at last" is what matters, and how we do it no longer disturbs us, though we do know how to give this pervasive society of ours, some respectability.

Are we willing to face the truth or will we continue to allow cynicism to pervert the very purposes for which the honourable Shah Commission was appointed. "Patronage" may indeed be laudable but a time has come for the common Indian to demand that equity and justice be meted out. But then he also knows the carving of the Indian in power— even those sitting today in the highest Courts of the land.

In fact as the book is going to the press one foreign dignitary has attempted to express an opinion on the domestic affairs of India. He has even gone so far as to tell us that "Ingratitude is fatal : it killed Julius Caesar." They do not realize that this very minute India may be seething with pain and guilt while they rejoice over the regalia of authority.

Most of the things that occurred during the emergency have taken place on a miniature scale ever since 1947. The emergency only made it that much easier. Doomsday is not far off unless the Indian is interested in knowing why we have made a mockery of our institutions.

This is no time to be euphoric but a time to take a shot of truth serum to enable us to spit it all out.

This book attempts, in the first place, to lay bare the facts and present the salient points brought out by the Shah Commission of Inquiry in a readable form. The whole narrative falls into a visible pattern. Each chapter is introduced in a few lines followed by actual case studies and affidavits; the rear-end is brought up by extracts from the cross-examination made during the Commission's sittings.

What we do learn from the tragic events and some not so tragic, but high-handed and capricious in the pages that follow, and what they will teach us . . . only time will tell. One thing is certain. The law governing the Commission of Inquiries Act, 1952 only provides for persons to be prosecuted for perjury and a good few public servants and others not so distinguished as to belong to that elite class, already belong to this undistinguished category.

For the present, one must seek some solace in Justice Shah's words of judicial eloquence:

This is a tall order . . . .
Unless officers and the people of India
develop a strong civic sense, things like
this, possibly worse, may happen !

1 Not Killing the Goose ...
That Lays the Golden Eggs

For the first time in India's 5000 years of history Indira Gandhi was astounded by the unbecoming honesty of an honourable Judge in her home state's High Court. Here was the Prime Minister of India, and Nehru's daughter being told politely but firmly by a State High Court Justice that she was not above the law of the land. Indira was furious at the sheer audacity of the Judge when someone advised her to be more sanguine about the whole episode.

Indira appealed to the Supreme Court hoping that the Superior Judge would understand the Indira concept of Democracy . . . which means paying lip service to it. Supreme Court Judge Iyer did not see merit in that argument. Well all was over for poor Indira, as if the whole rug of the Nehru Dynasty had been pulled from right under her feet, when Indira Gandhi's son Sanjay whom Cambridge (her father's Alma Mater) would not touch with a barge pole and Doon School had chucked out earlier gets worried at his bleak future and persuades his mother to forget the "whole damned business of Democracy."

Thereafter MISA is effectively used which generally came to be known as MAINTENANCE OF INDIRA SANJAY AGENCY.

The wonder that is Indira still continues to sanctify these monstrously cruel actions of hers, by saying "I was compelled to take these distasteful steps in the interests of India". But soon after by proclamation she ordered that no court can entertain petitions of arrest and with all

51407

her opposition behind bars she managed to get a law passed by her rubber-stamp Parliament which has no parallel in civilized jurisprudence, and which puts her and all her cronies above the law for any crime they may have committed, while in office, for the rest of their lives.

There are some Indians who believe a reckoning still has to be made by the "Court of the Almighty", but Indira felt "legislation to cover this could wait for another occasion." The events that follow here point out to the standard of morality of public servants.

I—EVENTS BETWEEN JUNE 12-25, 1975

In the election petition filed by Raj Narain, against Indira Gandhi, the Allahabad High Court pronounced its judgement on June 12, 1975. The relevant portion of the order of Justice J.M.L. Sinha of Allahabad High Court is reproduced below:

In view of my findings . . . this petition is allowed and the election of Smt. Indira Nehru Gandhi respondent No. 1, to the Lok Sabha is declared void.

The Court further ruled :

The respondent No. 1 accordingly stands disqualified for a period of six years from the date of this order, as provided in section 8A of the Representation of the People Act.

As regards the operation of the above order, the Court ruled:

. . . The operation of the said order is accordingly stayed for a period of twenty days. On the expiry of the said period of 20 days or as soon as an appeal is filed in the Supreme Court, whichever takes place earlier, this order shall cease to carry effect.

Dated 12-6-75   Sd/- J.M.L.S.

The above said judgement and the Order of the Allahabad High Court unseating Indira Gandhi, the then Prime Minister, from the Lok Sabha led to the manifestation of varying political reactions mostly through demonstrations, rallies and public meetings. New Delhi was the main venue of such activities in which most of the States, particularly those adjoining Delhi, participated. The post-judgement scene in Delhi and some of the adjoining States is described in the following paragraphs.

Bhawanimal, the then Inspector General of Police, Delhi,

has stated :

> ... There is no denying the fact that there had been
> a spurt of activity in the wake of the announcement
> of Justice Sinha's verdict. Several demonstrations,
> rallies and public meetings were organised between
> June 12 and 25. Most of these were in favour of the
> former Prime Minister while a few were directed
> against her. All this did generate tension but no unto-
> ward incident occurred during this period. We had full
> grip over the situation.

Krishan Chand, the then Lt. Governor, Delhi, has mentioned in his statement to the Commission that soon after the
pronouncement of the Allahabad High Court judgement against
Indira Gandhi on June 12, 1975, he had been called to the
Prime Minister's house but he sent Navin Chawla, his secretary, instead. He has further stated :

> ... I learnt from Navin Chawla that in order to
> cope with the law and order situation that might
> develop from the threatened opposition rallies, it had
> been decided to organise rallies in support of the
> Prime Minister and for this purpose people had to
> be collected from various places. I was also told that
> public utility services would also be mobilised for the
> purpose. These services included NDMC, DTC and
> DESU.

The records of Delhi Transport Corporation (hereinafter
referred to as DTC) show that *1761* DTC buses were requisitioned by the AICC/DPCC for organising the pro-PM rallies
from June 12 to 25, 1975. The relevant portion from the statement of J.R. Anand who had been working as Traffic Manager
in DTC since April 1974 till he was placed under suspension
in September 1977 is reproduced below :

> ... These buses were mostly booked under my orders
> as Traffic Manager as I was the competent autho-
> rity to do so. I did this in pursuance of the deci-
> sion taken by the Chairman, DTC, who was also the
> Lt. Governor, namely Krishan Chand, in a meet-
> ing held at Raj Niwas, that full cooperation should be

given by DTC by arranging buses to carry people who were taking part in rallies to be organised to express solidarity to the then Prime Minister.

As per DTC Rules for special hire by private parties, an application in prescribed proforma accompanied by advance payment is required. However, this formality was not observed in the case of the bookings mentioned above made by AICC. The buses were booked on the basis of telephonic instructions of Navin Chawla, the then Secretary to the Lt. Governor.

In the case of heavy number of buses booked on June 12 and 25, the buses had to be withdrawn from the scheduled operations, thus affecting the normal services. The number of buses booked during the period June 12 to 25, 1975, on special hire, was much above the normal booking allowed for private parties which is, as per instructions, 5 buses per Depot. The total thus comes about 95 buses a day which was far exceeded in the present case. This heavy booking adversely affected the normal operations of the DTC and caused much inconvenience to the commuters.

An amount of about Rs. 4 lakhs on account of special hire charges of the buses is still outstanding against the AICC and DPCC for the last about two years.

The two major rallies organised at New Delhi in favour of Indira Gandhi took place on June 12 and 20, 1975. Government organisations like Delhi Transport Corporation, New Delhi Municipal Committee, Delhi Electric Supply Undertaking participated in these rallies.

S.P. Goel, Asstt. Engineer I(P-2), NDMC stated that :

... On June, 12, 1975 at about 12 noon when the Allahabad High Court decision in the election petition against the former Prime Minister, Mrs. Indira Gandhi was announced, I was asked by A.P. Gupta, Assistant Engineer that the Chief Engineer V.P. Chetal had ordered that the entire labour force of the Civil Engineering Deptt. of NDMC should go to the Prime Minister's house, to express their support to her. Consequently at about 2 P.M., the entire labour force was sent to the P.M.'s house in Municipal Vehicles.

Vehicle No. DLL 1690 which was under the charge of Shri A.P. Gupta, A.E. was used in taking the labourers to P.M. house. . . .

At the P.M. house I saw that a large number of NDMC workers were present. . . . I saw that the Municipal officers including P.N. Behl, V.P. Chetal and B.R. Verma and all the Municipal Engineers were present there. V.P. Chetal on the instructions of Arjun Das, MMC, was guiding about 30 workers to finish the working of stage raising and barricading quickly. He was also inciting the other NDMC workers who were a part of the rally to raise slogans in support of the P.M. . . . . The entire labour force was kept there throughout the day. In the evening they were served milk, bread and other eatables which are meant for the poor people under 'Nutrition Scheme' of the NDMC. The entire labour force was being sent to Prime Minister's house, daily from from June 12, 1975 to June 25 1975 during working hours and the entire Municipal work (except some emergent work) was suspended.

Devi Singh, painter, NDMC has further added:

Asstt. Engineer B.R. Sharma told the employees that they will have to join the procession in ease they are interested in their service as these were orders of P.N. Behl. Out of fear, the employees joined the procession and were taken to P.M.'s house in Government truck. At the P.M.'s house, almost all the NDMC employees were present under the leadership of P.N. Behl and Arjun Das.

After June 12 also, the employees were taken to P.M.'s house almost daily for which telephone calls used to be received from Head Office every morning and according to these orders employees were sent in the trucks. The persons who used to ring from Head Office were Baldev Sharma, Member, Mahesh Gupta and Shri P.N. Behl. Sometimes, the orders were received that the attendance will also be taken at the town hall.

A note dated November 11, 1977 from Y.K. Malhotra, Municipal Engineer (E) regarding participation of NDMC in the rallies held at P.M.'s house between June 12 and 25, 1975 also throws some light on the subject. The relevant portion of this note is reproduced below:

> ... As per log book of the truck of School Lane Enquiry, it has been stated that the truck had gone to Prime Minister's house for carrying labour on 12.6.75, 18.6.75 and 19.6.75 and on 20.6.75 the truck had gone to Boat Club.

It is also borne out from the records of DTC that Government employees were pressed into service for organising these rallies. A number of buses deputed in connection with these rallies were required to report to the Government servants including some senior officers. An extract from the statement of Jaswant Singh, Depot Manager, DTC, giving the names/designations of such officials, number of buses which were deputed to report to them and the relevant dates, is reproduced below :

Name of the Officer and designation	Date of report	No. of buses reported
S.H.O., Police Stn. Faridabad	12.6.75	26
Meenaxi Dutta, S.D.M.	12.6.75	2
S.P. New Delhi Parliament	12.6.75	2
Street Police Station	16.6.75	2
K.D. Nayyar	26.6.75	4
S.H.O., Police Station Gurgaon	12.6.75	99
S.H.O., Police Station, Rai	12.6.75	95
Bakshi Singh Gill,		
Dy. S.P. Enforcement	12.6.75	16
Director of Transport	12.6.75	34
B.L. Anand, S.D.M.	12.6.75	1
Sareen, Sadar Bazar		
Police Station	12.6.75	1
Sareen, Dy. Director,		
Delhi Administration, Delhi	17.6.75	2
Hayalan, PA to Chief		
Secy., U.P.	19.6.75	60
PA to Chief Minister, Bihar	20.6.75	40

Participation in the rallies was not confined to Delhi alone but to quote Krishan Chand, the then Lt. Governor, Delhi:

...some neighbouring States like Haryana, Rajasthan, Western U.P. also sent contingents for the purpose. All these arrangements were made under instructions from the P.M.'s house conveyed through
Dhawan and the P.M. was kept informed about the
developments from time to time.

It is seen from the records of DTC that a number of buses
were deputed to make trips outside the Union Territory of
Delhi. According to law, buses going outside the Union Territory of Delhi are required to be issued a special permit from
the State Transport Authority for this purpose. It is also provided in Rule 9 of the terms and conditions for hiring of DTC
buses that in case the buses are to be utilised outside the
Union Territory of Delhi beyond the scheduled routes "special
permits for such purposes shall have to be obtained from State
Motor Transport Controller, Delhi, by the party requiring the
buses at his cost." The Secretary, State Transport Authority,
Delhi, has informed this Commission vide his letter No. 12783/
STC/77 dated November 28, 1977 that :

> ...as per records maintained in this office no
> contract carriage permits were issued to the D.T.C.
> for carrying contract parties outside the Union Terri-
> tory of Delhi or to any private parties for use of the
> D.T.C. vehicles outside the Union Territory of Delhi
> during the period from June 12, 1975 to June 25,
> 1975.

J.R. Anand the then Traffic Manager has made the following statement in this regard:

> A number of buses booked by AICC through the
> Secretary to L.G. during this period were sent outside
> the territory of Delhi. Under the Motor Vehicles Act,
> a route permit has to be obtained for sending vehicles
> outside Union Territory of Delhi which was not done
> in this case. At a high level meeting at the Raj Niwas,
> it was decided that the buses should be sent to the
> neighbouring Districts of Haryana and U.P. and the
> instructions to allow the busse to pass the barriers
> had been given. In order to ensure that the buses
> reach their destinations in the neighbouring States,
> the officers of the DTC were also deployed to accom-

pany the buses. I had also been assured by Navin
Chawla that the police authorities and the State
Transport authorities had been properly briefed and
instructed to ensure that the buses cross the borders
without any route permits.

Raj Roop Singh, the then Inspector, SHO, New Industrial
Township, Faridabad stated :

> I received a telephonic message from the police Hqrs
> Gurgaon to the effect that as informed by the D.C.
> Gurgaon about 100 DTC buses will be arriving from
> Delhi for carrying people from Faridabad to Delhi for
> the purpose of rallies in favour of Indira Gandhi.
> I was told that the buses will report to the police
> station and that on demand from the Labour Inspec-
> tors, Officers of Industries Department and other
> Govt. Agencies, I should permit them to take the
> buses with them.

The type of instructions given at higher levels of administration in Haryana for organising the rally on June 12 at
New Delhi is mainly borne out from the statement of N.K.
Garg, the then District Magistrate, Rohtak. The relevant
portions of his statement are reproduced below :

> On 12.6.1975, Bansi Lal, the then Chief Minister
> rang me up from Haryana Bhawan, New Delhi round
> about at 10.30 A.M. and informed that the Prime Minis-
> ter has been unseated in the Allahabad High Court
> Judgment. He desired that truck-loads of people, as
> many as possible, be sent from 2.30 P.M. onwards to
> the P.M.'s house. In this connection, I should contact
> the local MLA Lala Kishan Das who would muster the
> Congress workers etc.

> He also directed that the persons should raise slogans
> like 'judiciary murdabad', 'Justice Jagmohan Lal murda-
> bad', 'Desh Ki Neta, Indira Gandhi'. I immediately
> got in touch with Kishan Das and conveyed the whole
> thing. I then called S. H. Mohan, SSP and asked him
> that he should make an effort to get as many trucks
> as possible for taking these people to Delhi. Around
> 11.15 A.M. I got another call, this time Dalbir Singh,

the then Deputy Minister for Shipping in the Central
Cabinet, conveying a similar message.

S.H. Mohan the then SSP Rohtak has stated that he
was called by DM Rohtak to his residential office and given
the above instructions at about 11 A.M. He has further stated
that :

> ... I came back to my office and asked Chandu Lal,
> Inspector City Rohtak to get in touch with Truck
> Union/Operators Union and arrange for as many
> trucks as possible, also they should report to the
> Tehsildar Rohtak. Later on, I was told by the
> Inspector that not many trucks could be made avail-
> able as the notice was very short, however, 20 to 30
> trucks had been arranged. Here I would like to add
> that arranging trucks for political rallies in the State
> had become a routine affair, and police was always
> put to a lot of inconvenience and embarrassment by
> such unreasonable demand but since these orders were
> routed through the District Magistrate, they were by
> and large complicd with. Such demands became freq-
> uent after June 12, 1975.

M.K. Miglani, who was holding the office of District
Magistrate, Gurgaon, in June 1975, has confirmed in his
statement that instructions from Bansi Lal, the then Chief
Minister of Haryana were received to the effect that all assis-
tance should be provided in organising the people to come to
Delhi on June 12, 1975 to participate in the pro-Indira rally.
He also learnt that DTC buses were expected from Delhi to
carry the people. He told the local leaders to get in touch with
Ranjit Issar, SDM who was present there, in case they requir-
ed any assistance.

A local rally organised by the DTC employees on June 13,
1975 is also worth mentioning here. As per out-shedding schedule of DTC for the morning shift of June 13, 1975, the
number of buses sent out for plying on the routes was "NIL."
J.R. Anand the then Traffic Manager has thrown light on
this in the following words :

> On June 13, 1975, not a single bus could be out-
> shedded from the Depots of the Corporation as the

operational staff who reported for duty did not take
out the buses but went to the then P.M.'s house to
participate in a rally. For going and coming back from
the P.M.'s house, they used the DTC buses. No action
against the staff who did not work on this day was
taken. Actually it was learnt that this was pre-planned
by the DTC Union leaders under the orders of the then
Chairman DTC, Krishan Chand and, therefore, there
was no question of taking any action.

N. K. Garg, the then District Magistrate, Rohtak stated :

Again on June 17, 1975, Bansi Lal rang me and desired
that the District Administration should make another
all-out grand effort to see that large number of people
converged from my district to Delhi to participate in a
rally being organised in support of Indira Gandhi at
the Boat Club, Delhi on June 20, 1975. He explained
that the rally was a prestigious, personal and crucial
affair, and the Distt. Administration must not lag
behind in this task.

I contacted the SSP and asked that he should be able
to take necessary and appropriate action for providing
the transport. I then issued directions to the SDMs and
Tehsildars to mobilise the maximum manpower that
could be mustered as used to be the usual practice. As
far as I can recollect Rohtak was able to send about
150 truck-loads of people.

S. H. Mohan, S.S.P. Rohtak made a statement to this effect :

On around 17/18.6.1975, Garg again rang me and said
that Bansi Lal had desired that we should make
arrangements for vehicles to transport people from
Rohtak for participating in a rally being organised in
support of Indira Gandhi at the Boat Club, New Delhi
on June 20, 1975. A target of about 400 trucks had
been fixed for Distt. Rohtak. I again had to direct the
police officials under me to contact the truck operators
etc., and mobilise the maximum number that could be
available. These vehicles were to report to the various
sub-Divisions of Rohtak as chalked out by the Distt.
Administration. Ultimately we were able to mobilise
about 150-200 trucks, which reported to the various
Revenue Officers.

M.K. Miglani, the then District Magistrate, Gurgaon, has also confirmed having received similar instructions from Bansi Lal in regard to June 20, 1975 Rally at New Delhi. He has further stated that:

> . . . I then passed instructions personally to the SDMs Gurgaon and Ballabhgarh to liase and coordinate with the local police/Congress leaders for making arrangements to send trucks to the villages; to send people for the rally on the appointed date.

The state of affairs in this regard was not very different in the State of Punjab as it appears from the statement of R. S. Talwar the then Chief Secretary of Punjab State.

As regards the State of Uttar Pradesh, the information received from Northern Railway shows that three special trains were arranged one each from Varanasi, Lucknow and Kanpur on June 19, 1975 arriving at New Delhi/Delhi on June 20, 1975. Two of these special trains had been booked by known Congressmen. As regards the third special train, information received from S.S. Rana, Addl. C.O.P.S. (C) vide his letter No. 63-TT/6613/Extra rush dated November 29, 1977:

> . . . The identity of the party requisitioning the special ex Varanasi is not available on file but the special was arranged for the Congress delegates.

For return journey from New Delhi, only two special trains were sent on June 21, 1975. According to the above quoted letter of S.S. Rana:

> The special train from New Delhi to Lucknow was in the name of the Congress delegates and the special train between New Delhi and Varanasi was in the name of Chottey Lal Gupta with Congress delegates. As per information available on our file, no security was deposited at New Delhi by any one of them and the specials were arranged at railway convenience in order to clear very heavy return rush of Congress delegates who could not have been cleared in the normal train services.

During the hearing of a case relating to the complaint of Mangal Bihari an IAS officer of Rajasthan before this Commission, Damodar Maurya, General Secretary, Rajasthan State Electricity Board Workers' Union deposed that

Hari Deo Joshi the then Chief Minister of Rajasthan had told him and the MPs and MLAs of Rajasthan on June 16, 1975 at New Delhi that one lakh persons from Rajasthan should participate in the grand rally at New Delhi on June 20, 1975. Hari Deo Joshi the then Chief Minister of Rajasthan stated in his testimony before the Commission that not more than 5 to 7 thousand persons could have possibly come from Rajasthan to participate in this rally. He further stated that he had assured that transport arrangements will be made. The Rajasthan State Electricity Board records show that 58 trucks of the Board had been ordered to be placed at the disposal of the Workers' Union on payment for transporting the Electricity Board employees to Delhi on this account.

The records also show that no payment of hire charges has been made so far by the Workers' Union on the plea that the trucks had been deputed by Board's top management and the Chief Minister of Rajasthan and, therefore, the hire charges should also be recovered from them. On June 22, 1975, the opposition parties had organised a rally which was to be addressed by Jayaprakash Narayan. The concern that it had caused in the official circles is expressed in the statement of Krishan Chand, the Lt. Governor who has stated that:

> ... I was advised on 22nd evening that the Delhi Administration should be alert and keep ready for dealing with the situation which might develop on the following day as a result of the speeches of Jayaprakash Narayan and the opposition leaders. Several meetings were also held in the Home Ministry to consider as to how best the situation developing from the speeches of Jayaprakash Narayan could be dealt with.

R.G. Jamalabad, Commercial Manager (Plg. & Coord), Indian Airlines Corporation, New Delhi, has stated that:

> ... As seen from Reservation Chart for Service IC-410 ex-Patna, for June 22, 1975, J. Narayan was booked to travel on this flight from Patna to Delhi. He could not make the trip to Delhi by air as the flight was cancelled ex-Calcutta. ...

It is also learnt from Acting Station Manager, Patna that the flight IC-410 was progressively delayed on June 22, 1975 and subsequently cancelled at 16.30 hrs ex-Calcutta.

Justice Shah : *We are governed by our own laws, not American laws.*

Counsel Lekhi : *But My Lord she does not understand the Constitution. . . .For Indira Gandhi Emergency was cooked abroad and served at home. . . . (laughter)*

Justice Shah : *The rules require you to receive an application. . . was there any application made by AICC. . . . ?*

D.T.C. Traffic Manager Anand : *But Sir we have never followed rules now or then.*

Justice Shah : *Did you give instructions for 34 vehicles to be sent to Indira Gandhi's residence ?*

U.S. Shrivastav Director, Delhi Transport : *I do not remember.*

Counsel Lekhi : *Can he remember who was the then Prime Minister of India?*

Justice Shah : *The order is from the superior officer that buses crossing interstate boundaries should not be checked. . . .Was the direction proper?*

District Magistrate Garg : *That was the practice in the State.*

Justice Shah : *(visibly disturbed) You mean to say. . . goods and persons were the same thing to the DM. . . ?*
(*the witness does not really understand the significance of the honourable judge's remark*).

Justice Shah : *What did you understand by the word "assistance". . .?*

District Magistrate Miglani : *It was natural. . .*

Justice Shah : *I don't find it natural . . . . You break all the laws on the movement of vehicles from one state to another, and then. . .*

District Magistrate Miglani : *This Sir . . . was a part of the law in Haryana. . . . .*

II—EVENTS BETWEEN JUNE 23-25, 1975

In the wake of the Allahabad High Court judgement on June 12, 1975, while the non-Communist Opposition Parties organised a number of rallies and processions to press their demand for the resignation of the then Prime Minister Indira Gandhi, some of the Chief Ministers were present in Delhi from June 22 onwards. In this connection, J. Vengal Rao, Chief Minister of Andhra Pradesh, has stated as follows :

... I went to Delhi on 22nd of June, 1975. This was in pursuance of a telephonic message I received from Shri R. K. Dhawan, Additional Private Secretary to the then Prime Minister. I was requested to be available in Delhi at the time when the Supreme Court judgement on the appeal filed by the then Prime Minister would be pronounced.

Krishan Chand, who functioned as Lt. Governor of the Union Territory of Delhi from October 4, 1974 to March 31, 1977, has stated :

... it was expected that JP rally will take place on the 24th. On 23rd evening, I was given an indication by Shri R. K. Dhawan that the Opposition leaders might have to be taken into custody after the rally on the 24th. Lists of prominent political leaders to be arrested were prepared by SP (CID) at P. M.'s House. I was also shown the lists. Changes in the lists continued to be made from time to time as a result of continued discussions at P. M.'s house, but I did not see the final list. The Opposition rally did not take place on the 24th and was announced to take place on the 25th and therefore the action plan for 24th was stayed.

On the 24th June, Justice Iyer pronounced his judgement granting conditional stay and declaring that
Smt. Indira Gandhi could not continue as a Member of
Parliament but could continue as Prime Minister. The
exact import of this judgement was not realised at first
and the All India Radio in its Hindi broadcast at
4 P.M. gave the factual details of judgement of Justice
Iyer, namely, Mrs. Gandhi could not continue to avail
of the full privileges of an M.P. and that she could not
vote in the Parliament. I was present in the P.M.'s
House when a copy of the judgement was received by
the P.M. Many copies were typed out there itself for
supplying to Ministers and others coming there. I
remember that Shri Dhawan also brought to the notice
of the then Information and Broadcasting Minister,
Shri I. K. Gujral, that emphasis should be given to the
continuance of Mrs. Gandhi as the Prime Minister.
Immediately, the broadcast in English gave this version
presumably on the orders of Shri I. K. Gujral.

The statement of Krishan Chand has been corroborated by
S. C. Bhatt, Director of News, New Services Division, All
India Radio. As stated by him :

At about the same time the Director of News received
an urgent call from the Minister of I & B, Shri I. K.
Gujral, who was afterwards in frequent touch with
him on the telephone. A news item based on Shri
Trakroo's telephone despatch was to be broadcast in
the 1600 hours English bulletin as well as the special
Hindi bulletin at 1602 hours and copy given to the
Hindi Editor for translation. Obviously, the pattern
about partial stay was to be used. Just about a minute
or two before 4 P.M., the Director of News sent word
to the News room that the fourth (news not yet
received) pattern should be used and he would be
coming down with a story given to him (obviously by
the Minister) which could be used as a flash, if there
was still time. This was what actually happened in so
far as the English bulletin broadcast at 4 P.M. was
concerned, i.e. the bulletin began by saying word is
still awaited from the Supreme Court and after some
background came the flash item which presented the

judgement in a very favourable light.

Krishan Chand the then Lt. Governor of the Union Territory of Delhi, has further stated that

> after the import of the judgement was fully realised, it was decided to take drastic action against the Opposition leaders as soon as there were tangible signs of any effort on their part to dislodge the Prime Minister from her office. It was decided by the P.M. that action would be taken on the 25th June after the Opposition rally.

In this connection, it is also pertinent to mention that round about lunch hour on June 25, 1975, six new telephones with secraphones were ordered to be installed in P.M.'s office, as stated by Sitansu K. Roy, Deputy Director General (MS), P & T Directorate.

J. Vengal Rao, Chief Minister of Andhra Pradesh, has stated that :

> On the 24th June when I was in Delhi, a telephonic message was received from Mr. Dhawan requesting me to meet the then Prime Minister on the 25th. I met the then Prime Minister, who informed me that, having regard to the prevailing conditions and the contemplated country-wide agitation, it had been decided to take strong, deterrent action. The then Prime Minister informed me that as this was sure to cause resentment and as there was a possibility of some violent reaction, it would be necessary to take all preventive action including arrests of persons who are likely to cause disturbance.

> I was also requested to pass on the message to the Chief Minister of Karnataka who could not be present. Both of us were asked to be available at the telephone during the night when the final decision of the Goverment of India could be communicated to us by Shri Dhawan. As no regular commercial flights were available and as an IAF plane was making a trip to Bangalore with some officers, arrangements were made for my travel by that plane. I met the Chief Minister of Karnataka at Bangalore, apprised

him of what the Prime Minister wanted me to tell
him and in the evening reached Hyderabad by the
same plane.

As stated by Sqn Ldr O.D. Sharma, ADC to the then Chief
of Air Staff, Air Chief Marshal O.P. Mehra :

> On 25th June, 1975, as far as I can recollect, in the
> morning near about 9 A.M., I received instructions
> from Air Chief Marshal O.P. Mehra to escort Shri
> Vengal Rao, Chief Minister of Andhra Pradesh to
> Palam Airport where an aircraft was waiting to air-
> lift him to Hyderabad via Bangalore. Accordingly, I
> contacted Shri Vengal Rao at Andhra Pradesh House
> and took him to Palam Airport where Wing Com-
> mander P.K. Mani was waiting near TU-124 V. 643
> Aircraft and told him that he may take the Chief
> Minister to Hyderabad via Bangalore. I might have
> reached the aircraft around 10 A.M.

Wg Cdr P.K. Mani has stated :

> At about 09.30 hrs, the Team arrived and they were
> emplaned. At about 10.00 hrs. Sqn Ldr O.D. Sharma
> arrived in the Comn Sqn accompanied by the Chief
> Minister of Andhra Pradesh, Mr. VENGAL RAO and
> his Security Officer. I was briefed by Sqn Ldr O.D.
> Sharma that I was to drop the Team at Bangalore. I
> was to wait for the Chief Minister to finish his work
> at Bangalore and then drop him at Dindigul and
> thereafter to return to Delhi. I undertook the task as
> briefed except that I deplaned the Chief Minister at
> Hyderabad instead of Dindigul due to bad weather at
> Dindigul. Initially the sortie was entered as a VIP
> commitment. It was later changed to a training flight
> as per instructions from Air HQ.

J. Vengal Rao has further stated that at Hyderabad since
the Chief Secretary, I.G. of Police and D.I.G. (Intelligence)
were away from Headquarters, he informed the Secretary to
the Chief Minister and S.P. (Special Branch) :

> that the Government of India were contemplating a
> strong and deterrent line of action and as this was
> expected to produce resentment and opposition, it

would be desirable to initiate preventive action including dentention of people who were likely to create trouble. I asked them to be ready to initiate action as soon as we heard from New Delhi. The intention was that the District Authorities should be alerted to be ready and also that from the available information at the State level, having regard to the recent developments in the political and law and order situation, a list of people, who might have to be taken into preventive custody under MISA, should be kept ready. By about 11 that night, Shri Dhawan conveyed the decision of the Government of India and I asked the officers concerned to take necessary action.

P. C. Sethi, former Chief Minister of Madhya Pradesh, has stated that :

On 25.6.75, I went to No. 1, Safdarjang Road, the residence of the then Prime Minister, Mrs. Indira Gandhi. There at about 9.30 A.M.-10.00 A.M. Shri Om Mehta, who was the then Minister of State in the Ministry of Home Affairs, gave me guidelines on the basis of which certain persons were to be detained on the night of 25.6.75/26.6.75. These guidelines suggested that persons with communal backgrounds, members of banned organisations, smugglers, persons with violent records, etc. should be detained under the Defence of India Rules. Mrs. Gandhi was also present at that time when these instructions were given.

Attempts were also being made at that time to contact Shri Harideo Joshi who was the then Chief Minister of Rajasthan. Apparently, they were not successful; so I was requested to go to Banswara where Shri Joshi was attending his son's marriage. An Air Force plane had been arranged (who arranged it, I do not know). I flew in it from Delhi to Halwara and motored down to Banswara, gave Shri Joshi the message and in the same Air Force plane I returned to Bhopal, reaching Bhopal at 3.30 P.M.-4 P.M. on 25.6.1975. The message to Shri Joshi was the same as given to me, i.e. he was given the guidelines for carrying out detentions on 25.6.1975 evening under the DIR.

On reaching Bhopal, I convened a meeting of the senior officials like Chief Secretary, Inspector-General of Police, Home Secretary, etc. and passed on to them the instructions of the Government of India received through Shri Om Mehta. Accordingly, the officers prepared the lists of persons to be detained and the detentions were effected the same night.

As stated by Flt. Lt. V.K. Khandelwal:

I was detailed as navigator of HS-748 Aircraft of Air Headquarters Communication Squadron on June 25, 1975. I was asked by the Captain of the aircraft to file a clearance from Delhi to Banswara. At that time, no further programme nor the passenger details were known to the Captain or crew of the aircraft.

At about 09.45 hours, Flt. Lt. Shah, the ADC to the CAS brought two gentlemen to the aircraft (who were the passengers) and introduced one of them as Shri P.C. Sethi. The other man was the security man.

After getting airborne, I asked the captain for our further programme. I was told that we will have to go, wherever Shri Sethi asks us to go.

In this connection, a report received from A.N. Thyagarajan, Deputy Secretary (Air-I), Government of India, Ministry of Defence, is reproduced below :

...instructions for the airlifting of the Chief Ministers appear to have been given by the then Chief of Air Staff. The Chief of Air Staff at that time was Air Chief Marshal O.P. Mehra .... The conveyance of the above mentioned Chief Ministers has not been reflected in the records of the Unit and therefore no bills have been preferred .... The clearance for the use of IAF aircraft by non-entitled persons is cleared individually in the Ministry and a Govt. sanction is issued to cover each individual flight. In these cases no Govt. letter has been issued.

S.K. Mishra, who functioned as Principal Secretary to the Chief Minister, Haryana, from June 1968 to December 1975 has stated that :

On 25.6.75, some time between 12 and 2 P.M. Shri Bansi Lal rang me from Delhi a few times and wanted me to pass on the following instructions/messages :

that Shri Banar Singh, ADIG/CID, should be asked immediately to draw up a list of persons who are pre-judicial to the security of the State;

that the DCs were to be asked to remain at Hqrs. and available on telephones as some important develop-ment was expected that day;

that Deputy Commissioner, Gurgaon, Shri M.K. Mig-lani, was to be asked to reserve huts at Sohna Tourist Complex for two VIPs who were to reach there on the night of 25th/26th June, 1975. Also proper security arrangements be made. In this connection, the DC should get in touch with Lt. Governor, Delhi, for further instructions;

Deputy Commissioner, Rohtak, Shri N.K. Garg be asked to depute some police officer to proceed to Delhi and contact the Lt. Governor for taking further action;

that Chief Secretary Shri Bhambri be informed about the messages to be passed on to the DCs. C.S. be also asked to meet the Chief Minister along with IGP around 9.30 P.M. when the Chief Minister returns from Delhi.

... At about 10 P.M. Shri Bansi Lal rang me on his return and asked that I should immediately come to his residence. On reaching there I found that Shri B.D. Gupta, the then Irrigation and Power Minister was pre-sent. Shri Bansi Lal then informed me that emergency was to be promulgated that night and I should imme-diately call over the Chief Secretary. He then told me that Shri Jayaprakash Narayan and Shri Morarji Desai were to be confined at Sohna Tourist Complex, where-as Shri Raj Narain and some other top leaders were to be lodged at District Jail, Rohtak.

Regarding the rally on the June 25, 1975, Krishan Chand, the then Lt. Governor of Delhi, has stated that :

The opposition rally was held on the 25th afternoon.
I reached PM's house in the evening. I went to Mr.
Dhawan's room where Shri Om Mehta and Shri Bansi
Lal were also present. I was given definite instructions
by Shri Om Mehta that Shri Jayaprakash Narayan and
other top opposition leaders were to be taken into
custody after the rally. At the Prime Minister's House
Shri Bajwa, SP (Special Branch) gave me the revised
list of the leaders to be taken into custody. This list
had been approved by Shri Om Mehta, according to
Shri Bajwa. All necessary arrangements in connection
with the impending arrests were discussed in the
meeting in Shri R.K. Dhawan's room. I was specially
advised that Shri Jayaprakash Narayan and Shri
Morarji Desai should be lodged suitably in a Rest
House in Haryana. I was also advised about discon-
necting of electricity to the Press.

J.K. Kohli, who functioned as Chief Secretary, Delhi
Administration, during this period, has stated that at about
7 P.M. on June 25, he was summoned by the Lt. Governor,
Delhi, and when he reached Raj Niwas, Delhi, at 7.30 P.M.
Navin Chawla, Secretary to Lt. Governor, Delhi, was there.
As stated by him :

The Lieut. Governor told me that the Prime Minister
had instructed him (Lieut. Governor) to arrange the
arrests of top Opposition leaders then present in Delhi,
and some other members of the non-CPI parties
by the next morning. The Lieut. Governor said that
the likely number of these arrests would be about 200.
The Lieut. Governor instructed me to proceed
immediately to the Tihar Jail so that the jail authorities could make suitable arrangements for the new
prisoners to be received there by the next morning.
At the same time, the Lieut. Governor instructed me
not to divulge to the Jail authorities the nature of the
new prisoners. . . .He suggested that I should tell the
jail authorities that about 200 Naga political prisoners
were likely to be transferred to the Tihar Jail by the
next morning.

The statement of J.K. Kohli has been corroborated by

R.N. Sharma, the then Superintendent of Central Jail Tihar.

Simultaneously, efforts were also under way to ensure that some important newspapers were prevented from bringing out the morning editions on June 26. B.N. Mehrotra, ex-General Manager, Delhi Electric Supply Undertaking, has stated that he was called to Raj Niwas around 9.30-10.00 P.M. on June 25, 1975, and told by the Lt. Governor that :

> for certain security reasons supply of electricity to all the newspaper printing presses in Delhi is required to be disconnected at 2 A.M. on the night between 25th and 26th June, 1975. I tried to explain to him that this is a tall order not capable of being implemented at such short notice specially because the newspaper printing presses are not confined to any one area but are spread over the entire city and get their electricity from different distribution sources.

> I further explained to him that some newspapers like *Statesman, Hindustan Times* etc. are outside DESU area of supply as those are fed by New Delhi Municipal Committee and electricity to those newspapers cannot be disconnected by DESU. Shri Navin Chawla mentioned that these are orders from Prime Minister's house and have got to be carried out. To quote the specific orders I was given . . .Do whatever you may have to but electricity must be disconnected at 2 A.M.

Mehrotra thereafter met the IG of Police, Delhi, and P. S. Bhinder, DIG, and after doing the needful at 2 A.M. he immediately reported compliance to Raj Niwas where Navin Chawla was available at that time.

From the statements of officers, it appears that efforts to prevent publication of newspapers were made in certain other places also.

N. P. Mathur, who functioned as Chief Commissioner Chandigarh, during that period has stated that :

> I received a telephone call on the night of 25th June 1975 at about 11.30 P.M. from Shri Zail Singh, the then Chief Minister of Punjab, asking me to lock up *The Tribune* and its Editor, Shri Madhavan Nair. I told

him that I was not aware of any grounds calling for this action nor were any grounds mentioned by him to me. He told me that emergency was being promulgated and as such the publication of newspapers had to be stopped.

J. S. Bawa, the then DIG, CID, Punjab, has stated that about 11.00 P.M. on June 25, 1975 he was summoned by the Chief Minister of Punjab. When he reached there, the Chief Minister mentioned to him that Emergency was being imposed and that newspapers might carry inflammatory and prejudicial material leading to or provoking breach of peace. It was pointed out to him that the *Tribune* was published from Chandigarh Union Territory and the vernacular newspapers published from Jullundur were printed quite early in the night. CM directed that vigilance should nevertheless be exercised in regard to newspapers published in Punjab.

H. G. Devasahayam, the then Deputy Commissioner, Chandigarh, has also mentioned that :

> As far as I remember the only instruction received during that night from Delhi was that the *Tribune* which is published from Chandigarh should not come out with facts about the various arrests that were taking place during the night. Accordingly, one DSP along with a small Police force was sent to the *Tribune* office in the small hours of 26th June to advise them that they should not bring out the news regarding the arrests of the top opposition leaders in the day's paper. This was complied with by the Tribune authorities.

S. C. Varma, the then Addl. Chief Secretary, Government of Madhya Pradesh, has stated that P. C. Sethi, the then Chief Minister of Madhya Pradesh, told him around 9 P.M. on June 25, 1975 that :

> internal emergency was being declared and that the formal declaration may be made on the following morning. He directed that suitable action should be taken to apprehend persons considered to be hazardous to public peace as there may be disturbances consequent upon declaration of emergency. He clari-

fied that even the MPs and the MLAs could be detained. He also mentioned that efforts be made to see that the news about the arrests should not appear in newspapers at Bhopal and other important places.

Narendra Prasad, the then S. P., Bhopal, has mentioned in his statement that :

> In pursuance of the orders of the Government conveyed by the Home Secretary and the IGP, Madhya Pradesh, on the night of 25th June, 1975, Police parties were despatched to various presses in Bhopal city to take possession of the copies of the newspapers which were due for circulation on 26.6.1975. The action was hardly completed when another order came in, requiring us to restore the copies to the concerned presses with due apologies, and it was promptly done.

In a d.o. letter sent vide No. 1/SSB-PF/77 dated September 2, 1977, S. S. Bajwa, the then IGP Haryana, wrote to A. Banerji, Home Secretary, Government of Haryana that he went to the residence of Bansi Lal on the evening of June 25, 1975 where he had been called to report by S.D. Bhambri. When he entered the room, Bansi Lal was "in an ecstatic state of mind. He was restive. He would sit down, lie down on his sides or abruptly stand up to approach a telephone with great alacrity and eagerness and show of extreme self-importance, I believe, due to the new accretion to his power." Bansi Lal observed that Emergency had been promulgated and wanted to know whether the Police Deptt. was in a position to enforce it. According to Bajwa :

> These discussions were interspersed by Shri Bansi Lal speaking to Shri Sanjay Gandhi at Delhi on the telephone. Even though all the talk could not be comprehended, it was clear that these two were very close to each other and of one mind as regards the promulgation of Emergency; that he was against somebody who was then it appeared in the Prime Minister's House. It seemed that while these two were in favour of complete (perhaps temporary) closure of the newspapers, that person thought it right only to impose censorship. Shri Bansi Lal remarked: "Throw him out he is spoiling the game...

...He thinks too much of himself as a lawyer although
he knows next to nothing. ... Push him out and send
him by the first plane."

S.K. Mishra, the then Principal Secretary to CM Haryana,
has stated that when he went to the residence of Shri Bansi Lal,
at 10 P.M. a "number of calls" were received by Shri Bansi Lal:

I recollect one such call came from the Prime Minister
asking him to get in touch with Giani Zail Singh, the
CM Punjab. I recollect that this call was before the
I.G. and the C.S. arrived. There was another call
which I guess was from the P.M.'s house. Shri Bansi
Lal was telling the other person, on the other end
that "legal luminary creating hurdle be thrown out."
He also made a couple of calls to Giani Zail Singh.

S.D. Bhambri, Chief Secretary, Haryana, has stated that
at about 10.30 P.M. he was informed by the Chief Minister
that "internal emergency was going to be declared all over
the country." He has further stated that :

The Chief Minister had before him a typed list of
persons who, he said, "were to be detained, for which
purpose instructions should be sent by me to field..."
After the arrival of Shri Bajwa, the communication
with me ceased and the CM directed his observations
and instructions exclusively to him. ... There were
again telephonic conversations with the P.M.'s house
in Delhi and in one of these conversations the C.M.
made critical comments about Shri S.S. Ray and his
role in the consultations being held in Delhi.

While preparations were going on in Haryana, and other
States, Indira Gandhi, the then Prime Minister of India,
came to see the President at the Rashtrapati Bhavan, round
about 5.00 P.M. on June 25, 1975. As stated by A.M. Abdul
Hamid, Press Secretary to the President of India, Rashtrapati Bhavan, New Delhi,

Round about 5.00 P.M. (at this distance of time, I do
not remember the exact time) I was informed by
ADC to the President, the former Prime Minister,
Smt. Indira Gandhi, has come to meet the President.

I went down to the ADCs Room and I was given
to understand that Smt. Indira Gandhi and Shri
Siddhartha Shankar Ray were closeted with the
President. I went back to my room and after sometime
(may be about 30 minutes) I learnt that they had left
Rashtrapati Bhavan.

S.L. Khurana, who functioned as Home Secretary, Govt. of
India, during the relevant period, has stated that on June,
25, 1975,

At about 6 P.M. Shri Om Mehta, the then Minister
of State in the Ministry of Home Affairs, sent for me
and asked me if it would be possible to get a copy of
the notification pertaining to the proclamation of
External Emergency 1971.... When I asked him about
the need for it, he replied that there was nothing
significant about it and that he just wanted to have a
look at it.

Subsequently, Khurana took a copy of the notification to
the residence of the then Prime Minister and gave it to Om
Mehta who was present there.

K. Brahmananda Reddy, the then Union Minister of Home
Affairs, Government of India, has stated that :

I received a call from the then Prime Minister's
house at about 10.30 P.M. over the phone on the night
of 25th June, 1975 and was asked to go over to her
house. Since I had already sent away the staff car, a
car was sent for me from the Prime Minister's house.
The Prime Minister told me that in view of the
deteriorating Law and Order situation it was felt
necessary to impose Internal Emergency. I told her
that there was already an Emergency on and so it may
be all right if the powers available under that Emergency were availed of to deal with the situation. On
this she said she would consult others and send for
me if need be. After that I came away to my house.
After about half an hour I received another call from
the Prime Minister's house and was asked to go over
to the house. A car also was sent. Accordingly I went
again. When I arrived at Prime Minister's house

and went into the visitors' room Shri Siddhartha
Shankar Ray came in and discussed about the Article
352 and said promulgation of Internal Emergency
would be preferable to meet the situation. The Prime
Minister then came in and said that my earlier suggestion had been examined and found that Internal Emergency may still be necessary. I told her that she knew
best what was good for the country and that she
could take a decision. After that I came away to my
house.

He has further stated that :

After a few minutes a letter to the President of the
Republic making reference to the telephonic conversation which the then Prime Minister had with him
was signed by me appending the Proclamation of
Emergency for his assent.

The letter sent by K. Brahmananda Reddy to the President
of India is reproduced below :

Top Secret   **HOME MINISTER**
                                     INDIA
                              June 25, 1975

Dear President,

    With reference to your telephonic conversation
with the Prime Minister, I am sending the appropriate
Proclamation for your assent.

With kind regards,

                            Yours sincerely,
                                 Sd/-
                        (K. Brahmananda Reddy)

Shri Fakhruddin Ali Ahmed,
President of India,
New Delhi.

    The letter sent by K. Brahmananda Reddy was on a plain
sheet of paper and without any correspondence number. No
office copy of this letter is available in the Ministry of Home
Affairs.

Akhtar Alam, who functioned as Special Assistant to the President of India, has stated that :

> On 25th June, 1975 at about 10 P.M. I received a telephone call from the Prime Minister's house most probably from Shri R. K. Dhawan—that an important letter for the President of India is coming.
>
> The letter came to my house at about 10.30 P.M. through a messenger. I immediately contacted the President. He asked me to bring the letter to Rashtrapati Bhavan and I submitted it to him by 10.45 P.M. After reading it he asked me to call Shri K. Balachandran his Secretary. I accordingly contacted Shri Balachandran and also Shri Nilakantan, Deputy Secretary to the President dealing with such matters. Both came within 10 minutes or so.
>
> Around 11.20 P.M. or so Shri R.K. Dhawan came and he brought with him some papers. Round about that time, as I was not feeling well and since both the Secretary and the Deputy Secretary to the President were already there I left for my house.
>
> Next morning when I met the President in his study between 10.30-11.00 A.M. he gave me the Prime Minister's letter and asked me to keep it with myself as it was a very important communication. Accordingly, I kept it with me till the close of February, 1977 when I handed it over to Shri Balachandran. I may have mentioned to Shri Balachandran on 26th that the letter had been received from the Prime Minister but I do not have a full recollection of my conversation. (The letter was given to me by the President as stated above).

As stated by K. Balachandran, former Secretary to the President of India :

> At about 11.15 P.M. on 25.6.75, I received a telephone call from Rashtrapati Bhavan saying that the President desired to see me urgently. In about ten minutes time I reached Rashtrapati Bhavan and went to the President who was in his private sitting room on the first floor. He held a letter in his hand which

he asked me to go through.

The letter was marked "TOP SECRET" and was from the Prime Minister Smt. Indira Gandhi. She began by recalling a discussion she had with the President earlier in the day and said that as she has explained to him then, she had received information regarding imminent danger to the security of India due to internal disturbances. She stated that if the President was satisfied on this score, a Proclamation under Article 352 (1) of the Constitution had become necessary. She added she was enclosing a copy of the draft Proclamation for the President's consideration. (As a matter of fact, however, there was no draft Proclamation enclosed with the letter.)

The Prime Minister also stated in her letter that she would have liked to consult the Cabinet on the subject but it had not been possible to do so owing to shortage of time and as the matter was extremely urgent. She said she was therefore permitting a departure from the Transaction of Business Rules, in exercise of her powers under Rule 12 thereof.

After I had carefully gone through the letter in the President's presence, he asked me what I thought about it. I told him that in my opinion, for more than one reason, it would be constitutionally impermissible for him to act in the manner suggested in the letter. At this, he wanted to consult the Constitution and I went out to get my office room opened. Shri S. Nilakantan, Deputy Secretary in the President's Secretariat had come by that time and after a brief discussion among ourselves regarding the constitutional provisions, I went back to the President with a copy of the Constitution.

I explained to the President that in the exercise of his constitutional powers, he had to act on the advice of his Council of Ministers and therefore his personal satisfaction in these matters would not arise. The letter from the Prime Minister indicated that the Cabinet had not considered the matter; moreover, it was worded in such a manner as would make it appear that the decision to declare the Emergency was that of the President based on his personal satisfaction. The President apparently saw the force of this argument and wanted to contact the Prime Minister on the telephone. Thereupon, I withdrew from his room and went over to the office room across the corridor.

After a wait of about ten minutes I went back to the President's room when the President told me that during my absence Shri R.K. Dhawan, Addl. Private Secretary to the Prime Minister had come with the draft of the Proclamation of Emergency for his signature. He also told me that he had signed the Proclamation and given the same to Shri Dhawan who took it back with him, along with the Prime Minister's letter.

The next day Shri Akhtar Alam, Special Assistant to the President, told me on the telephone that a revised letter had been received from the Prime Minister. It was subsequently passed over to me and I kept it in the file.

The revised letter of the Prime Minister available in the records of the Rashtrapati Bhawan is reproduced below. It does not bear any correspondence number.

TOP SECRET   PRIME MINISTER   NEW DELHI
INDIA   JUNE 25, 1975

Dear Rashtrapatiji,

As already explained to you a little while ago, information has reached us which indicates that there is an imminent danger to the security of India being threatened by internal disturbance. The matter is extremely urgent.

I would have liked to have taken this to Cabinet but unfortunately this is not possible tonight. I am therefore, condoning or permitting a departure from the Government of India (Transaction of Business) Rules 1961, as amended up-to-date by virtue of my powers under 12 thereof. I shall mention the matter to the

Cabinet first thing tomorrow morning.

In the circumstances and in case you are so satisfied, a requisite Proclamation under Article 352 (1) has become necessary. I am enclosing a copy of the draft Proclamation for your consideration. As you are aware, under Article 352 (3) even when there is an imminent danger of such a threat as mentioned by me, the necessary Proclamation under Article 352(1) can be issued.

I recommend that such a Proclamation should be issued tonight, however late it may be, and all arrangements will be made to make it public as early as possible thereafter.
With kind regards,

Yours sincerely,
Sd/- Indira Gandhi.

PROCLAMATION OF EMERGENCY

In exercise of the powers conferred by Clause 1 of Article 352 of the Constitution, I, Fakhruddin Ali Ahmed, President of India, by this Proclamation declare that a grave emergency exists whereby the security of India is threatened by internal disturbance.

New Delhi June 25th 1979.   PRESIDENT

P.N. Dhar, the then Secretary to the Prime Minister, has stated in his affidavit that during the night of June 25 and 26, 1975, he received a telephonic message from the Prime Minister's house that he should come to No. 1 Safdarjang Road, as soon as he could. As stated by him:

I came to know of the declaration of the Emergency first time during the night of 25th and 26th June 1975 ...When I reached No. I Safdarjang Road, I found Shri H.Y. Sharada Prasad and Smt. Maya Ray sitting in the waiting room. After a little while, Shri Sharada Prasad and I were called into the main drawing room where the then Prime Minister Smt. Indira Gandhi was sitting with Sri D.K. Barooah and Shri Siddhartha Shankar Ray.

Smt. Indira Gandhi informed us that a decision had been taken to declare Emergency and she handed over to us the draft of a speech which she was to broadcast to the nation. We read the speech and a few changes were made. We were also told that there would be a Cabinet Meeting early in the morning. We left the house after the draft was typed out and arrangements were made for Hindi translation of the speech. As far as I can recollect, I must have reached No. 1, Safdarjang Road around 11.30 P.M. on 25th June, 1975.

B. D. Pande, who functioned as Cabinet Secretary during the period has stated in his affidavit that he did not know anything about the proclamation of Emergency till the morning of June 26, 1975. As stated by him :

When I left the office on the evening of 25th June, it was to me a day like any another day. At about 4.30 A.M. on the morning of 26th June, 1975, my RAX telephone rang, which was attended to by my son. This was a call from the then P.M.'s house. I took the phone and was told that I was to attend a Cabinet meeting at 6 A.M. at 1, Akbar Road. I asked him whether the Ministers had been informed or I was to inform the Ministers. I was told that they were taking steps to inform the Ministers.

I went to 1, Safdarjang Road, a few minutes before 6 A.M. Some Ministers had come and some were coming. Some of them asked me what the Cabinet meeting was about ? I told them that I myself did not know about it.

Then one Minister came—I have forgotten his name— who had seen a very early morning P. T. I. teleprinter message containing reports about the arrests of Shri Morarji Desai, Jayaprakash Narayan and some others. It was only then that I learnt the action that had been taken. It also appeared that this was the first time that some of the Ministers came to know of this. Just

about that time, Shri Om Mehta was seen walking
from 1, Safdarjang Road into 1, Akbar Road for the
Cabinet meeting followed by the Prime Minister. The
Cabinet meeting perhaps lasted for 15 to 20 minutes.
The proceedings of the meeting are contained in the
minutes. There were no detailed discussions, but only
some clarifications were sought. The Cabinet approved the promulgation of emergency and thereafter the
Cabinet meeting ended.

Atma Jayaram, the then Director, Intelligence Bureau, has
stated that :

As far as I can recall it was sometime during the day
following the night on which some arrests were made
by the Delhi Police. Early that morning, I received
reports that a number of arrests had been made during
the night. It was only after I went to the office that
day that I gained more detailed knowledge about these
events from my staff. It was, I think, a good deal later
in the day that I came to know about the declaration
of the Emergency.

S. L. Khurana, who took over as Home Secretary Government of India, on June 23, 1975, has stated that :

At about 10. 30 to 11. 00 P.M. I received a phone
call at Rajasthan House from the then Lt. Governor,
Delhi, requesting for some additional police force.
When questioned about the need for it, he replied that
he was apprehending some deterioration in the communal situation. I, thereupon, asked him to send the
requisitions alongwith the detailed reasons for consideration in the Ministry. . . . At about 3 A.M. I
received a phone call from the Chief Minister, Rajasthan. He wanted some clarification about the arrests
which he had been advised to make. "By whom?" I
asked. He did not disclose the source. I told him that
as Home Secretary I had nothing to communicate to
him. If he, therefore, required any clarification, he
would have to refer the matter to the source which
had advised him about these arrests. I, however, felt
perturbed about these developments and wanted to
know the factual position. I, therefore, tried to get in

touch with MMHA and H.M. but there was no response from their residences.

About an hour later, I received another call. This
time, it was from Shri N.P. Mathur, Chief Commissioner, Chandigarh. He wanted to know if he was
required to act upon the advice of Giani Zail Singh,
Chief Minister, Punjab, and seize all the copies of
the local daily newspaper. I also told him that as
Home Secretary I had no instructions to give him. It
was for him to discuss the matter further with Gianiji
and use his discretion. I again went back to bed but
couldn't sleep as I was feeling very restless.

At about 6 A.M. I was informed from the Prime Minister's house a Cabinet meeting was being held that
time at No. 1, Akbar Road and that I was also required
to be in attendance. As it was already past six, I had
a hurried wash and left immediately thereafter. I
must have reached No. 1 Akbar Road by about 6.30
A.M. The meeting was already being held. I am not
aware of what preceded my arrival. Only one or two
points were raised when I was there. As far as I can
recollect, they related to the period for which the
emergency would remain in force. It was perhaps
replied that it would depend upon the internal situation in the country but it could not be for a very
long time. The Cabinet then gave it ex-post facto
approval and the meeting adjourned at about
6.45 A.M.

I was then called by the Prime Minister and Home
Minister and was given the proclamation duly signed
by the President. I was told to inform the State
Governments immediately and issue instructions to
them to ensure that law and order was maintained
at all costs.

H.R. Gokhale, former Minister for Law and Justice, has
stated that:

I came to know of the proclamation of the emergency for the first time at the Cabinet meeting held
on the morning of 26th June, 1975. I had no know-

ledge whatsoever about it before. I was not consulted with regard to the proclamation of emergency at any time before nor was the proclamation vetted by me or by my Ministry. In fact, on the 26th June, 1975 when I came to know about it, the proclamation had already been issued on the previous night.

In this connection, an extract from letter No. SECY (LA)-1025/77 dated Nov. 19, 1977 received from the Ministry of Law is reproduced below :

The records of this Department and also of the Legislative Department do not indicate that the draft proclamation of emergency was either prepared by or shown to this Ministry before it was sent to the President.

Regarding the Cabinet meeting on June 26, 1975, a report received from the Joint Secretary to the Cabinet in this connection is reproduced below :

A meeting of the Cabinet was convened at 6 A.M. on Thursday the 26th June 1975 at No. 1, Akbar Road. No written note of this meeting was circulated, and no agenda, or notes on the agenda items, were circulated. According to a note recorded by the Under Secretary, Cabinet, on 7.8.1975, the then Cabinet Secretary was asked by the PM's Sectt., between 4-4.30 A.M. on the 26th June to convene a Cabinet meeting at 6 A.M. The concerned Under Secretary came to the office around 5 A.M. and the Ministers were informed on phone about the Cabinet meeting.

The Cabinet meeting in question was attended by eight Ministers, including the Prime Minister. Five Ministers of State holding independent charge of their Ministries and the Minister of State in the Ministry of Home Affairs were also present. Nine Cabinet Ministers were not in station at that time.

The Minutes recorded and issued read as follows :

The Cabinet considered the present situation and approved the promulgation of Emergency under Article 352 of the Constitution on the ground of existence of grave emergency threatening the security of India by internal disturbance. It was further decided that the necessary rules may be framed immediately to implement these decisions, and brought before the Cabinet as soon as possible. Necessary instructions to the State Governments and other appropriate measures may be taken forthwith.

Some of the special features of the proclamation of Emergency gathered from official records are as under :

> On the economic front, as revealed by the Economic Survey 1975-76, a Govt. of India publication, the prices had started falling well prior to June 25, 1975, The whole-sale price index had declined by 7.4 per cent between the 3rd December, 1974 and the last week of March, 1975. The All-India Consumer Index had also on balance shown a declining trend since November, 1974. The number of man-days lost due to strikes and lock-outs had also fallen steeply from February 1975 onwards as per statistics furnished by the Ministry of Labour.

> On the law & order front, the fortnightly reports sent by the Governors of various States to the President of India and by the Chief Secretaries of the various State Governments to the Union Home Secretary indicate that the law & order situation on the eve of the declaration of Emergency was under control all over the country.

In reply to a questionnaire sent by this Commission, the Ministry of Home Affairs, Government of India, have intimated that :

> no reports from the State Governments were received indicating any significant deterioration in the law and order situation in the period immediately preceding the proclamation of Emergency;

> the Home Ministry, at no time, prepared any contingency plan prior to June 25, 1975 with regard to the imposition of Internal Emergency; no steps were taken to mobilise Central

Police Reserves for any possible law and order break-down before the declaration of Emergency on the 25th June, 1975.

No paper was received from the Intelligence Bureau in the Ministry of Home Affairs between 12th and 25th June, 1975, suggesting that the internal situation in the country warranted the imposition of Internal Emergency.

The Ministry of Home Affairs, at no stage made any recommendation to the Prime Minister that the internal situation in the country warranted the imposition of Internal Emergency.

During the period of Emergency, the Ministry of Home Affairs were not aware of any communication having been sent by the Prime Minister to the President regarding the imposition of Emergency.

It seems from the letter . . . that the decision to recommend the imposition of Internal Emergency was taken by the then Prime Minister herself.

A report received from the Cabinet Secretariat further confirms the view that there had been no extraordinary developments on the law and order front during the three months preceding the proclamation of Emergency. To quote an extract from the report received from the Cabinet Secretariat vide D.O.No. 50/7/1/77—CF dated November 11, 1977 :

We had scrutinised the agenda notes and the minutes of the meeting of the Cabinet and the Cabinet Committee on Political Affairs for three months prior to the imposition of Emergency and did not find any item which was related to the declaration of the emergency or the internal situation which may have warranted a proclamation of emergency.

As stated in her letter to the President, Indira Gandhi, the then Prime Minister, had invoked Rule 12 of the Government of India (Transaction of Business) Rules 1961 and by virtue of power vested in her under this rule she had condoned a departure from the Government of India (Transaction of

Business) Rules, 1961.

In this connection, an enquiry from the Cabinet Secretariat has revealed the following :

> The business of the Government is transacted in accordance with the Transaction of Business Rules and the Allocation of Business Rules, both of which have been promulgated under Article 77 of the Constitution. The Allocation of Business Rules provides that the business of the Government shall be transacted in the Ministries, Departments, Secretariats and Offices specified in the First Schedule to these rules. The distribution of subjects among the departments is specified in the Second Schedule to these rules. While the President can on the advice of the Prime Minister, change the allocation of business between departments, nothing in the rules seems to provide for the Prime Minister's Secretariat transacting any business allotted to a particular Ministry.
>
> By virtue of entry 27 under the Home Ministry, matters relating to the emergency provisions of the Constitution (other than financial emergency) are to be dealt in the Home Ministry. This, read with Rule 3 of the Transaction of Business Rules, therefore, requires that all business pertaining to the emergency provisions shall be transacted in the Home Ministry, with cases relating to the proclamation of emergency being brought before the Cabinet.
>
> The normal procedure for submission of cases to the Cabinet is for the Ministry concerned to send a Note for the Cabinet to the Cabinet Secretariat. This note contains the proposal needing Cabinet approval and should have the approval of the Minister concerned. Thereafter the item is placed before the Cabinet and approval, if accorded, is conveyed to the Ministry by the Cabinet Secretariat. If the item is short, the Cabinet Secretariat obtains the approval of the Prime Minister under Rule 12 of the Transaction of Business Rules, and thereafter, authorises the Ministry concerned to proceed further in the matter.

Since the Home Ministry has been allotted the work
relating to the emergency provisions of the Constitution, proposals relating to the proclamation of emergency should normally originate from that Ministry.
This would be particularly so when the emergency is
to be declared on grounds of internal disturbances,
as the Home Ministry deals with the Intelligence
Bureau, Preventive Detention and National Integration. It is the Home Ministry which is in touch with
the State Governments on matters relating to law
and order. The Cabinet Secretariat did not, however, receive any proposals from the Home Ministry
in respect of the Proclamation issued on the 25th of
June.

While the Director, Intelligence Bureau, the Home
Secretary, the Cabinet Secretary and the Secretary to
the Prime Minister had not been taken into confidence, Shri R.K. Dhawan, the then Addl. Private
Secretary to the Prime Minister appears to have been
associated with the preparations and promulgation of
the Emergency from the early stages.

Om Mehta, the then Minister of State in the Ministry
of Home Affairs appears to have been taken into
confidence much earlier than K. Brahmananda Reddy,
the then Union Minister for Home Affairs who was
informed for the first time at about 10.30 P.M. on June
25, 1975 regarding the intended proclamation of the
Emergency.

While the Lt. Governor, Delhi, and the Chief Ministers of Haryana, Punjab, Madhya Pradesh, Rajasthan,
Karnataka, Andhra Pradesh, Bihar and West Bengal
had been given advance intimation by the Prime Minister's house about certain intended actions, no such advance information was given to the Governments of
Uttar Pradesh, Orissa, Kerala, Tamil Nadu, Maharashtra, Gujarat, Assam, Meghalaya, Dadra & Nagar
Haveli (UT), Tripura, Sikkim, Himachal Pradesh,
Arunachal Pradesh, Lakshadweep (UT), Pondicherry
etc.

H. N. Bahuguna, the then Chief Minister of Uttar

Pradesh has stated that while he was having breakfast along with Uma Shanker Dixit and Keshav Dev Malviya on the morning of June 26, 1975, at his residence at Lucknow :

> one of my Assistants rushed into the room and told us that he had just heard over the All India Radio that a state of Emergency had been declared in the country. Soon after this, at about 9.00 A.M., the Chief Secretary Shri B. D. Sanwal, informed me that official intimation about the declaration of Emergency had been received. The Central Govenment Ministers Shri Dixit and Shri Malviya as also Shri Tripathi, who had also by then joined us, were as surprised as I was about the promulgation of Emergency. It was apparent that they also did not have any prior knowledge.

In reply to a questionnaire sent from the Shah Commission I. K. Gujral, the then Minister of State for Information & Broadcasting, has informed the Commission that :

> On the 26th and 27th June 1975, the following incidents took place :

> Immediately after the Cabinet meeting at 1, Akbar Road on the morning of 26th June 1975 Shri Sanjay Gandhi asked me to arrange to show to him radio news bulletins before they were broadcast. I told him that was not possible. I repeated my reply to the Prime Minister who was standing nearby. She agreed. She however deputed an officer of the Prime Minister's Secretariat Shri P. N. Behl to the All India Radio to scrutinise the news bulletins.

> In the morning I was called to the Prime Minister's house. When I reached there around 11 A.M. I found that the Prime Minister had left but Shri Sanjay Gandhi came into the room and said brusquely that the Ministry of Information and Broadcasting was not being properly managed and that the broadcast of the Prime Minister's address (earlier in the morning) had not been covered on all channels. I took exception to his remarks and told him that if he wished to talk to me he would have to be "civil and polite". I added that my association with the Prime Minister and the

Congress had started before he was born. I told him that he had no business to interfere in the work of my Ministry which I intended to manage as I thought best. Thereafter I left the Prime Minister's house.

On 27th June 1975 Shri Mohd. Yunus asked me over the RAX phone from the Prime Minister's house to lock up the B.B.C. office and to expel the B.B.C. correspondent because he had heard the B.B.C. reporting house arrest of some senior Ministers. I told him that it was not my Ministry's function to do so. At the same time I called for monitored report of the B.B.C. broadcast and discovered that there had been no such report. I sent a copy of the monitored version to the Prime Minister.

Gujral has further intimated that

On the evening of 27th June 1975 the then Prime Minister Shrimati Indira Gandhi sent for me and told me that she had decided to change my portfolio, as she felt that the Ministry needed a "different and firmer handling in the changed circumstances."

Justice Shah	:	*Who are people prejudicial to the security of the State ?*
Assistant Deputy	:	*Political activists . . .*
Inspector General		
of Police (CID)		
Banar Singh		
Justice Shah	:	*Who are Political activists ?*
Banar Singh	:	*Politicians popular with the masses . . . .*
Justice Shah	:	*Members of the Opposition but not the ruling Party.*
		It is said you were very close to the then Chief Minister of Haryana Bansi Lal . .
Banar Singh	:	*He liked me . . .*
Justice Shah	:	*You were a junior officer of the Police in Haryana . . .*
		Wasn't that surprising . . . ?
Banar Singh	:	*Policemen are never surprised . . .*
Former Minister	:	*Sir . . . in those days all we knew could*
of Rajasthan		*best be summed up thus :*
Mohan Changani		

Desh Ki Neta—*Indira Gandhi,*
Youth Ke Neta—*Sanjay Gandhi,*
Mahilaon Ki Neta—*Maneka Gandhi,*
Bacchon Ke Neta—*Rahul Gandhi,*
Bhar Men Jaye—*Mahatma Gandhi.*

Nation's leader—*Indira Gandhi,*
Youth's leader—*Sanjay Gandhi,*
Women's leader—*Maneka Gandhi,*
Children's leader—*Rahul Gandhi,*
To hell with—*Mahatma Gandhi.*

III—ARRESTS AND DETENTIONS

On the night intervening June 25 and 26, 1975, when the emergency was promulgated, arrests/detentions of a large number of persons were effected in Delhi city as well as in a number of States. Regarding arrests and detentions in Delhi, Sushil Kumar, the then District Magistrate, Delhi, has stated that :

At a meeting of the senior officers held late in the evening of 25.6.75 at Raj Niwas attended by S/Shri J.K. Kohli, Chief Secretary, Bhawani Mal, IGP, P.S. Bhinder, D.I.G., K S. Bajwa, S.P. (SB) Navin Chawla, Secretary to L.G. and myself, Shri Krishan Chand, the then L.G. told us that it had been decided to arrest a number of opposition and other leaders along with their important followers who were then in Delhi in the early hours of 26.6.75 including all those leaders who were then attending the public meeting at Ram Lila grounds like S/Shri J.P. Narayan, Morarji Desai, Charan Singh, Raj Narain, Ashok Mehta, Sikander Bakht and Piloo Mody etc.

He informed us that similar action was being taken in other States also as a part of country-wide arrests of all opposition leaders and their important followers simultaneously according to the decision of the Government in this behalf. The L.G. desired that the arrests should be made with complete surprise so as not to allow any opportunity to the persons to go underground and to prevent leakage of any information pertaining to the proposed arrests.

The L.G. gave me orders to issue warrants under MISA in respect of all the persons to be arrested. I had, while pointing out the difficulties involved in taking action under MISA in the very short time available when according to the procedure necessary information will have to be made available by the police authorities in respect of all the persons proposed to be arrested and in regard to getting the office opened at that late hour when everybody would have gone home, proposed that the arrests be made under the ordinary laws in pursuance of the Government's decision.

However, I was overruled by the L.G. and ordered to issue detention orders as it was considered necessary to make all the arrests under MISA only, and it was stated that it will be difficult to arrest leaders of the status of S/Shri J.P. Narayan, Morarji Desai and Ch. Charan Singh and their important followers under the provisions of the Criminal Procedure Code. It was also mentioned that it had been decided to send the important leaders outside Delhi immediately after arrest, which course of action would not be possible in case of their arrest under the Cr. P.C. Since they will then have to be produced before the court next day when at the time of their production before the magistrates, there is likely to be gathering of large crowds with the possibility of demonstrations resulting in ugly law and order situations.

Thereafter, arrangements were made to get the office opened and to locate the relevant papers dealing with use of MISA. While I along with the additional district magistrates was thus attending to the work of getting the necessary forms ready and preparing the detention orders in receipt of names and other data about the persons proposed to be detained from police officials, I started getting repeated telephone calls from the L.G., Secretary to L.G. and the Chief Secretary who were all presumably in Raj Niwas as also from Shri R.K. Dhawan from the Prime Minister's residence, each one asking me to issue the detention warrants without any delay as it was considered imperative that all the arrests are made expeditiously and simultaneously all over the city so that none of

the persons proposed to be arrested gets any tip-off
and makes good his escape.

As I felt that too much pressure was being applied
on me through these telephone calls every few minutes,
I went over to the Prime Minister's House along with
Shri S.L. Arora, seniormost ADM and met Shri R.K.
Dhawan, Additional P.S. to the P.M. and explained
to him that some delay is inevitable in the issue of
warrants and that I had already pointed this out to
the L.G. at the meeting in Raj Niwas that for the
arrests to be made under MISA, prescribed procedure
has to be observed which takes time but that I had
been over-ruled by the L.G.

I put my signature on major part of these warrants
after they were filled in, but as the time was running
out and there was great pressure on me from Raj
Niwas and P.M's House to expeditiously hand over
MISA warrants to the police authorities, in some cases,
forms were signed by me and given to other persons
available for filling up the names and other details . . . .
In the circumstances, some blank or incomplete warrants were probably taken away by police authoritiies
and filled in later on.

Regarding the use of MISA warrants, J.K. Kohli has
stated that :

I telephoned the Secretary (Law & Judicial) and
asked him to come to the Raj Niwas. When Secretary
(L&J) reached the Raj Niwas, I had a separate discussion with him and asked him whether the MISA
warrants could be issued on cyclostyled forms. He
opined that there was no specific provision prohibiting use of cyclostyled forms for MISA warrants but
the courts generally did not like such practice. I
apprised the Lt. Governor of this opinion and told
him that Secretary (L&J) was available in the Drawing room of the Raj Niwas for consultation. . . .
Secretary (L&J) remained in the Raj Niwas till the
next morning but was never called in by the Lt.
Governor for any consultation.

Rajni Kant, Secretary (L & J), Delhi Administration has mentioned in his affidavit :

> I was awakened by my son from my sleep at about 11.30 P.M. in the night of 25th June, 1975 which is now rightly remembered as black night to tell me that the then Chief Secretary (Shri J. K. Kohli) wanted to talk to me from the Raj Niwas. I was asked by Shri Kohli on phone to reach the Raj Niwas immediately . . . I found Shri Navin Chawla, Special Assistant to the Lt. Governor sitting on the chair and Shri Kohli standing in the office room. Shri Chawla enquired from me in how many days the grounds of detention needed to be furnished to a detenu. I explained the procedure and thereafter I was asked to go and wait in the drawing room. I waited there all alone till about 5 A.M. Perhaps by then the drama was over. While sitting in the drawing room I could see the Chief Secretary going up and down.

In the background of the enquiry made from me about the procedure of detention and from the movement of the Chief Secretary I could imagine that something serious was transpiring. Next morning I came to know from other sources that almost all the important leaders of opposition had been detained during the night. I then felt that I might have been the Law Secretary of the Administration but indeed I was not amongst its confidants.

As a result of a series of operations that night, the Delhi Police detained 67 persons under MISA which included the following :

Shri Jaya Prakash Narayan,
Shri Morarji Desai,
Shri Charan Singh,
Shri Chandra Shekhar,
Shri Ram Dhan,
Shri Sikandar Bakht,
Shri Raj Narain,
Shri Piloo Modi,
Shri Biju Patnaik.

Action under MISA, however, did not remain confined to Delhi city alone. Similar action was taken in the neighbouring States also. Banar Singh, the then ADIG/CID, Haryana, has stated that in response to a request made by S. K. Mishra, Private Secretary to C. M., Haryana, he had given "a list of important political activists and others whose activities could be considered prejudicial to the maintenance of law and order in the State", to S. K. Mishra by the evening of June 25, 1975.

Banar Singh has further stated that S. S. Bajwa, IGP Haryana, directed him at 6.30 P.M. on June 25, 1975 to be available in his office till he returned to the office after meeting Bansi Lal, the then Chief Minister of Haryana. As stated by him :

> Shri Bajwa returned to the office at around midnight and called me to his room. He told me that emergency is going to be promulgated in the country that very night and that about 70 persons in the State are going to be detained under MISA. I saw hand-written pencil scribbled note at his table from which he read out the names. Keeping a mental note of the list which I had given to Shri Mishra, it appeared that there was change in about 10/15 names. I did not mention to him at any stage that I had furnished a list of 70 persons to Shri Mishra earlier. The I.G. did not ask my comments on these 70 names nor did I consider it necessary and proper to offer any comments. He further told me that he would personally pass the messages to arrest to the concerned District Ss. P. He asked me to stay in office till further orders . . . .

> At about 5 A.M. Shri Bajwa called me and instructed while leaving the office that I should keep him informed about the progress of arrests made in various districts as soon as the messages are received.

In Andhra Pradesh also, detentions under MISA were made on the night intervening June 25 and 26, 1975. As stated by J. Vengal Rao, Chief Minister of Andhra Pradesh :

> In actual fact, upto 8 A.M. on 26th June, only 11 persons were taken into custody. After receipt of offi-

cial version of proclamation of Emergency on 26th June, the guidelines issued by the Government of India were communicated to the appropriate District authorities. In all, only 36 persons were detained under MISA till the evening of 26th.

On June 26, 1975, in file No. HD-63-SWM75 of Special Section of the Home Department, Government of Karnataka, G. V. K. Rao, Chief Secretary, noted as follow :

Shri Kohli, Chief Secretary of Delhi, telephoned to me at about 7.30 A.M. this morning, and requested that Shri L. K. Advani, Shri A. B. Vajpayee, Shri S. N. Mishra, Shri Madhu Dandavate, Shri Samar Guha, and Shri Subramanyan Swamy, who were in Bangalore, may be arrested, and that this had the concurrence of the Prime Minister. I immediately contacted the IGP, and requested him to take immediate necessary action. I also contacted Shri S. L. Khurana, Home Secretary to the Govt. of India, who confirmed the instruction. He also informed me that the President of India had issued a Proclamation under Article 352, declaring a State of Emergency on the ground that the security of India is threatened by internal disturbance.

The matter was reported to the Chief Minister, and a meeting was held by him, along with the Home Secretary and IGP.

M. L. Chandrashekar, who was then Commissioner of Police, Bangalore City, has stated that :

On 26th June, 1975 . . . round about 8 A. M. I had telephonic message from my Inspector General of Police, (Shri C. V. S. Rao) that the following persons may be arrested :

(1) Shri L. K. Advani
(2) Shri A. B. Vajpayee
(3) Shri S. N. Mishra
(4) Shri Madhu Dandavate

Accordingly I have taken action . . .

M. L. Chandrashekar, the then Commissioner of Police,

Bangalore, reported compliance with this action to the Home Department, Government of Karnataka, Bangalore, in his secret letter No. SB/280/MISC/75 dated June 26th, 1975, and said that he had passed the detention order against the above mentioned leaders "after scrutinising the material placed before me and satisfying myself regarding the need for their detention. They have been apprehended and sent to the Central Jail, Bangalore."

It appears that the grounds of detention had not been made available to Karnataka Government till June 28, 1975, as would be evident from the following Crash Wireless Message from Home Secretary Bangalore, to Home Secretary, New Delhi:

> No. HD 148 SPD 75 DT 28th June, 1975 following for Sr. A.C. Sen Deputy Secretary from Sri B.S. Hanuman. Reference our telephone conversation on the morning of June 28th, four persons namely SR (1) Atal Bihari Vajpayee M.P. (2) Shyam Nandan Mishra M.P. (3) Shri Lal K. Advani, M.P. and (4) Sri Madhu Dandavate M.P. detained under MISA on 26th June, 75 as already reported(.) As regards grounds Sri Vital Naik being deputed to Delhi this evening(.) please give him all help(.)

In Madhya Pradesh, most of the arrests on the night intervening June 25-26, 1975, were made under section 151 Cr. P.C and subsequently, all these arrests were converted into detentions under the MISA. In this connection, it would be relevant to quote the Wireless Message sent by the Chief Secretary, Bhopal, Government of Madhya Pradesh to all District Magistrates and Ss.P. on June 26, 1975, which is as under :

> F. No. 38-2/75/X-I(.) You must have heard on the All India Radio that Government of India have declared Emergency under article 352 of the Constitution. Detailed instructions from Government of India are awaited. Last night instructions were issued to you to make Preventive arrests. In most of the districts arrests have been made under section 151 Criminal Procedure Code. It is necessary to convert these arrests into detention under MISA. Further arrests

are also to be made under MISA. Please take all precautionary steps emanating with proclamation of emergency namely protection of vital installations, guarding of vulnerable points, security of VIPS, supply of essential articles etc. Further instructions will be issued as and when received from Government of India(.)

In Rajasthan, directive to use MISA against certain categories of political workers was issued telephonically to all the DMs on June 26, in the following words :

Selected top leaders of non-CPI opposition parties and most prominent student leaders be arrested and detained under Sub-Clause(II) of clause (A) of Sub-section (1) of Section 3 of the Maintenance of Internal Security Act, 1971. The number of arrests should not be too large, but should be selective. Details be furnished to Home Department.

Justice Shah	: *Who gave you the list of names . . .?*
Lt. Governor of Delhi, Krishan Chand	: *Mr. Bajwa . . .*
Justice Shah	: *What did your conscience tell you . . .?*
Krishan Chand	: (*unashamedly*) *There was no question of conscience then Sir . . . .*
Justice Shah	: *Somebody had to apply his mind . . .*
Krishan Chand	: *Somebody had to be out of his mind to question the P.M.*
Justice Shah	: *Do you know what her satisfaction was . . . since under law the Magistrates have to be satisfied, if they are signing the orders.*
Krishan Chand	: *She was the Central Government.*
Justice Shah	: *You are a Senior I.C.S. officer . . . the authority has to be vested in some officer of the Central Government.*
Krishan Chand	: *Sir . . . there was no time for these . . .*
Justice Shah	: (*a little disturbed*) *There was no satisfaction . . .* (*pause . . . witness trying to understand the significance of the remark*) *They are opposition leaders and they had to be arrested.*
Krishan Chand	: *We were tools of the Government . . . it was not in our hand.*
Justice Shah	: *In the language of law you were persuaded to pass the order without following the law.* (*laughter*)
Justice Shah	: *Was this merely an eyewash . . . a make believe?*
Krishan Chand	: (*without remorse or guilt*) *I did not apply my mind to anything . . .*
Justice Shah	: *You were participating in a conspiracy to deprive a number of citizens of their liberty . . .*
Chief Secretary of Delhi, J.K. Kohli	: *I did not think of it . . .*
Justice Shah	: *I dare say you did not . . . . I want to know why you did not ?*
Justice Shah	: *. . . J.P. was a dying man when you visited him in detention.*

J.K. Kohli	: *Om Mehta (Minister of State for Home affairs) told us there will be 2 orders: the first one was for conditional release on 30 days' parole, and the second one for unconditional release. If JP accepted the first letter, then we should report the matter to the PM.*
Justice Shah	: *Even then you did not have sufficient humanity to give him the second letter. He was almost a dying man . . . . .*
Chief Secretary Kohli	: *I was relieved that Government had decided to release him.*
Justice Shah	: *Don't pay too much attention to so called legal niceties.*
Senior Superintendent of Police M.L. Bhanot	: *After serving the order of parole Mr. Kohli rang up Delhi immediately and talked to R.K. Dhawan :*

Bhai Sahib, Voh Kam Ho Gaya,
Koyi Etraz Nahin Kiya.
Doosre Order Ki Zarurat Nahi Pari.
Ham Aaj He Vapas Aa Jayenge . . .

Dear brother, that job has been accomplished.
He did not raise any objections.
We did not need the other order.
We shall come back today itself . . .

1 Get Appointed now. . .And Pay Later

The names Navin Chawla, Bhinder, Jagmohan, Krishan Chand, N.K. Singh, S.R. Mehta, and D. Sen meant quite something not too long ago. Some said the names symbolised the Government of Indira and others felt they epitomized the arrogance of power. People envied them and they in turn despised them. An interesting combination and all that was missing was a ready system of selection as these "dedicated" public servants had to waste a good few years of their precious lives proving their usefulness.

The Reserve Bank of India, the State Bank of India, Punjab National Bank, Air India, Indian Airlines Corporation, International Airports Authority of India, India Tourism Development Corporation and Delhi Transport Corporation are fairly large organisations with assets running into crores. The appointment of the Chief Executive Officer in any one of these corporations by law has to be through a Public Enterprises Selection Board (PESB) and Administrative Committee of the Cabinet (ACC), consisting of the Prime Minister, Home Minister and the Minister concerned. For Indira all this was cumbersome and time-consuming and she decided to do away with it.

The big question to be answered is—What is the appointment for and for whom? If what is intended is not the country's welfare but one's own future, then the question needs no further answer. Whether they were or what they were not intended to be may be an interesting thought, but one thing is clear it pays to be not only ambitious and loyal but also dishonest and pliable.

IV—THE RESERVE BANK OF INDIA

S. Jagannathan, the then Governor of the Reserve Bank had to be relieved before the expiry of his tenure as he had to assume the office of Executive Director on the Board of the International Monetary Fund on behalf of India, Bangladesh and Ceylon as early as possible. Therefore, pending selection of the successor of Jagannathan, it was decided to appoint N. C. Sen Gupta, the then Secretary of the Department of Banking to hold office as Governor of the Reserve Bank for a period of three months. Accordingly, Sen Gupta was appointed as Governor, Reserve Bank, for a term of three months with effect from the close of business on May 19, 1975. Under the Rules of the Business of the Government, the appointment of any person as a Governor of the Reserve Bank, requires the approval of the Appointments Committee of the Cabinet, which consists of the Prime Minister, the Home Minister and the Minister concerned (in this case, the Finance Minister).

The background, qualifications and calibre essential in any suitable individual for this important post were discussed by C. Subramaniam, the then Finance Minister, in his Top-Secret Note dated July 29, 1975 to the Prime Minister.

> We have appointed Shri Sen Gupta as Governor of the Reserve Bank of India for a period of three months which ends on August 18, 1975. This short-term appointment was made to give the Government time to identify a suitable person for the post.

> In assessing the suitablity of an individual we have to keep in mind the functions which the Governor has to

discharge and the leadership he has to provide to the Reserve Bank of India as the Central Bank of the country.

The Bank has to regulate the monetary system, ensure monetary stability and particularly to operate the currency and credit system of the country.

The Indian monetary system cannot function in isolation. It is part of the International monetary system and is affected by changes that are taking place in the field. It is, therefore, necessary for the nation's Central Banking Institution to be aware of these changes and take appropriate action within our system.

The Bank has also the obligation and the right to transact Central and State Government business relating to monetary and banking operations, including the public debt.

The Governor of the Reserve Bank of India should be a person capable of providing leadership in all these areas. He will have to participate in many international Conferences of Financial and Banking Experts and also in the meeting of the international, financial and banking institutions.

Particularly in a difficult monetary situation we would expect the Reserve Bank of India to be the main guide for the Government in the formulation of their monetary and fiscal policies. Of late, there has been a feeling that this leadership has not been forthcoming from the Reserve Bank of India. It is necessary to rectify this situation and ultimately this depends upon the competence of the Governor.

It is in this context that we have to scan the following list of possible candidates for this job and make a final choice.

Subramaniam further discussed briefly the names and qualifications of various persons among others (I.G. Patel, K.N. Prasad, S.R. Sen and M.G. Kaul) whom he considered suitable for appointment as Governor of the Reserve Bank of India.

Thereafter he added :

P.M. has in this connection mentioned the name of
Shri K.R. Puri, Chairman, L.I.C. I have examined
his suitability for the post very carefully. He is an
ordinary graduate and as such lacks an adequate
academic background. He has been in the field of
insurance throughout his career and therefore his experience has been in a very limited area of specializa-
tion unconnected with Banking and Finance.

These are the names for consideration and if she so
wishes, P.M. may send for me for discussions so that
an early decision may be taken.

As indicated above, N.C. Sen Gupta was appointed as
Governor, Reserve Bank of India for a term of three months
with effect from the close of business on May 19, 1975. His
term would have ended on August 19, 1975. On the previous
day, namely August 18, 1975, the then Finance Minister minuted in the concerned file of the Department of Banking as
under :

Shri K.R. Puri now Chairman, L.I.C., may be appointed as Governor of Reserve Bank for a period of 1
year. This has the concurrence of the Prime Minister.
In view of the fact, Shri Sen Gupta's term expires
tomorrow orders of appointment may issue immediately and A.C.C. kept informed. Shri Puri may take
charge tomorrow.

Pursuant to the then Finance Minister's orders contained
in the minute extracted above, a notification dated August 18,
1975 appointing K.R. Puri as Governor of the Reserve Bank
for a term of one year with effect from the close of business on
August 19, 1975, was issued.

Thereafter on August 20, 1975, M.G. Balasubramaniam the
then Additional Secretary in the Department of Banking wrote
to U.C. Agarwal, Establishment Officer, Department of
Personnel & Admn. Reforms, who functions as the Secretary
to the Appointments Committee of the Cabinet as under :

... It has since been decided with the approval of
the Prime Minister to appoint Shri K.R. Puri, (Chairman, Life Insurance Corporation of India) as Governor

of the Reserve Bank of India for a period of one year ...

It would be seen from the facts narrated above that a person whom the Finance Minister considered unfit for the post was appointed Governor of the Reserve Bank without the prior approval of the Appointments Committee of the Cabinet.

V—THE STATE BANK OF INDIA

T. R. Varadachary was appointed as Chairman & Managing Director of State Bank of India in August, 1976 replacing R. K. Talwar whose tenure as Chairman & Managing Director would normally have ended on February 28, 1977.

Government's decision in this regard is reflected in the notes extracted below :

Copy   *Secret*

OFFICE OF THE MINISTER OF REVENUE & BANKING

Sub : Shri R. K. Talwar, Chairman, State Bank of India—Term of appointment.

Shri R. K. Talwar was appointed Chairman, State Bank of India with effect from 1.3.1969 for a term of 5 years. The term was extended by a further period of 3 years and comes to an end on 28.2.1977. It has been the Government's intention that his term of appointment should be curtailed and he be asked to vacate office. As the State Bank of India Act provided only for removal from office which could be only as a punishment, the State Bank of India Act has been recently amended to provide for the Government, if it so chooses, to terminate the term by giving allowance in lieu thereof. Accordingly, it is proposed to terminate, in terms of Sub-Section (IA) of Section 20 of the Act, the term of appointment of Shri Talwar as at the close of business on the 30th June 1976 and pay him 3 months' salary and allowances in lieu of notice.

In the vacancy caused it is proposed, that Shri T. R. Varadachary at present Managing Director, State Bank of India, be appointed Chairman, with effect from July 1, 1976 till 28-2-1977, i.e. till such time as he would have served as Managing Director of State Bank India.

Sd/-

(Pranab Mukherjee)
Minister of Revenue & Banking

Prime Minister of India

U. O. No. 350(S)/MRB/76 dated 24.6.1976

PM has approved.

Sd/- P. N. Dhar
Secretary to the Prime Minister
21.7.76

The order may be effective from 4th August, 1976.
Sd/- Pranab Mukerjee
24.7.76

As is seen from the extract above, the then Minister of Revenue & Banking had ordered on 24.7.76 that appointment of Varadachary as Chairman of State Bank should be effective from August 4, 1976. Pursuant to that the Department of Banking issued a notification dated July 30, 1977 appointing Varadachary as Chairman to the State Bank of India for the period commencing August 4, 1976 and ending with February 28, 1977. A copy of this notification was also endorsed to the Establishment Officer in the Department of Personnel & Administrative Reforms, Government of India.

On November 12, 1975, the then Chairman, State Bank of India, R. K. Talwar had forwarded a note to Varadachary requesting for his comments on certain matters indicative of improprieties on the part of Varadachary. The then Chairman had also brought to the notice of the Central Board of the State Bank for discussion at the Board's meeting on 30.3.76 a memorandum dealing with the alleged improprieties on Varadachary's part. As desired by N. C. Sen Gupta, the then Secretary, Department of Banking and P. K. Mukherjee, the then Minister for Revenue & Banking, M. G. Bala-subramanian, the then Additional Secretary, Department of Banking, who was a member of the Central Board of the State Bank, met the then Chairman, State Bank and advised him not to bring this subject for discussion before the Board. The matter was not accordingly brought before the Board's meeting held on March 30, 1976.

There is nothing on record to show that Government examined the matter further and satisfied itself that Varadachary was not guilty of any impropriety, as alleged by the then Chairman before deciding to appoint him (Varadachary) as Chairman of the State Bank.

Under clause (a) of sub-Section (1) of Section 19 of the State Bank of India Act 1955, the Chairman of the State Bank is to be appointed by the Central Government in consultation with the Reserve Bank of India. There is no evidence of such consultation with the Reserve Bank either orally or in writing in the Department of Banking File No. F. 8/7/76 BO.I. dealing with the subject.

Under the procedure prescribed the appointment of the Chairman, State Bank of India requires the approval of the Appointments Committee of the Cabinet. In this case, the only communication to the Secretariat of the Appointments Committee of the Cabinet is the endorsement of a copy of the Notification appointing Varadachary as Chairman of the State Bank of India to the Establishment Officer, Department of Personnel and Administrative Reforms, who acts as Secretary to the Appointments Committee of the Cabinet.

As for the manner and background of the appointment of Varadachary and his own conduct as Chairman of the Bank, we cannot do better than quote from a note which he forwarded to the Prime Minister under cover of his letter dated April 30, 1977. The relevant portion of the note reads as under :

I had heard that before my appointment as Chairman of the Bank, Shri Sanjay Gandhi was against the proposal and had desired that the chairman of some other nationalised bank should be appointed and was actually working towards that purpose. Therefore, there was no question of my having any regard or sense of obligation to him. In point of fact my first meeting with Shri Sanjay Gandhi took place at the instance of the former Minister for Revenue Banking to lodge my claim that I should not be superseded and an outsider brought in my place. During the meeting, I proposed against such a move to supersede me and he made certain unkind remarks about me and the Bank, which I defended to the best of my ability.

After my appointment as Chairman, I called on the Minister at his residence where I happened to meet the Chairman of the Delhi Small Industries Development Corporation. In the course of conversation, he explained to me the Trans-Jamuna Project and sought the Bank's assistance to rehabilitate the poor settlers of the colonies which I readily agreed to. He also invited me to attend the Inauguration function of 3 colonies on the following day.

Shri Sanjay Gandhi was the Chief Guest at this function and in his inaugural address he mentioned that the Bank had agreed to help the resettlers. He also requested me to keep him informed of the progress of the Bank's efforts in the rehabilitation programme. I apprised the Minister of the developments and sought his directions. He advised me that I should keep him and Shri Sanjay Gandhi informed from time to time in view of the importance attached to the project. The financing of economic and resettlement activities in these colonies is very much within the ambit of the Bank's normal development activities even constituting part of established priorities.

Another occasion when I was directed by the Minister to meet Shri Sanjay Gandhi was in the following circumstances. An officer of the Bank attached to the Bombay Local Head Office, who was at one time Union President, was transferred out of Bombay in the normal course during my predecessor's time. To my utter surprise, a communication was received by the Bank from the Deparment of Banking that the Minister desired the transfer to be withheld. Thereupon, I took up the matter with the Minister and strongly defended the action of my predecessor and expressed the view that it was not desirable for the Government to interfere in the routine administration of the Bank, particularly relating to the transfer of this officer, whose activities incidentally were suspect. The Minister advised me to explain the whole matter to Shri Sanjay Gandhi. Accordingly, I called on Shri Sanjay Gandhi and maintained my stand, and also wrote to the Government that the action of the Bank was proper and should stand. The matter was not pursued by the Government.

On another occasion, when I went to apprise Shri Sanjay Gandhi regarding the progress of rehabilitation assistance given in the Trans-Jamuna colonies (in the circumstances explained earlier), I was told by him that the former Prime Minister was impressed with the potential obtaining in Mauritius for industrial and economic collaboration with India and to take advantage of this potential, the authorities felt that the Indian Banking presence should be strengthened by the State Bank of India establishing its offices over there. In consultation with the Minister, I deputed two officers of the Bank to Mauritius to make an on the spot assessment and submit a report. The report was forwarded to the Department of Banking with the Bank's views.

On another occasion when I met Shri Sanjay Gandhi again in relation to the Resettlement Project he enquired whether the Bank could examine the feasibility of starting a new type of banking organisation to attract investments and deposits from expatriate Indians who have settled abroad. This too was discussed by me with Minister and he felt that the State Bank of India could profitably undertake such a study. Accordingly a study was undertaken by the Bank and a report was submitted to Government.

It would be seen from the above that, as per his own statement, Varadachary had met Sanjay Gandhi to ensure his appointment as Chairman of the State Bank of India and that

he had various other meetings with Sanjay Gandhi during
which he had consulted/taken instructions from Sanjay Gandhi
on various matters regarding the functioning of the State Bank,
including staff matters. As per Varadachary's statement, most
of these meetings were at the instance of the then Minister
for Revenue & Banking.

VI—THE PUNJAB NATIONAL BANK

P.L. Tandon's term as Chairman and Managing Director of the Punjab National Bank was due to expire on July 31, 1975. Under clause 3 (a) and 5, read with clause 8 of the Nationalisation schemes, the Chairman and Managing Director of a Nationalised Bank is appointed by the Central Government after consultation with the Reserve Bank. In the Government itself, the appointment requires the approval of the Appointments Committee of the Cabinet. Accordingly, on May 12, 1975, the then Secretary, Department of Banking wrote to the then Governor, Reserve Bank, inter alia, seeking the Reserve Bank's views in this regard. The Reserve Bank recommended, through their letter dated May 14, 1975, that O.P. Gupta who was then Deputy General Manager "be considered seriously" to succeed Tandon as Chairman and Managing Director.

The then Finance Minister agreed with the Reserve Bank's recommendation (which incidentally was in accordance with P.L. Tandon's own views) that O.P. Gupta should succeed Tandon as the Chairman and Managing Director. Accordingly, the Department of Banking submitted a note to the Appointments Committee of the Cabinet on May 30, 1975 seeking the Appointments Committee of the Cabinet's approval to O.P. Gupta's appointment as Chairman and Managing Director of the Punjab National Bank for a period of one year with effect from August 1, 1975. When the matter was still pending before the Appointments Commitee of the Cabinet, the then Additional Secretary, M.G. Balasubramaniam, in the Department of Banking minuted as under on July 15, 1975 :

> The file has been returned from P.M.'s office for submission of revised proposals. I have spoken to Governor, R.B.I.

Further he recorded the following note on July 21, 1975 :

I enquired of the Governor when I met him in Calcutta
on 19th July, 1975 about R.B.I.'s Report to us regarding Government's proposal to appoint Shri T.R. Tuli
of New Bank of India as Chairman, Punjab National
Bank about which I had spoken to him over the phone
on 15th July, 1975. Governor told me that he was
under the impression that I would be writing to him
about this to enable R.B.I. to send a reply. When I
told him that my understanding was different, he
promised to write to me after he reaches Bombay on
21st evening.

The Chairman and Managing Director is to be appointed by Government after consultation with RBI and
RBI has been consulted. Please put up this file for
F.M.'s orders *today itself* whether he should send a
revised note to A.C.C. or issue the orders and inform
the E.C. to keep the A.C.C. appraised.

It is seen from this minute that the Government had by
then decided to appoint T.R. Tuli of New Bank of India as
Chairman of Punjab National Bank. The consultation with
the Reserve Bank, at any rate was on July 21, 1975 and could
only have been oral because the written response of the
Governor, Reserve Bank, which is quoted below is contained
in his letter dated July 22, 1975 :

As desired by you, I made enquiries about Shri T.R.
Tuli, at present Chairman of the New Bank of India.
Shri Tuli's date of birth is 1st October, 1913. He
has thus completed 61 years. He is a matriculate.
However, he has done very good work in the New
Bank with which he has been associated practically
since its inception. The growth of the Bank is due to
a considerable extent to his dynamism and leadership.
Whether he would do equally well when he goes to a far
bigger Bank with a regular hierarchy is a matter for
consideration. He looks fit for the new assignment but
he will necessarily have to adapt himself to a greater
degree of decentralization and delegation than to what
he has been accustomed to so far in his personally run
bank.

Dr. Hazari was consulted and he has no objection to the proposed appointment.

It would appear from this letter that the Reserve Bank was not very happy with this choice.

On July 21, 1975 a note was recorded by D.M. Suthankar, the then Director in the Department of Banking seeking the then Finance Minister's orders, inter alia, as to whether a notification appointing T.R. Tuli as Chairman and Managing Director may be issued straightaway and the Establishment Officer requested to keep the Appointments Committee of the Cabinet apprised or whether a revised note may be sent to the Appointments Committee of the Cabinet for obtaining their approval to the revised proposal.

The then Finance Minister minuted on July 22, 1975 that Tuli may be appointed straightaway for a period of one year and sought the then Prime Minister's approval to this. The then Prime Minister approved the proposal on July 24, 1975 and Tuli accordingly was appointed Chairman and Managing Director of Punjab National Bank vide notification dated July 31, 1975 issued in this regard. Thereafter, M.G. Balasubramaniam the then Additional Secretary in the Department of Banking wrote as under to U.C. Agarwal, Establishment Officer, who functions as the Secretary to the Appointments Committee of the Cabinet:

> Please refer to our Note for the Appointments Committee of the Cabinet regarding the appointment of a new incumbent in the place of Shri P.L. Tandon, former Chairman and Managing Director, Punjab National Bank; sent to you vide this Department' O.M. of even number dated May 31, 1975.
>
> It has since been decided with the approval of the Prime Minister to appoint Shri T.R. Tuli (Chairman, New Bank of India Ltd.), as the Chairman and Managing Director of Punjab National Bank, for a period of one year with effect from August 1, 1975, on a salary of Rs. 3500/- per month in the approved scale of Rs. 3,500-125-4,000 Home Minister has also been kept suitably informed by Finance Minister's office.

The relevant Government notifications have already
been issued on July 31, 1975, copies of which have been
separately endorsed to you. Perhaps, you may consider
recording the information suitably in the office of the
Appointments Committee of the Cabinet.

VII—NATIONAL HERALD

Associated Journals Limited, a Company publishing three dailies namely *National Herald, Nav Jivan* and *Quomi Aawaz*, imported printing machinery for its Lucknow Unit on deferred payment basis guaranteed by Vijaya Bank Ltd. It required funds to the extent of Rs. 10 lakhs for payment of Customs duty and demurrage.

In March 1976, P.C. Sethi, the then Minister of Chemicals and Fertilisers summoned T.R. Tuli, the then Chairman of Punjab National Bank. Subsequent events narrated by Tul are :

I was Chairman of Punjab National Bank from 1st August, 1975 to 31st July, 1977.

In early March 1976 I was called by Shri P.C. Sethi, the then Minister of Petroleum & Chemicals at his residence and asked to help Associated Journals Limited by advancing money to enable them to take delivery of the machinery lying at Bombay Port on payment of the custom duty and demurrage charges. Thereafter, Col. B.H. Zaidi, Chairman and Managing Director, Associated Journals Ltd. and his accountant met me in the office two-three times to explain the requirements and also suggested that the amount now being advanced would be paid off from the term loan of Rs. 15 lakhs to be later advanced by the bank against the security of mortgage of building known as 'Herald House' on Bahadur Shah Zafar Marg, New Delhi.

Since *National Herald* published by Associated Journals Ltd. was connected with the then Prime Minister, it must have weighed a little at my mind to deal with the case on the priority basis expeditiously.

Thereafter the Company addressed a letter to the Manager, Parliament Street Branch of the Bank as under :

We are separately submitting the proposal directly to your Head Office for a term loan of Rs. 15 lakhs against mortgage of our building known as "Herald House" situated at 5-A, Bahadurshah Zafar Marg, New Delhi, to be repaid by us over a period of 5 years which has been principally agreed to by your Head Office authorities. Pending sanction and disbursement of this loan to us you are requested to allow us an overdraft of Rs. 9,00,000/- in our current account and remit Rs. 10,00,000/- to the Vijaya Bank Ltd., Connaught Circus, behind Rivoli Cinema, New Delhi for payment of custom duty of Rs. 7,00,000/- and demurrage of Rs, 3,00,000/- direct by them in respect of machinery which has been imported by us under deferred payment guarantee (schedule attached) furnished by them on our behalf. Cheque for Rs. 1,70,000/- on R.B.I. deposited today in our account with you.

This letter was jointly signed by Col. Zaidi and Dhan Singh, Chairman and Managing Director and Accountant respectively of the Company.

L.D. Adlakha, Regional Manager, Maharashtra and Goa, who was at that time Branch Manager of Parliament Street Branch of the Bank states inter alia as under in his affidavit before the Commission :

I was Manager of Parliament Street, New Delhi Branch of Punjab National Bank from February 1976 to September, 1976.

T.R. Tuli, the then Chairman of the Punjab National Bank called me in his chamber sometime in the month of March 1976 and introduced me to Col. B.H. Zaidi, the then Chairman and Managing Director of Associated Journals Ltd. Tuli told me that

Associated Journals Ltd. wanted to have a Term-loan of Rs. 15 lakhs against mortgage of building known as "Herald House" situated at Bahadurshah Zafar Marg, New Delhi. He told me that the party had to make immediate payment of customs duty and demurrage charges for the machinery imported through Vijaya Bank on deferred payment basis. He, therefore, directed me to grant a clean overdraft of Rs. 8.3 lakhs and the balance amount of Rs. 1,70,000/- would be paid by the party itself by depositing a cheque in the account to be opened with the Branch. The debtor party opened a current account with the Bank on 20th March, 1976. A cheque of Rs. 10 lakhs was issued by the Bank on 22nd March, in favour of Vijaya Bank Ltd. resulting in a net clean overdraft of Rs. 8,29,500/- after the adjustment of cash and cheque deposits totalling Rs. 1,70,500/- by the party.

Associated Journals Ltd. was a new account with the Branch and before granting the temporary clean overdraft I had no occasion to assess the financial or other credit worthiness of the party, as is required to be done in all such cases. This was because I acted under the instructions of Shri T.R. Tuli, former Chairman. It was not within my power to grant such a clean overdraft. During my entire career of 34 years in the Bank I never granted clean overdraft of such an amount without any security or margin. However, my action was confirmed by the Board in its meeting dated the 14th June, 76.

As per the understanding with the Associated Journals Ltd., the clean overdraft was to be adjusted and secured against the mortgage of "Herald House" as per Company's letter dated 20.3.1976 and received by me on 22nd March, 1976.

Adlakha sent a letter dated April 8, 1976 to Head Office for confirmation of his action of granting a clean overdraft of Rs. 8,30,000/- which reads as under :

Re : Associated Journals Ltd.

Paid-up capital   Rs. 51,64,480

Reserves & Surplus   Rs. Nil
Accumulated Losses   Rs. 47,45,995. 36
Loss for the year   Rs. 8,00,457.34

(As per B/S as at 31.3.1975)

The above named company publishes a daily newspaper *National Herald*. It imported printing machinery for its Lucknow unit through Vijaya Bank Limited on deferred payment basis and was in urgent need of financial assistance to pay for Customs Duty and demurrage amounting to Rs. 10 lakhs to get the machinery cleared. We, therefore, at the Company's request and under approval of our worthy Chairman, permitted a clean overdraft of Rs.8,30,000/- on 22.3. 1976 to meet the aforesaid expenditure. The balance amount of Rs.1,30,000/- has been met by the company from its own resources.

The company proposes to raise a Term Loan of Rs. 15 lakhs from us against mortgage of its building known as 'HERALD HOUSE' on Bahadurshah Zafar Marg, New Delhi out of which the aforesaid clean overdraft of Rs. 8,30,000/- together with interest thereon is to be adjusted. The company has been requested to furnish to us the information required for compilation of the proposal for a Term Loan of Rs. 15 lakhs which is awaited.

A copy of the Company's Balance-Sheet as at 31.3.1975 together with a list of Directors is enclosed.

Pending submission of the proposal for a Term-Loan of Rs. 15 lakhs and its consideration by the authorities, we request that our action in allowing a clean overdraft of Rs. 8,30,000/- as aforesaid, may kindly be confirmed.

Developments after submitting above proposals are stated by Adlakha in his statement as under :

That on being asked by the Bank to put up a proposal for a term loan of Rs. 15 lakhs the debtor party informed the Bank, vide its letter dated 26th April, 1976 that "due to some technical difficulties we are not in a position to offer the Herald House as security. Hence we are arranging to repay the said sum within a short period." It further informed us that "Remission Committee of the Bombay Port Trust had sanctioned Rs. 3,21,229.62 against the total demurrage of Rs. 6,50, 854.62 paid by us on 81 cases of Volga Rotary Machine. The said amount would be deposited with the Bank when it is received.

That Associated Journals Ltd., however, did not deposit this amount inspite of our writing many letters to them and till I remained the Manager of Parliament Street, New Delhi Branch, the said party did not repay the amount to the Bank nor was any payment made by them towards interest. On our asking for repayment of our dues the party informed us that they are negotiating with Syndicate Bank, Inderprastha Branch and the said Bank is sanctioning a term loan to them against the second mortgage of "Herald House." Then, immediately we wrote to Syndicate Bank to know whether such a loan is being sanctioned by them to Associated Journals Ltd. and in reply Syndicate Bank wrote back to us as per their letter No. 5854/253/ General dated 16.6.1976 that sanction of loan to the above party is being considered by them.

Syndicate Bank, vide their letter No.6570/253/General dated August 16, 1976 informed us that the request of the company for term loan has not been considered by their Head Office due to tight resources position of the Bank. On our again writing to the party for repayment of our dues and showing Syndicate Bank's letter, the party informed us that they are still negotiating with Syndicate Bank and are hopeful to get the term loan of Rs. 10 lakhs sanctioned from their Head Office. Syndiate Bank also informed us vide their letter No. 6933/253/ General dated September 23, 1976 that "a Term Loan to liquidate the liabilities of Rs.8,30,000/- with Punjab National Bank has been sanctioned to the above Company." Further they informed that they are shortly arranging the loan and remit the proceeds to liquidate the said loan with Punjab National Bank.

In the meanwhile, Central Intelligence Section of Credit Administration of Punjab National Bank analysed the financial position of Associated Journals Limited and states as under in its report dated April 16, 1976 :

> Reg : *Analytical Assesssment of financial position of the Company as per Balance Sheet as at 31. 3. 1975.*

The Company publishes a daily newspaper entitled *"National Herald"*. As at 31. 3. 75 it has an authorised capital of Rs. 1.00 crores, divided into 50,000 Pref. shares of Rs. 100/- each and 5.00 lakhs Equity Shares of Rs. 10/- each. As at the same date its Paid-Up Capital stood at Rs. 51.64 lakhs and Reserves & Surplus amounted to Rs. 6.77 lakhs.

While Revenue from circulation (1974-75 Rs. 43.15 lakhs, 1973-74 Rs. 32.99 lakhs) and Sales of Newsprint etc. (1974-75 Rs.3.27 lakhs, 1973-74 Rs. 2.43 lakhs) have gone up by Rs. 10.16 lakhs and Rs. 0.84 lakhs respectively. The revenue from advertisements (1974-75 Rs. 669.52 lakhs, 1973-74 Rs. 72.48 lakhs) has come down by Rs. 2.96 lakhs as compared to the previous year. The company has incurred a heavier loss of Rs. 10.63 lakhs in the year 1974-75 against a loss of Rs. 9.33 lakhs suffered in the year 1973-74.

It is reported that the financial results have been adverse due to :

(a)   abnormal scarcity of newsprint & its exhorbitant prices,

(b)   reduction in newsprint quota, and

(c)   increase in wage bill

The working of the company for the period under report cannot be considered as satisfactory.

Deferred Liabilities (including gratuity Rs. 15.66 lakhs) aggregate to Rs. 28.62 lakhs against Net Worth of Rs. 10.95 lakhs. The Debit Equity ratio works out to 1 : 0.38 and cannot be considered as satisfactory.

As at 31.3.75 the accumulated losses stand at a figure of Rs. 47.46 lakhs against paid-up Capital (Rs. 51.64

lakhs) and Reserves & Surplus (Rs. 6.77 lakhs) aggregating to Rs. 58.41 lakhs. This shows that not only
the whole of Reserves & Surplus stands wiped off, but
Paid-up Capital to the extent of Rs. 40.69 lakhs also
stands eroded.

Current Assets aggregate to Rs. 71.76 lakhs against
Current Liabilities of Rs. 65.68 lakhs, leaving thereby
a sum of Rs. 6.08 lakhs for Working Capital requirements. The ratio of Current Liabilities to Current
Assets works out to 1 : 1.09 against 1 : 1.31 in the
previous year and cannot be considered as entirely
satisfactory. To augment its liquid resources, the
Company raised unsecured loans of Rs. 10.47 lakhs by
way of Deposits from its Agents and the public.

A note was also prepared by Assistant General Manager on
June 5, 1976 which reads as under :

*Regarding Associated Journals Limited—B O Parlia-
ment Street New Delhi*

Paid up	51.64
Reserves & Surplus	6.77
Misc. Exp. & Losses	47.46

(B/S as at 31.3.75)

	31.3.75	31.4.74 (Rs. lakhs)
Circulation Revenue	43.15	32.99
Advertisement revenue	69.52	72.48
Sale of newsprint etc.	3.27	2.43
	115.94	107.90
Losses	10.63	9.33

The above company publishes a daily newspaper *Natio-
nal Herald.* It had discussions with the Manager, B.
O. Parliament Street, New Delhi and indicated an in-
tention to apply to our bank for raising a Term-loan of
Rs. 15 lakhs against mortgage of its building "Herald
House" on Bahadurshah Zafar Marg, New Delhi.

It had imported printing machinery for its Lucknow
unit through Vijaya Bank Ltd. on deferred payment

basis. In order to pay customs duty and demurrage amounting to Rs. 10 lacs, the company had requested for financial assistance to that extent. The Branch Manager states that with your approval he was permitted a clean overdraft of Rs. 8.30 lacs on 22.3.76 to the company to enable them to meet the aforesaid expenditure. The balance of Rs. 1.30 lacs has been met by the company from its own resources.

At the time of requesting for the loan of Rs, 8.30 lacs the company had proposed to return this amount out of the proceeds of the proposed Term-loan of Rs. 15 lacs against their property 'HERALD HOUSE'.

The company, after sometime, informed the Branch Manager that due to some technical difficulties they were not in a position to offer the said property as security and had stated that they were arranging to repay our loan of Rs. 8.30 lacs within a very short period. They also informed that they were expecting a payment of Rs. 3.21 lacs from the Bombay Port Trust being the amount remitted by the Remission Committee of the B.P.T. out of demurrage of Rs. 6.51 lacs paid by the company on machine and that the said amount would be deposited with our bank on receipt, in their loan account. The said amount has not yet been deposited in their account.

The ccmpany has now intimated that they were negotiating with Syndicate Bank I.P. Estate, New Delhi for raising a loan against renewal of II mortgage charge on the building, and that they are hopeful of getting the loan very shortly. As soon as the loan is sanctioned from that bank they shall pay our dues. We may put up the matter to the Board for confirmation.

Sd/-K. C. Mehra
Asstt. General Manager 'C'

This note along with report of Credit Administration Section dated April 16, 1976 was put up before Tuli, the then Chairman on June 7, 1976. Tuli saw it on the same day with the comment "Board" presumably directing that it be put up before the Board of Directors for approval. However, these papers were not included in the original agenda despatched on June 7, 1976, for the Board's meeting to be held at Srinagar on June, 12 and 14, 1976. Additional items received by the Board Department after the despatch of the original agenda are, as per Bank's normal practice, sent to the directors as supplementary items. However, in this case the matter relating to approval of the loan to the Company was only placed on Board's table on June 14, 1976. It would appear, therefore, that the directors could not have had adequate time to study the proposal especially in the light of the report of the Control Intelligence Section of Credit Administration Section.

It may be stated here that the Regional Manager of the Bank had expressed concern in his letters dated 12.5.76 and 15.6.76 which read as under:—

Inter-Office

Ref : 3/PSND/A: SRS
DT. MAY 12, 1976

Shri L. D. Adhlakha,
Manager,
B.O. Parliament Street, New Delhi.

REG : Monthly statement of irregular OD a/cs as on 30.4.1976

On going through the above statement we observe that M/s Associated Journals Ltd. have been allowed clean overdraft facility to the extent of Rs. 8,29,500/- on 20.3.76. Please let us know the circumstances under which clean overdraft facility has been allowed to this party to such a great extent. Also get your action confirmed for allowing this facility much beyond your personal loaning powers from our Loans Section and get the account adjusted as early as possible.

Sd/-Illegible
Manager

Inter-Office

The Manager,
Parliament Street,   1 PSND/L/1817
New Delhi

Ref :   Your endorsement dated 27.5.76 on letter
        addressed to M/s Associated Journals Ltd.—

Reg :   A/c M/s Associated Journals Limited—Clean
        Overdraft of Rs. 8.30 lakhs.

While referring to your letter dated 31.5.76 we note
the borrowers are now negotiating with the Syndicate
Bank for sanction of Term-loan. This is likely to take
some time, and meanwhile, clean overdraft of 8.30 lakhs
cannot be allowed to outstand indefinitely. You are,
as such, requested to call on the officials of the
company personally to work out suitable repayment
programme which should be submitted to us for
approval. Meanwhile, concerted efforts should be
made to effect recovery of bank dues.

We would like to know whether the sum of Rs. 3,25,
229.62 has been received from the company towards
reduction of indebtedness to the Bank, as stated in
your letter dated 27.5.76.

Sd/-
Regional Manager

It is clear from Adlakha's affidavit referred to above that
the sum of Rs. 3,25,229.62 was not deposited by the Company,
contrary to the undertaking made by them in this regard.

Coming to the Syndicate Bank it is seen that they had
originally turned down the proposal of the Company for
granting a Term Loan against mortgage of Herald House
stating that "the request of the company for a term loan has
not been considered by our Head Office due to tight resources
position of the Bank".

Thereafter, Mohamed Yunus Special Envoy to Indira
Gandhi, the then Prime Minister and Managing Director of
the Company wrote to the Head Office of Syndicate Bank and
also appears to have spoken to the Regional Development
Manager of Syndicate Bank at New Delhi, who thereupon
sent the following Telex message to Head Office.

To Sri HN Rao General Manager KHO

From Sri PSV Mallya R D M ND

Reg : Associated Journals Limited—I P Estate Branch Please Refer to letter 20th August of Mohd. Yunus, Managing Director of the Company who Incidentally is a Special Envoy of the Prime Minister Stop You May Kindly Reconsider Your Decision in view of the Facts Explained by Mohd. Yunus Stop

:::: R D M ND ::::

Thereupon Head Office of the Syndicate Bank sanctioned Term Loan of Rs. 9.40 lakhs on September 20, 1976. The loan was on the security of a sound second mortgage of the land and building sof the Company and was subject, inter-alia, to the condition that all the directors of the company should guarantee the loan in their individual capacity.

It is significant to add that the Term Loan to the Company by the Syndicate Bank has not so far materialised.

M/s R.K. Khanna & Company, Chartered Accountants, who audited the accounts of the Punjab National Bank for the relevant period wrote to the Chief, Credit Administration of the Bank vide their letter dated April 18, 1977 that:

Ref : Loan of Associated Journals Ltd. Branch Parliament Street.

The branch auditors have suggested that the loan of Rs. 9.24 lakhs be classified as "Bad & Doubtful Debts". After considering all the facts we feel that provision for full amount should be made. As such please make the necessary provision.

The sum of Rs. 9.24 lakhs referred to above is made up of the principal sum of Rs. 8.30 lakhs and interest upto 31.12.76. It is seen from the statement of account furnished by the Bank that the balance outstanding in this account, after giving credit for Rs. 20,000/- paid by the Company towards interest is Rs. 10,23,507. 90p. as on Oct. 31, 1977.

It has further been confirmed by the Head Office of the Bank, after a scrutiny of all overdraft facility cases of Rs. 55 lakhs and above allowed by them, that there was no other case, where a party new to the Bank was granted a clean overdraft facility without any security during the period under review.

VIII—KRSMA CHEMICALS

KRSMA Chemicals Private Limited (hereinafter referred to as the Company) was incorporated as a Company on the 23rd day of October 1975. The balance sheet of the company as on August 31, 1976 shows that the authorised, issued and paid up capital of the company stood at Rs. 4 lakhs. S.P. Mehta and Rajinder Paul, Directors of the Company, held one share of Rs. 100/- each and the other shares were held by Sat Mehta (brother of Om Mehta, the then Minister of State in the Ministry of Home Affairs) and B. L. Kohli, both of whom are sons-in-law of S. P. Mehta, since deceased.

S. P. Mehta and one other person called on T. R. Tuli some time in September 1976. What transpired next is given below in Tuli's words :

> Sometime towards the close of September 1976, Shri Kumar, Personal Assistant of Shri Pranab Mukherjee, the then Minister of Revenue and Banking, came to me with Shri S. P. Mehta, Director of KRSMA Chemicals Pvt. Ltd. Shri Kumar introduced Shri Mehta as the father-in-law of Shri Sat Mehta, brother of Shri Om Mehta, the then Minister of State for Home Affairs. Shri Kumar further requested me to get three Foreign Letters of Credit opened without any margin on behalf of KRSMA Chemicals Pvt. Ltd. as the company was holding import licence. Since the party was related to Shri Om Mehta and was brought by Shri Kumar, I asked the Regional Manager Shri D. P. Nayyar, who incidentally happened to be at the Head Office, to get the needful done expeditiously.

I had no occasion to assess the financial soundness of the company or its directors except that the directors were highly connected and as per Shri Kumar, they were very well experienced in the line.

D. P. Nayyar accordingly accompanied the two gentlemen to the office of K. N. Vali, the then Branch Manager of the Parliament Street Branch of the Bank. The events thereafter as narrated by Vali are :

I took over as Manager of Parliament Street Branch on 16.9.1976.

In the last week of September 1976, Shri D. P. Nayyar Regional Manager of Delhi Region came to my office with two gentlemen one of them was introduced to me as Shri S. P. Mehta, Director, KRSMA Chemicals Pvt. Ltd. Shri Nayyar told me that these two gentlemen had met Shri T. R. Tuli, the then Chairman. Shri Nayyar informed me that Shri Tuli had instructed him to take Shri Mehta and the other gentleman to me and asked to open three Foreign Letters of Credit without any margin in favour of KRSMA Chemicals Pvt. Ltd. Shri S. S. Jolly, Manager (Foreign Exchange) of the Branch was also present when Shri Nayyar conveyed directions of Shri T· R. Tuli to this effect.

Shri S. P. Mehta then gave me a letter of 28.9.76 which inter-alia stated that "as already sanctioned by your Chairman we are enclosing herewith three applications for opening letters of credit by cable without margin of unit Tochi."

The letter coupled with oral instructions of Chairman conveyed by Shri D. P. Nayyar, Regional Manager to me constituted approval of the Head Office. Accordingly, three Foreign Letters of Credit of the value of Rs. 9.30 lakhs were opened by cable on behalf of the company in the branch.

At the time of opening of three foreign letters of credit, the borrower company, nor any Director had any previous dealings with our branch. Neither I knew Shri Surinder Paul Mehta nor the other director. I had no previous knowledge about the financial standing of KRSMA Chemicals Pvt. Ltd.

The normal procedure followed by the Bank in case of
any prospective borrower is to take a loan application
in the prescribed form accompanied by the statement
of assets and liabilities and previous experience, on
the basis of which the proposal is appraised by the
Branch after ascertaining the credit worthiness of the
borrower and the viability of the proposal. Unless
the bank is satisfied about the credit worthiness of the
borrower and the viability of the project no foreign
letter of credit is opened without any margin. All
this procedure takes a period of two to three weeks to
get the proposal compiled, processed and sanctioned
by higher authorities.

In the case of KRSMA Chemicals Pvt. Ltd. normal
procedure was not followed as I was under the instructions from Shri Nayyar, Regional Manager, immediately to establish three foreign letters of credit amounting to Rs. 9.30 lakhs without any margin and then to
send the case to him for confirmation.

I may also state here that the party was having business activities at a place which falls within the command area of our Faridabad Office. But for the aforesaid exceptional circumstances the proposal should
have normally emanated from Faridabad Branch.

During the course of conversation with me, Shri S.P.
Mehta, Director of the Company, disclosed that he was
a close relation of Shri Om Mehta, the then Minister
of State for Home Affairs and intimate friend of Shri
Pranab Mukherjee, the then Minister of Revenue and
Banking.

Shri S.S. Jolly, Manager, Foreign Exchange, of the
Branch was also incidentally present, when Shri Mehta
spoke of his connections and friendship with Shri
Mehta and Pranab Mukherjee respectively.

This is corroborated by S.S. Jolly, Manager (Foreign
Exchange Department) of Parliament Street Branch of the
Bank, who has stated as under :

I am posted as Manager (Foreign Exchange Department) in Parliament Street Branch since January 1975.

Shri Nayyar also instructed me to see that no inconvenience was caused to any of these gentlemen and the work was done expeditiously.

Since the instructions of the Chairman were conveyed by Shri Nayyar, Regional Manager, a note was prepared by my Section for establishment of three Foreign Letters of Credit totalling to Rs. 9.30 lakhs, wherein it was inter-alia stated that "the transaction reportedly carries the approval of the Chairman. Loan Section shall be advised to send a regular case to R.M. for confirmation after the Letters of Credit were established." My Section carried out the instructions of the Chairman expeditiously and three Foreign Letters of Credit were opened next day by cable.

On October 11, 1976, K.N. Vali addressed a letter to the Regional Manager, which inter-alia stated :

We have already opened 3 L/Cs aggregating Rs. 9,30,000/- without margin for the import of chemicals under your instructions. This may please be confirmed.

Subsequent developments as per Vali's statement are as under :

Later the documents covering the imported goods under the two foreign Letters of Credit were received on 10.12.1976 and 20th December, 1976 which the party failed to retire. Thereafter notices were served upon the party for retirement of the documents and the payment of the bank dues. The party showed its inability to retire them on the plea of credit squeeze in the market. It first came forward with a proposal to deposit 20 per cent margin if the bank agreed to take delivery of all goods by paying custom duty, demurrage and other charges. To our surprise, the party backed out from its own proposal and came forward with a request to reduce the margin from 20 per cent to 10 per cent. Even this commitment was not honoured. Shri S.P. Mehta vide his letter dated 1.4.77 offered to deposit Title Deeds of a house property purchased for Rs. 2.20 lakhs by way of equitable mortgage in lieu of margin. This property did not stand in his name and as such he backed out from his commitment.

KRSMA Chemicals Pvt. Ltd. appears to have run into serious financial trouble which is evident from the testimony of Rajinder Paul, Director (since resigned on September 23, 1977). Paul in his statement inter-alia stated :

> Returns of sales tax for the quarter ending 31st March and 30th June 1977 were filed by me without depositing dues of the Sales Tax Department. I was reminding Shri S.P. Mehta frequently, practically every week for providing the funds to enable me to deposit money to the Sales Tax Department. Non-payment of sales tax dues was causing me anxiety and embarrassment as I was being reminded by the authorities concerned time and again.

> In the month of July/August 1977, I came to know from the market that Asian Paints Ltd. had instituted a criminal case against S.P. Mehta for non-payment of their dues. I was very upset to know about this and when I asked him as to why dues of Asian Paints had not been settled, he told me that Dr. Reddy owed him some money and this amount was to be adjusted against the payment of Asian Paints. He further told me that since Dr. Reddy is not traceable, he has not settled their accounts. The above developments caused me embarrassment, anxiety and uneasiness and I tendered my resignation from the Directorship of the Company.

The Bank was thus left with no option but to take delivery of goods, which is clear from the further part of Vali's statement:

> Under the circumstances by the party, there was no option left for the bank but to safeguard its own money by taking delivery of the goods by making payment of custom duty, demurrage etc., totalling to Rs. 9.15 Lakhs and to keep the stock in its own possession.

> The average cost of the N.C. Cotton and MEK imported under licences covered by the aforesaid two foreign

letters of credit comes to Rs. 34.60 and Rs. 14.40 per kg respectively. The prevailing prices of N.C. Cotton & MEK according to the market quotations available are around Rs. 25 and Rs. 11.50 per kg respectively. As the position stands today, the bank is likely to suffer a loss of about Rs. 4.5 lakhs in this transaction. During my career of over 30 years of service in Bank, I never allowed any such letter of credit facility without margin in my personal power.

Thus, it is seen that the decision to open letters of credit without margin and without following normal procedures and safeguards, has caused a loss of about Rs. 4.5 lakhs to the Punjab National Bank.

IX—MARUTI LIMITED

Maruti Limited is a Company incorporated under the Companies Act, 1956, on the fourth day of June, 1971. The Company applied in 1971 to the Punjab National Bank for certain cash credit and other facilities. At that time, the paid up share capital of the company was Rs. 3 lakhs apart from the share application money of Rs. 12.65 lakhs. On January 6, 1972, the Bank allowed a Inland Letter of Credit-cum-Fixed Loan facility of Rs. 30 lakhs only to the Company on the hypothecation of tool room plant, machines and equipment, subject to various terms and conditions which included stipulation that the facility should be guaranteed by at least two of the Company Directors, one of whom must be either M. A. Chidambaram or V. R. Mohan.

In May, 1974, Maruti Limited enjoyed two cash credit facilities of Rs. 30 lakhs and Rs. 60 lakhs respectively from Punjab National Bank subject inter-alia to the stipulation that total outstanding should not exceed Rs. 75 lakhs at any one time. This stipulation was, however, removed in March 1975. With this, the Company's total limit amounted to Rs. 90 lakhs but additional limit of Rs. 15 lakhs was only meant as a bridging facility for a period of six months only or till proposed public issue of shares in the Company, whichever was earlier.

Thus when T. R. Tuli took over as Chairman and Managing Director of the Punjab National Bank in August 1975, Maruti Limited already enjoyed the total facility of Rs. 90 lakhs subject to the stipulation that the additional facility of Rs. 15 lakhs would be withdrawn at the end of the period of six months referred to above. It is seen from the statement furnished by the Bank that cash credit account for Rs. 30 lakhs started becoming irregular from May 1974 and the cash credit account for Rs. 60 lakhs became irregular from October of the same year. The Bank had been asking the company from time to time to regularise its accounts.

In accordance with its normal practice in dealing with irregular accounts, the Bank started charging penal interest on the cash credit accounts to the extent to which they were in excess of the allowed limits.

After protracted correspondence Maruti Limited wrote to the Chairman of the Punjab National Bank on September 15, 1976, with reference to the discussions which J. K. Pahuja of the Company had with the Bank. In that letter the Company wrote that it had incurred heavy losses, mainly due to interest cost and requested the Bank to waive the penal interest and also to reduce the rate of interest to the maximum extent possible. In their turn the Company agreed to regularise the accounts by making a lump sum payment of Rs. 5 lakhs and monthly remittances of the order of Rs. 1 lakh. Based on this the then Assistant General Manager (Credit) wrote a note recommending to the Board that :

penal interest amounting to Rs. 67, 272.17 P. already charged in the accounts may be refunded and that it may be waived for the future.

the rate of interest may be reduced from $15\frac{1}{2}$ per cent to 14 per cent per annum.

This recommendation was endorsed by his superior officers and submitted to the Board of which Tuli was Chairman, and approved by the Board at its meeting held on October 6, 1976. The concession in interest of $1\frac{1}{2}$ per cent per annum allowed to the Company from 1.10.1976 to 31.3.1977 amounted to Rs. 70, 347.65 P.

It is further seen that the Company failed to keep up its commitment regarding recurring payments of Rs. 1 lakh each for and from April 1977, and that, accordingly, the refund of penal interest allowed has been recovered on May 31, 1977. The facility of the concessional interest rate was also withdrawn on the same day.

Justice Shah	: *Do you know why you were selected . . .?*
Former Chairman	: *No.*
T. R. Tuli	
Justice Shah	: *As a banker of 40 years experience is it advisable to lend monies to a company without security?*
T. R. Tuli	: *I did not have a look at their balance sheet*
Justice Shah	: *Why not . . . You would be unfit to be a banker . . . .*
	Is it true that P. C. Sethi called you . . . ?
T. R. Tuli	: *He said please help them . . .*
Justice Shah	: *Ministers ask you . . . ?*
T. R. Tuli	: *Yes and that is a big consideration. When the Minister says . . . it has to be done.*
Justice Shah	: *Have you met Sanjay Gandhi?*
T. R. Tuli	: *I met him in connection with Maruti . . . .*
Justice Shah	: *Is it true that soon after your appointment you went over to the P.M.'s house to thank him for the appointment?*
T. R. Tuli	: *No . . . Not him . . .*
Justice Shah	: *Do you know that the records show that you visited the PM's house on 21 occasions? How many times did you see the Finance Minister . . . ?*
T. R. Tuli	: *You mean Mr. Subramaniam . . . once to thank him.*
Justice Shah	: *Mr. P. K. Mookerjee . . .?*
T. R Tuli	: *8 to 10 times.*
Counsel Kandalawala	: *As far as you are concerned . . . you did not have a scrap of paper before you gave 10 lacs . . .*
T. R. Tuli	: *It was a Bridging loan . . . Banks give a lot of them.*
Khandalawala	: *Yes . . . over which no bridges have been built.*
	It seems you have a predilection for ministerial authority.
	. . . In Shakespearean language . . .
	To be in the Punjab National Bank or not to be in the Punjab National Bank.
T. R. Tuli	: *I don't follow it . . . I am only a matriculate.*

X—INTERNATIONAL AIRPORTS AUTHORITY OF INDIA

The post of Chairman, International Airports Authority of India, fell vacant w.e.f. October 1, 1975 consequent to the completion of tenure by Air Marshal Y.V. Malse. B.S. Das, whole time Member, IAAI, was appointed to look after the current duties of the post of Chairman in addition to this own duties, pending the selection of a regular Chairman. In order to fill the post, the Ministry was on the look out for the selection of an internal candidate. Therefore, they confined enquiry to the two Dy. Managing Directors of the Indian Airlines, senior officers working in the IAAI as also in the Directorate of Civil Aviation and the Department of Tourism.

The Ministry forwarded to the Public Enterprises Selection Board the names of B. S. Das, Member, IAAI, B. S. Gidwani, Addl. Director General of Tourism, and A. K. Sarkar, Dy Director General Civil Aviation. The matter was considered by the PESB at its meeting held on December 4, 1975. After considering the suitability of the candidate possessing the requisite qualifiations, the PESB short listed the following five persons for further assessment of their candidates.

1. B. S. Das, Acting Chairman, International Airport Authority of India, New Delhi.

2. A. K. Sarkar, Dy Director General of Civil Aviation, New Delhi.

3. Air Marshal H.C. Dewan, Vice Chief Air Staff, New Delhi.

4. Air Marshal H Moolgavkar, Air Officer Commanding in-Chief, Western Command.

5. B. S. Gidwani, Additional Director General of Tourism.

The Board recommended B. S. Das, as the most suitable person for the appointment as Chairman, IAAI. The recommendation of the PESB was accepted by the then Minister for Tourism and Civil Aviation and the Establishment Officer was approached on December 24, 1974 to seek the approval of the Appointments Committee of the Cabinet for the appointment of B. S. Das, as Chairman, IAAI. While seeking the approval of the ACC for appointment of Das, the Ministry sent only his CR dossiers and particulars of none of the other candidates considered by the PESB were forwarded.

For no apparent valid reasons and deviating from the procedure of selection of officers for top level executive post in the Public Sector Undertakings on the recommendation of the PESB, the Appointment Committee of the Cabinet chose to disagree with the recommendation of the PESB and did not approve the proposal to the appointment of B.S. Das as Chairman.

Instead the Committee desired that Air Marshal H. C. Dewan be appointed to the post. Air Marshal H. C. Dewan had been interviewed by the PESB but not found suitable. His selection came as a surprise to the Ministry and the Secretary, Ministry of Tourism and Civil Aviation recorded that "evidently there is a disparity of criteria as between PESB, and ACC, because the former had interviewed Air Marshal Dewan but not recommended him." The then Minister of Tourism and Civil Aviation, Raj Bahadur, however, chose to ignore the Secretary's noting and desired that the decision of the ACC should be complied with.

XI—INDIA TOURISM DEVELOPMENT CORPORATION

The post of Chairman-cum-Managing Director of India Tourism and Development Corporation fell vacant consequent on the expiry of the contract of M.S. Sundara on April 14, 1976 As desired by the Minister of Tourism and Civil Avation, the public Enterprises Selection Board was requested to recommend suitable names for the post of Chairman-cum-MD of ITDC. According to Resolution No. 5(1)/74 of Bureau of Public Enterprises dated August 5, 1974 the Board will have the responsibility for selecting persons for appointment against the top level appointments—viz. Part time Chairman, Full time Chairman and Managing Directors for all Public Sector Corporations, including recommendations for extending the terms of an existing incumbent. According to this Resolution, no such appointment extension will be made save on the Board's recommendations.

The PESB met on July 25, 1976 and after considering the suitability of Lt. Gen. J.T. Satarawala, R. Krishnan, Maj. Gen. R.D.R Anand, M.L. Gaind, V.B. Khanna, B.S. Das and Ajit Singh, the Board recommended the following persons in the order given, as suitable for the post of Chairman-cum-MD, ITDC,—

(1) Ajit Singh
(2) B.S. Das

The recommendation of the PESB was conveyed to the Ministry on August 9, 1976. Accordingly, a draft letter requesting the Establishment Officer to obtain the approval of the Appoitments Committee of the Cabinet to the appointment of Ajit Singh as Chairman-cum-MD of ITDC was prepared by the Ministry and put up to the Secretary and the Minister before issue. The Secretary N.K. Mukherji agreed to the proposal and marked the file to Minister for approval. The Minister, Raj Bahadur desired that "the Minister of State may also see the proposal first."

The Minister of State Surindra Pal Singh disagreed with the proposal and mentioned that Lt. Gen. J.T. Satarawala would be the best choice. He stated that in his opinion to bring out a change at the top most level in ITDC at that particular juncture would be detrimental to the national interest. Disregarding the age factor the Minister of State commented that Lt. Gen. Satarawala is in very good physical condition and is quite capable of shouldering the onerous and heavy responsibility of looking after the affairs of the ITDC.

The Minister Raj Bahadur, agreed with the Minister for State's assessment of the matter and proposed Gen. Satarawala's name for the post. Accordingly, a revised draft was prepared urgently and the matter was dealt with by a Joint Secy. in the absence of the Secretary who was on tour on August 19, 1976. The Appointments Committee of the Cabinet approved the appointment of Gen. Satarawala who had been consi dered by the PSEB but not recommended for appointment.

XII—AIR INDIA AND INDIAN AIRLINES CORPORATION

It has been alleged in a statement filed by N.S. Bhatnagar then special assistant to Raj Bahadur, that on February 9, 1976 he received a telephone call from R.K. Dhawan, Additional Private Secretary to the then Prime Minister who gave him a list of names for the two Boards which should be recommended to the Appointments Committee of the Cabinet. Bhatnagar has alleged in his statements that Dhawan informed Bhatnagar that the names have been suggested by the former Prime Minister and also that he should not mention these names to N.K. Mukherji, Secretary of the Ministry at that time.

The list of names allegedly suggested by Dhawan for the two Boards was different from the original proposal of the Ministry of Tourism and Civil Aviation. In the case of Air-India, the names of S.Y. Ranade and K.G. Appuswamy had been dropped and instead the names of Air Chief Marshal H. Moolgavkar, Air Marshal H. C Dewan, M. S. Sundra, and S.K. Kooka had been added. For the Board of Indian Airlines the list as allegedly "dictated" by Dhawan was also different from that of the original Ministry recommendation as it replaced S. Y Ranade and V. Satyamurty with four other names which were Air Chief Marshal Moolgavkar. M. S. Sundra, Air Marshal Dewan and Captain A. M. Kapoor.

...Dhawan advised Bhatnagar to send the proposal under his own signature when told that the Minister was away on tour. When Bhatnagar reportedly protested that he was not competent to do so, Mr Dhawan "gave vent to his anger". However, as Mr Raj Bahadur returned the same evening the incident was reported to him by Mr Bhatnagar and Mr Raj Bahadur sent a fresh proposal for the reconstitution

of the two Boards under his own signature directly
to the then Prime Minister on February 10, 1976.
The new proposal had all the names allegedly "dictated" by Mr Dhawan.

The former Prime Minister gave her approval the
same evening. It has also been alleged that the new
proposal contained the names of some non-officials
—Air Chief Marshal Mehra and Mr Kooka in the
case of Air-India and Air Chief Marshal Mehra for
Indian Airlines. It has also been stated that Captain
Kapoor was junior to Mr Satyamurthy who had been
dropped.

. . .It has been alleged that the Ministry did not
consult the PESB nor the chairmen of the two Boards
before finalizing the proposal. It has also been noted
that instead of sending the proposal to the Establishment Officer it was sent directly to the Prime Minister,
bypassing the Appointments Committee of the
Cabinet.

. . .The approved names were notified on February
13, 1976 and on the same day the Establishment
Officer was requested to get the formal approval of the
Appointments Committee. This was communicated by
the Establishment Officer on February 27, 1976.

Air Chief Marshal Lal is reported to have protested
against the dropping of Mr Satyamurthy and the
inclusion of Captain Kapoor without prior consultion
with him to Mr Raj Bahadur. According to a statement made by Air Chief Marshal Lal, the Minister
seemed to be under considerable strain and said that
he was simply passing on instructions received from
the Prime Minister's household and that Mr Dhawan's
name was mentioned.

Air Chief Marshal Lal said that he resigned soon after the
new boards of Indian Airlines and Air India were announced.
The resignation was not accepted and instead he was asked to
go on leave. Later, his services were "terminated but I have
not yet received the termination order." He was asked to hand
over charge to A.H. Mehta.

XIII—THE BOEING DEAL

In connection with the proposal for augmentation of capacity in the Indian Airlines a special group was constituted "to study in depth operational capabilities, financial terms and economics of the aircraft available in the market and recommend the most suitable aircraft fleet composition and programme of induction" during the period of October 1976 to March 1979. The Committee dealt with the technical details, airport constraints and financial evaluation of the various types of aircraft viz., BAC-111 (84 seats), F-28 (80 seats) and Boeing-737 (126 seats). While F-27 and BAC-111 were subjected to proving flights on IA's selected routes to obtain first hand technical knowledge and operational performance figures, Boeing 737 was considered on the basis of technical data supplied by the manufacturers but without any route testing.

The report of the Committee was placed before the IA Board and in its meeting held on August 16, 1976, the Board considered an item styled 'Aircraft evalution study—to meet the demand on certain selected routes'. The Board decided that an Interline Committee consisting of Joint Secretary (Finance), Ministry of Tourism and Civil Aviation and the Managing Directors of Air India and Indian Airlines should study these proposals.

The Interline Committee had not finalised its views yet when on the morning of October 29, 1976, P.N. Dhar, the then Secretary to the Prime Minister Indira Gandhi spoke to N.K. Mukherji, the then Aviation Secretary, on telephone to say that "it was the then Prime Minister's impression that the Ministry of Tourism and Civil Aviation was obstructing the purchase of Boeing 737 aircraft by Indian Airlines." As per a reply prepared by N.K. Mukherji, P.N. Dhar asked the following two points:

(i) Was a proposal about purchase of aircraft by Indian Airlines pending with the Ministry, and if so, was its
consideration being unduly held up?

(ii) If was true that Boeing's offer carried a dead line for the
end of October, 1976 and would there be advantage in
availing of the concessions offered by issuing a letter of
intent by October 30?

After checking the facts available with the Ministry N.K.
Mukherji sent a reply, in writing, to P.N. Dhar on the same day
i.e., October 29, 1976, to the effect that there was no proposal
about purchase of aircraft by Indian Airlines pending with the
Ministry and that the Board of Directors of IA did consider
an item styled "Aircraft evaluation study—to meet demand on
certain selected routes" on August 16, 1976 and the matter was
referred to the sub-committee, which was expected to finalise its
view shortly. Regarding the dead-line of Boeing offer, it was
pointed out to P.N. Dhar "that the Minister took a meeting this
morning, in which it was decided to extend the dead-line up to
December 31, 1976, as this would give enough time for the
proposal to be processed through all stages, including PIB and
Cabinet.

On the same day i.e. October 29, 1976, N.K. Mukherji was sent
for by Raj Bahadur, the then Minister for Civil Aviation. A.H.
Mehta, Acting Chairman of Indian Airlines and Kripal Chand,
Director (Finance), Indian Airlines were already in the Minister's
room when Mukherji and his two Joint Secretaries entered the
room. According to Mukherji, the Minister enquired about the
progress made in processing the proposal of Indian Airlines
for purchase of 3 Boeing 737 aircraft. Mukherji explained
to him that in fact, there was no such proposal before the
Government, and that a proposal had been submitted by the
Management of Indian Airlines to its Board of Directors and
the Board had referred it to an Inter-line Committee for detailed examination and that it was premature to state that there
was any proposal pending in the Ministry of Tourism and
Civil Aviation.

A.H. Mehta said that as the latest offer from Boeing Company
was to expire on November 1, 1976 it was urgent that a letter of
intent be placed on the manufacturers before that date in order

that escalation in quoted costs should not arise. "Raj Bahadur also urged that a decision should be taken in this respect as quickly as possible."

N.K. Mukherji has stated that "while the discussion was taking place in the room of Raj Bahadur, a telephone call came and Raj Bahadur was heard to remark 'Yes, Dhawan Sahib, I am going into the matter with my officers who are with me.'"

Pending the receipt of the recommendations of the Interline Committee and the final decision of the IA Boards, the IA Management sent a letter on October 10, 1976 requesting for Permission to issue a letter of intent to the Boeing Company in respect of purchase of three Boeing-737 aircraft. In fact, as stated by N.K. Mukherjee, this letter was handed over at a meeting convened on October 30, 1976 in his room. The meeting was attended by representatives of Indian Airlines, Ministry of Finance and Planning Commission. After discussion it was agreed that the requisite letter of intent may be issued subject to the condition that it did not involve any commitment for purchase of aircraft. It was also decided that IA should request the other manufacturers to extend their respective deadlines upto the end of December 1976, but if they declined to do so, similar letter of intent may be issued to them also.

Kripal Chand, Director (Finance), Indian Airlines, has stated that sometime in the beginning of Oct. 1976 when he happened to be with the then Chairman and Managing Director, discussing with him certain points, discussed in the Interline Committee Meetings, Capt. A.M. Kapoor, Director of Operations had rung up A.H. Mehta and later on accompanied by Rajiv Gandhi came to the office of A.H. Mehta. "During their discussion a reference was also made to some aspects of the Boeing 737 aircraft". As far as Kripal Chand recollects, A.H. Mehta and Capt. Kapoor described the operational and technical superiority of the Boeing 737 aircraft. A.H. Mehta also mentioned that Boeing 737 aircraft was more economical. Mehta asked Kripal Chand to show the financial projections to Rajiv Gandhi.

On October 5, 1976, a Secret Note was prepared by Director CBI, D. Sen, regarding some allegations of corruption in respect of A.H. Mehta, the then acting Chairman of Indian Airlines. It is not known from the file as to what action was taken on this note. However, subsequently, on November 11, 1976 D. Sen, sent another note which opened with the following sentence: "I had intimated sometime back that as a result of confidential enquiry there appeared to be some truth in the following allegations against A.H. Mehta of the IAC". This note dated November 12, 1976 was marked to R.K. Dhawan P.S. to the then Prime Minister.

The Indian Airlines sent the proposal for purchase of three Boeing 737 to the Ministry on November 20, 1976. Subsequently, the Airlines Board at its meeting held on November 24, 1976 approved the action of the management in seeking Government's approval for purchase of the aircraft. The proposal, was however, opposed by A.C.M. O.P. Mehra on the ground that it was not based on any system study.

Kripal Chand has stated that they were all "upset at the decision of the PIB to defer the augmentation of capacity pending completion of the Total System study". According to him, after returning from the meeting, when they all went to the office of the Chairman and Managing Director to discuss further action A.H. Mehta remarked to the effect that "you technocrats have not been able to get the aircraft for me. Now I will get them for you".

N.K. Mukherjee has stated that "the then Minister for Tourism and Civil Aviation, K. Raghuramaiah, had more than once desired verbally that the case relating to the purchase of Boeing 737 aircraft for Indian Airlines should be processed urgently. On one occasion, he suggested that if I (N.K. Mukherji) felt any difficulty in dealing with the case, I could ask the Joint Secretary to submit the file direct to him (the Minister)". Mukherji assured the Minister that the case would be processed as quickly as possible and that he would find no difficulty in dealing with it when submitting the file to the Minister.

Raghuramaiah has stated that a few days after he took over as Minister of Tourism and Civil Aviation on Dec. 24, 1976 when he happened to go to the then Prime Minister's house to see the then Prime Minister Indira Gandhi in connection with some Parliamentary Affairs matter, R.K. Dhawan told him that there was a Boeing Purchase file which was being delayed in the Ministry and that he should look into it. According to

Raghuramaiah his "long association with the then Prime Minister and her method of functioning had convinced him that whenever Shri R.K. Dhawan said something it was as good as the then Prime Minister's saying so".

On receipt of PIB's recommendations N.K. Mukherji advised the Minister that these should be accepted. The noting on the file had brought out the point that, as informally advised by the Ministry of Finance, there had not been any case where an administrative Ministry had gone to the Cabinet for a decision against the recommendation of the PIB. However, the Minister overruled the Secretary's advice and directed that the matter may be immediately referred to the Cabinet recommending purchase of three Boeing 737 aircraft for Indian Airlines.

Kripal Chand has stated that in the absence of A.H. Mehta, who had gone abroad, he was "called to meet the Minister on a number of occasions when he required information with regard to certain matters regarding the dates upto which the offer of the Boeing Company was valid and a brief justification for the purchase of the three Boeing 737 aircraft". On February 8, 1977 the Minister called Kripal Chand and told him that the proposal had been finally cleared by the Cabinet. The Minister also instructed A.S Bhatnagar, Joint Secretary, Aviation, "to ensure that the formal approval was communicated to the Corporation the same day and the contract was signed immediately".

The Ministry's sanction for purchase of three Boeing 737 aircraft at a total project cost of Rs. 30.55 crores was issued to the Indian Airlines on the same day i.e. February 8, 1977 and was delivered to Kripal Chand by hand on the same day. In the sanction, it was mentioned inter alia that Indian Airlines should further negotiate with the sellers and try to obtain the best possible terms for the three aircraft. According to C.L. Dhingra, Deputy Secretary, Civil Aviation, the intention was to associate Joint Secretary (Finance) in the Ministry with the negotiating team. Even before the Ministry could inform Indian Airlines that Joint Secretary (Finance) will be the representative on the negotiating team, the Indian Airlines informed the Ministry, that they had signed the contract with the company on February 9, 1977 i.e., the day after the issue of the sanction and had obtained a further discount of $15,000 per aircraft. The Joint Secretary (Finance) was thus not associated with the negotiations with the Boeing Company.

It may be noted here that delivery schedule limit given by the Boeing Company expired on Feb. 7, 1977. On Feb. 7, 1977 Kripal Chand who under the instructions of the Minister had discussed the question of extension of dates of the offer for the sale of the aircraft with the representatives of Boeing Company had recorded a note to the effect that the representative of Boeing Company "categorically informed him that any further extension of dates was not possible". The position on Feb. 7, 1977 was that the delivery schedule was held firm upto Feb. 7, 1977 and price and concessions upto Feb. 15, 1977. The contract with the Boeing Company was signed by Indian Airlines on Feb. 9, 1977 even when the delivery schedule limit given by the Boeing Company had expired on Feb. 7, 1977.

XIV—DELHI TRANSPORT CORPORATION

U.S. Shrivastuv, IAS (UT-1960) was the Director of Transport, Delhi Administration and Member of the DTC on March 1, 1976. M. Ramkrishnayya, Secretary, Ministry of Shipping and Transport recorded a note on March 2, 1976 stating that the Minister of State informed him that the Lt. Governor, Delhi, rang him up requesting him to notify immediately U.S. Shrivastuv who was then Director of Transport, Delhi Administration, as Chairman DTC in place of A.N. Chawla. The Lt. Governor also said that this appointment had been cleared by the Prime Minister. The Secretary in his note to the Establishment Officer (E.O.) of Department of Personnel gave a background of the DTC and pointed out that "it is not clear whether the proposal to appoint Shri U.S. Shrivastuv as Chairman, DTC, is on a permanent footing or only on a temporary basis pending the selection of the competent Chairman and General Manager in accordance with the usual procedure in consultation with the PESB". The Secretary also pointed out that U.S. Shrivastuv was a junior officer only of a Director's rank and that the two representatives of the government on the DTC Board were of the rank of Joint Secretary and therefore some changes will have to be made in case U.S. Shrivastuv was appointed as Chairman of the DTC. The Secretary in his note had requested the E.O. for the orders of the ACC and the Prime Minister. The then Transport Minister G.S. Dhillon was out of station. He returned from tour the very next day— March 3, 1976, and in a note recorded on the office copy of the Secretary's note to the Department of Personnel took strong exception to the procedure adopted and the undue haste shown in the matter. In fact he wrote the following DO letter to the Prime Minister on March 4, 1976 :—

Confidential

March 4, 1976

My dear Prime Minister,

When I returned from a short tour yesterday evening, I saw a note to the ACC dated 2. 3. 1976 proposing the appointment of Shri U.S. Shrivastuv (IAS-UT-1960) at present Director of Transport, Delhi Administration, as Chairman of the Delhi Transport Corporation, in place of Shri A.N. Chawla. This note had been sent with the approval of the Minister of State in my Ministry, as the Lt. Governor, Delhi, had insisted that the notification of the appointment should be made immediately without waiting for my return in the head quarters the very next day. The Lt. Governor had also stated that the proposal had already been cleared by you. I am surprised at the procedure adopted by the Lt. Governor. I am not aware of the reasons for this kind of urgency. I have been unable to appreciate the manner in which the Lt. Governor mooted this proposal and obtained your clearance as stated by him without even mentioning to me. You know very well that I consult you on all important matters particularly before making formal proposals for sensitive appointments. I wish I was taken into confidence on this matter directly. You are aware of my views on such matters. I feel that the interest of good administration will be best served by following as far as possible correct and proper procedure leaving little scope for any type of criticism. Now that the proposal must have already reached you as the Chairman of the ACC, I request I may be allowed to discuss with you before final orders are passed.

            With kind regards,

                                  Your sincerely,
                                        Sd/—
                                  (G.S. Dhillon)

Shrimati Indira Gandhi,
Prime Minister of India,
NEW DELHI

Thereafter on May 15, 1976 the Transport Minister again recorded a note for the Prime Minister recalling his discussions with her regarding Chairmanship of the DTC in the first week of April 1976 just before his departure for the Inter-Parliamentary Union Meeting in Mexico. He also added that his proposal for combining the posts of the Chairman and the General Manager of the DTC appeared to meet her approval and that such an appointment should be in consultation with the PESB. In this letter, he also suggested three names which were in view including that of U.S. Shrivastuv but added that the Bureau of Public Enterprises may have some more names and that he proposed to ask the PESB to consider the names and send the Ministry a panel urgently for further action.

While on the one hand correspondence was going on from the Minister to the Prime Minister on the lines indicated above, the file initiated by the Secretary of the Department on March 2, 1976 in the absence of the Minister and marked to the ACC took the following course. On the ACC file on March 2, 1976 itself, the EO recorded a long note pointing out that there was a proposal to revise the scale of the Chairman to the level of Rs. 2500-3000 and that if the intention is to appoint Shrivastuv on a regular basis, the proposal may present the following difficulties:

i) Shri Shrivastuv is an officer of 1960 year of allotment. At present he is drawing pay in Selection Grade of the IAS. Officers of his seniority are not yet eligible to hold posts at the level of Joint Secretary under the Government of India. He would thus be junior to hold a post which may carry the scale of Rs. 2500-2700 or Rs. 2500-3000;

ii) The post of Vice-Chairman is already in the scale of Rs. 2500-2700 and may have to be kept unfilled or filled up at lower level;

iii) The post of Additional General Manager and Financial Adviser presently held by an officer of 1954 year of allotment from the Railway will have to be filled by a junior officer;

iv) The Board of Directors of the DTC at present have Government of India nominees of the level of

Joint Secretary. Shri Shrivastuv being of the rank of Director only, some changes may have to be made in the Government representatives.

The EO also proposed that in case the arrangement is to be a regular one, it would be desirable to combine the post of Chairman with the Managing Director and since the appointment would be in a public sector undertaking, it could be given a regular scale and

> if he is finally approved by the Public Enterprise Selection Board for appointment to this post on long term basis and Shri Shrivastuv also opts for permanent absorption in the undertaking.

The Cabinet Secretary has signed it on the same day namely March 2, 1976. The Home Minister K. Brahmananda Reddy has recorded

> I have no objection to the name but he seems to be only of a Director's rank. The rank may not matter as it is felt by the Lt. Governor that he is fit. However, PM may decide.

In PM's Secretariat, B.N. Tandon, Joint Secretary recorded the following internal note on March 19, 1976:

> On the advice of the Lt. Governor, Delhi, the Ministry of Shipping and Transport proposes to appoint Shri U.S. Shrivastuv, IAS (UT-1960) as Chairman DTC, in place of Shri A.N. Chawla. It is seen from the file that LG has obtained PM's clearance to the proposal.

EO has pointed out certain functional difficulties in the proposal arising out of the fact that U.S. Shrivastuv does not have the requisite seniority to be eligible for a post equivalent to that of a Joint Secretary. HM also has minuted as follows :

> I have no objection to the name but he seems to be only of a Director's rank. The rank may not matter as it is felt by LG that he is fit. However, PM may decide.

LG has presumably made this proposal in view of Shri U.S. Shrivastuv's long experience in the field of transport. EO himself has pointed out in his note that if the proposed arrangement is on a long-term basis it would be desirable to combine the post of Chairman with the Managing Director and considering Shri Shrivastuv's seniority he may be appointed to the combined post on a fixed salary of Rs. 2500/- p.m. He may be given a regular scale if he is finally approved by PESB for appointment to this post and he opts for permanent absorption in the undertaking.

It is understood that Shrivastuv is willing to be absorbed in this undertaking. He should, therefore, be screened by the PESB.

Indira Gandhi, the then Prime Minister recorded the following note on the internal file on June 3, 1976.

The Minister spoke to me yesterday and suggested that Shrivastuv be appointed.

Sd/- Indira Gandhi
3. 6. 1976

The Prime Minister has minuted as follows on June 3, 1976 on the ACC file :

Shri Shrivastuv has had long experience in transport and should therefore be appointed. His pay and conditions may be decided in consultation with the concerned department.

On the other hand on June 4, 1976, the Minister in the concerned file of the Ministry recorded a note :

I discussed this case with Prime Minister on 2.6.1976. She has approved the appointment of Shri U.S. Shrivastuv IAS (UT-1960) as wholetime Chairman of the DTC. This is to be notified immediately and ACC be informed.

The ACC was informed on June 5, 1976, the same date on which the notification appointing U.S. Shrivastuv as Chairman of the Corporation was issued.

3 Gallantry in the Land . . . of the Blessed Son

Yadav, Malik, Walia, Bhambri, Rangaraja, Chatterjee, Ghosh, Gupta, Venkatesh, Chakravorty, Jain and Mukherjee sound like common Indian names ranging from the Himalayas to Kanyakumari, but what about ANAND? Particularly when it happens to be AMTESH-WAR ANAND (mother-in-law of Sanjay Gandhi)—that we will soon get to know! Her husband knew it, but then he also knew when to die.

Krishnaswamy, Rajan, Cavle and Bhatnagar however, did not know the name M.A.R.U.T.I. also spells "May All Rules Upto Today be Inverted". They were asked to collect information on Maruti for a question in Parliament and they seriously went about their business of doing just that—only the result was shocking!

Justices Aggarwal and Lalit, Kishore Kumar, Sachar, Sewak Ram, Vishnu Dutt, Sinha, Sharma, Sahni, Chadha, Prabhatkar, Shah, Fateh Singh Gaekward, Bajaj, Tata, Godrej, John, J.P., Gayatri Devi, Rajmata of Gwalior are known names, but by any chance do they know the name Indira? Evidently not, since all of them learnt the real meaning of the name the hard way!

Sharma, Gaur, Mangal Bihari however were simple folk unable to understand the vagaries of the minds of people holding the reins of power. Nonconformity had become an ugly word and as the events unfold—it came to be nondescript too!

XV—INDIRA INTERNATIONAL

D.B. Ghosh, A.K. Chakravorty, R.C. Jain, S.K. Walia, R. Rangaraja, R.S. Gupta, C.S. Venkatesh, V.B. Bhambri and Asutosh Mukherjee were working as Inspectors in the Regional Office of Textile Committee Delhi during April-May 1976. S. N. Chatterjee was the Asstt. Inspecting Officer in the same office. The Inspectors working in the Textile Committee Office were required to inspect the textile materials meant for export. The intending exporters of cotton garments are required to obtain from the Textile Committee a certificate to the effect that the fabric from which the garments were made was mill-made or handloom. The Textile Committee is required to ensure that no garments which are made out of mill-made cloth are mis-declared as made from handloom fabric. During the same period, Sumer Singh Yadav and M.S. Malik were working as Custom Inspectors at Palam Airport and they used to deal with exports. Their duty included enforcing Export Trade Control Restrictions in the matter of exports and also ensuring that correct rates of 'draw back' are granted to the exporters. 'Draw back' is a refund of central excise duty to the exporter when the goods are exported out of the country, the rate varying depending on the incidence of duty on the item or raw material.

 S.S. Yadav has alleged that on April 22, 1976, he was directed by his Superintendent to draw samples from the consignment of 20 packages belonging to a firm, M/s Indira International, for determining whether the garments were actually of mill-made cloth as claimed by the exporter or of power-loom cloth. The shipping bills of these packages had already been examined on April 21, 1976 by M.S. Malik, the other Inspector, but the Superintendent doubting the declaration that the garments were made out of mill-made cloth, for drawback purposes, had not allowed the consignment to be exported on April 21, 1976 and had desired that the samples be shown on the next day. Representative samples were drawn by Yadav in whose opinion the samples were of power-loom cloth and the exporter had mis-declared the goods for obtaining illegal benefit of drawback which was @ 3.5% of FOB value on mill-made cotton garments and 1.6% of FOB value for power-loom cotton garments.

The clearing agents M/s Lee & Muirhead were asked to produce definite proof by showing mill cuttings of the cloth to substantiate the claim as was the prevailing practice. The clearing agents had no mill cuttings with them and they were asked to get in touch with the exporter for producing the same. S.K. Kapoor, the representative of the clearing agents, went out of the warehouse premises to contact the exporter and came back after a few minutes to inform that mill cuttings were not available. There was a heated altercation between Yadav and Kapoor. Yadav tried to explain to the clearing agent that M/s Indira International was cheating the Government by claiming higher rate of drawback by mis-declaring that the garments were made out of mill-cloth, though actually these were made out of power-loom cloth, and that the law required that the consignment should be seized.

The Manager of the Clearing Agents, Harish and two other representatives of the firm who had arrived at the scene started threatening Yadav with dire consequences. The Custom Officers were threatened that the consignment belonged to the mother-in-law of Sanjay Gandhi, son of the then Prime Minister, Indira Gandhi, and that "the officers will have to pay the price for the hold up of the consignment". The Customs authorities were overawed to the extent that the consignment was allowed to be exported without any action.

R.D. Bhatnagar, another Inspector in the Textile Committee, who had gone to M/s Indira International in connection with inspection, found Smt. Doddy, one of the proprietors of the firm, much annoyed and who allegedly threatened that if the shipments were rejected or delayed by the officers, she would see that drastic action was taken against the officers.

Sometime in the last week of May 1976, S.C. Suri, Inspecting Officer in the Textile Committee office received a telephone call from N.K. Singh, Special Assistant to the former Commerce Minister, requiring Suri to furnish within 30 minutes the addresses and date of posting of all the inspecting staff in the Textile Committee. N.K. Singh's orders were complied with immediately and the list was sent to him. N.K. Singh had earlier called Suri in his office and told him that the lots for export offered for inspection by Oriental Enterprise, a New Delhi firm of which Vinay Gupta was the proprietor, should be passed without any objection.

According to the statement of A.P. Mukherjee, DIG/CBI, sometime towards the end of May 1976, P.S. Bhinder, then DIG Delhi Police, informed him that he had received some information from the Prime Minister's house about corruption and harassment by some officers of the Excise/Customs/Export Promotion Council in the matter of export of garments by various exporters. Bhinder was informed that the Delhi Branch of CBI had no such information about corruption but Mukherjee checked up with other Units of CBI located in Delhi and finding that none of them had any information on the subject, he detailed a few officers to collect information about the system of inspection of garments meant for export, names of officers known to be indulging in corrupt practices, etc.

It appears that simultaneously Bhinder had also asked S.P. Anti-Corruption, Delhi Administration, to collect similar information and in this connection Ved Prakash, Inspector, Anti-Corruption Branch visited the office of the Textile Committee in Karol Bagh and made certain enquiries. He did not prepare any note in writing and passed on the information collected by him orally to his S.P., who, in turn, informed Bhinder. The team of officers detailed by A.P. Mukherjee, DIG/CBI, started collecting information on the lines suggested by him; but it appears that the Delhi Police did not have the patience to wait for the information which was being collected by the CBI team to ascertain the names of officers who were indulging in corrupt practices and A.P. Mukherjee was surprised to learn from his officers that a large number of employees belonging to the Textile Committee and Customs Department who were connected with clearance of garments for export had been detained by Delhi Police while his systematic collection of information regarding corruption was still continuing. In view of the fact that Delhi Police had already taken unilateral action the CBI officers were instructed by Mukherjee not to proceed further in the matter.

Delhi Police struck in the first week of June 1976. The concerned Superintendents of Police were supplied the names of the officers of the Textile Committee/Customs by Bhinder who ordered their immediate arrest and detention under MISA because they were indulging in corrupt practices and anti-Government activities. The SPs were also informed that the District Magistrate would give instructions to the concerned ADMs for issuing the detention orders under MISA, and that meantime "in accordance with the prevalent practice" the officers should be arrested under the preventive sections of the Criminal Procedure Code so that they did not evade arrest by going underground. The SPs passed on the orders to their SHOs after confirming with the concerned ADMs and the arrests followed.

Customs Inspectors Yadav and Malik were picked up from their office in the afternoon of June 1, 1976 by the Police on some false pretext and locked up. Textile Inspectors Walia, Bhambri, Rangaraja and Asstt. Inspecting Officer Chatterjee, were whisked away from their home in the late hours of the night on the same day. The other Inspectors Ghosh, Gupta, Venkatesh, Chakravorty, Jain and Mukherjee were arrested subsequently at the convenience of the police between June 2-5, 1976.

All these officers were initially arrested under the preventive sections of Criminal Procedure Code (108/151) on false and fabricated allegations. Inspector Yadav and Inspector Malik who were arrested from their office premises were alleged to have raised slogans protesting against the Emergency and plotting to overthrow the Government. Inspector Bhambri was charged with instigating the people against the Government in a public speech allegedly made at 5.30 in the morning on June 2, 1976 in Ajmal Khan Park, while actually he was picked up from his house, earlier at 12.30 at night and locked up at the police station. The other Inspectors were also arrested on similar false allegations.

All these respectable Government officers were handcuffed by the police while being taken to the Court or to the Jail. Some of them were made to travel in the public buses where

they were seen by the general public. After a mechanical production before the Magistrate where none of them was given a
hearing or permitted bail etc., they were sent to Tihar Jail.
Within a few days of their arrest the detention orders under
MISA were duly served on them at Tihar Jail. The grounds of
detention in the MISA orders in respect of the Textile Committee officers were that "in the course of inspection of textile
material meant for export the officers were showing undue
favour to the exporters by stamping the sub-standard textile
for export to foreign countries which is bringing bad name to
the country" and also that the officers "have been indulging in
malpractices and acting against the national interest". In
respect of the Customs Officers the grounds of detention were
that they were "conducting themselves in a manner prejudicial
to the maintenance of public order while working as Inspectors
in the Air Cargo Unit of Palam Airport." The charges under
Sections 108/151 Cr. P.C. on the basis of which these officers
were initially arrested were subsequently dropped in view of
their detention under MISA.

The authorities in power did not appear to have been satisfied with the mere detention of these officers under MISA.
The CBI was brought into the picture probably with a view to
justify their detention under MISA and to make cases of disproportionate assets against them. On June 8, 1976, the CBI
Director, D. Sen asked Y. Rajpal, DD-Intelligence, to get in
touch with Bhinder and arrange interrogation of the detenus in
Tihar Jail in order to collect intelligence regarding their corrupt activities. As per orders of D. Sen, the interrogation of
the arrested officers of Textile Committee/Customs was done
by CBI officers with the assistance of Inspector Ved Parkash of
Delhi Police, who was directed to do so under orders of
Bhinder.

According to Rajpal, the interrogation did not reveal anything specific against the officers who had been arrested. On
the other hand, it indicated that the Inspecting Officer S.C.
Suri, who, as mentioned earlier, had supplied the names of
officers of the Textile Committee to N.K. Singh, had formed a
coterie with a few favourite Inspectors and that the relations
between them and the arrested officers were not cordial. A
meeting was held in the room of D. Sen on June 11, 1976 where

Y. Rajpal and P.S. Bhinder were present. On enquiry from D. Sen, Bhinder informed him: "We are hundred percent convinced that these officers are corrupt though no documentary evidence is available". Y. Rajpal was asked to collect further evidence regarding the corrupt activities of the officers by keeping a watch. Y. Rajpal specifically asked D. Sen the usefulness of the watch since the suspects were already in jail, but Sen wanted the watch to be mounted to find out which persons came to meet the relatives of the arrested persons. Rajpal was also told that the cases would be registered in Delhi Branch after the intelligence enquiry was over. It was obvious that Sen had made up his mind to register cases against a few of these officers and Y. Rajpal recorded a note on the file to this effect on June 11, 1976 itself.

The SP of the Intelligence Unit was ordered to prepare a report on the enquiries so that cases could be registered in the Delhi Branch and searches taken as ordered by Director C.B.I. The S.P., R.K. Gupta, discussed the matter with A.B. Chaudhari, Joint Director, and a list of four officers was prepared, who on the basis of the interrogation conducted in Tihar Jail, had admitted having some moveable/immovable property. Nobody cared to verify whether possession of these properties amounted to disproportionate assests.

The orders to register cases immediately and follow it up by searches were conveyed to DIG CBI Delhi Branch on June 19, 1976. In accordance with these orders, cases of disproportionate assets under P.C. Act were registered against S.N. Chatterjee, Asutosh Mukherjee, Sumer Singh Yadav and M.S. Malik. While these persons were in jail, the CBI officers conducted searches of their residences in their absence.

In the case of M.S. Malik, after conducting the search of his residence, the CBI officers searched the house of his son-in-law also. Mrs. Mukerjee wife of Inspector A. Mukerjee was bedridden with a serious illness when the CBI party raided her residence.

It may be noted that while cases of disproportionate assets were registered against these four officers without any worthwhile verification, Director CBI did not agree to register cases against S.C. Suri and R.D. Bhatnagar against whom the Intelligence Unit had collected sufficient material and recommended registration of cases. On July 29, 1976, Y. Rajpal recorded a note to the effect that "sufficient evidence has been collected to register at least a PE for open enquiries" against Suri and Bhatnagar. The Joint Director A.B. Chaudhari suggested that "regular case should be registered against these two officers in Delhi Branch and searches will have to be conducted in these cases." The Director CBI asked Chaudhari to discuss the matter with him on August 8, 1976 and expressed the opinion that "the material available is not enough for registration of a case at this stage". The DD (I) was asked to continue the watch and submit further report. The verification continued and on October 27, 1976 the SP again recommended that a regular case should be registered against Suri. But, ultimately, it was decided that Suri and Bhatnagar should be reported to the Department for such necessary action as may be deemed fit by them. It may be recalled that it was S.C. Suri who had supplied the names of the Textile Comittee employees to N.K. Singh, the then Special Assistant to the Commerce Minister, before Delhi Police detained them under MISA.

At the time of their arrests or subsequently the officers had no knowledge whatsoever as to the real reasons why they had been arrested and detained under MISA. Their wives and relations were helplessly running from pillar to post to ascertain the reasons for their detention and also for seeking help in getting them released. These helpless ladies knocked at the doors of Krishan Chand, Lt. Governor Delhi, D.P. Chattopadhyaya, Minister for Commerce, N.K. Singh, the Minister's Special Assistant and other powerful personages. The reception they received from N.K. Singh was not too pleasant. It is significant that most of the ladies were under the impression that N.K. Singh was aware of the facts leading to their husbands' arrest.

Om Wati Yadav, wife of Custom Inspector Yadav, solicited the help of Qadam Singh, a resident of Gurgaon, in getting her husband released. Qadam Singh met Bhinder who informed him that he was helpless in the matter since the detention had been ordered by the ADM. When Qadam Singh met the ADM, he advised him to see Bhinder. Qadam Singh went to

Bhinder again who told him that "no person other than Sanjay Gandhi could help in the matter since Yadav had annoyed him by raising objections in consignment of garments exported by his mother-in-law." Qadam Singh could not meet Sanjay Gandhi there but when no help was forthcoming from any other quarter, he picked up courage and with the help of a Security Guard met Sanjay Gandhi in Maruti Factory and pleaded with him to take pity on the family of Yadav. Sanjay Gandhi enquired the particulars of the detenu and when told that he was the Custom Inspector working at Palam Airport, contemptuously remarked that "he needed to be taught a lesson."

Om Wati had also contacted another family friend, Surinder Mohan Vohra, an Inspector of Central Excise posted at Palam, and entreated him to use his good offices with Bhinder to get her husband released. Bhinder had come in contact with Inspector Vohra while he was posted as SSP Gurgaon, in connection with clearance of unaccompanied baggage of his wife who had been coming from abroad a few times during the year 1975-76. Vohra met Bhinder in his office and on his persistent requests for help in the matter, Bhinder told him that only Sanjay Gandhi could help because he was annoyed over the objection made by Yadav in respect of consignments of exports by his mother-in-law.

The wives of the detenus sent representations to the Prime Minister, the Home Minister, the Minister for State for Home Affairs and others. The representations were processed in the Ministry of Home Affairs, and it was felt by the MHA that the detenus being Government servants, the use of MISA for their detention for alleged corrupt practices was not covered by the law. In the case of Inspector A. Mukherjee, the Joint Secretary MHA, R.L. Misra, felt that it was "yet another case of abuse of MISA by the Delhi Administration, and if the detenu was guilty of any lapse in his performance of official duties, truly the concerned Ministry would be better informed about the same and least that could have been done was to consult the Ministry of Commerce before taking any action". It was also felt that "most likely the charge against Mukherjee was fabricated." The detention of Inspector Man Singh was also considered as "a gross misuse of MISA," and it was felt that the Government servant had been arrested without any cogent reasons.

On the representation of Rangaraja also it was pointed out that detention of Government servant under MISA for corruption is not valid and that it appeared "very doubtful whether the report received by the Delhi Administration in this regard was correct". In yet another case, that of Inspector D.B. Ghosh, R.L. Misra pointed out that "the Delhi Administration be advised to take suitable action against those responsible for misuse of emergency powers". All these representations were dealt with at the highest level in the Ministry of Home Affairs and the orders of K. Brahmananda Reddy, the then Home Minister, were obtained before Delhi Administration was advised to revoke the detention orders.

However, the L.G. Delhi Krishan Chand did not appear to be keen to comply with the instructions of the MHA. Whenever the case of a Textile Inspector was put up to him he would simply say that he had made up his mind that they were not to be released and that the Delhi Administration need not bother the about MHA's letters as he would take care of those. When the Home Secretary, Delhi Administration pointed out to him that the MHA had written letters asking the revocation, the L.G. did not appreciate this sort of advice and used to say sharply the responsibility was his and only his. When the detention orders of Inspector S.K. Walia were revoked by the L.G. on the advice of MHA on September 4, 1976, a note about another similar case was submitted for his orders but he ordered that in view of the identical nature of the grounds of detention in all these cases, it would be desirable to have them reviewed through the Screening Committee instead of taking up cases individually. Accordingly, the cases of Textile Inspectors were placed before the Screening Commeittee in its meeting held on November 16, 1976. When these came up for consideration before the committee P.S. Bhinder told the L.G. that he would like to speak to him about these cases in camera. Thereupon, both the L.G. and Bhinder went inside and returned after a couple of minutes when the L.G. said that these cases need not be reviewed for the present. In the proceedings of the meeting, however, it was recorded that the committee did not recommend revocation of detention in respect of the officers concerned.

Affidavit of Sumer Singh Yadav :

During my posting at Palam Airport the various duties and functions which I was obliged to perform were to enforce Import Trade Control restrictions in the matter of export from Palam Airport, New Delhi. In the aforesaid capacity I came into contact with a large number of exporters of goods from Palam Airport including M/s Maruti (P) Ltd., Gurgaon and M/s Indira International, C-56, Defence Colony, New Delhi. I knew that one of the Directors of M/s Indira International, aforesaid, was Amteshwar Anand, the mother-in-law of Sanjay Gandhi, the son of Indira Gandhi, the former Prime Minister of India. During the course of my duties and functions I also came into contact with a large number of Clearing Agents who were handling the shipments on behalf of the exporters.

In the aforesaid capacity I was deputed to examine a consignment of Petrol Savers manufactured and sought to be exported by M/s Maruti Pvt. Ltd., Gurgaon of which Sanjay Gandhi was the main person having interest in the said firm. The said consignment was covered by shipping bill No. 6851 of July, 1974 valued at Rs. 3,500/- being exported to Nepal involving foreign exchange. After some days M/s Maruti (P) Ltd., again filed a shipping bill No. 28286 dated July 27, 1974 for export of petrol savers to Thailand. I noticed that the value of the petrol savers given in the Customs and Bank documents was grossly under-declared with the ulterior motive of keeping in countries abroad foreign exchange, the difference between the 'real value, and the 'declared value'.

I pointed out this gross irregularity and violation of F.E.R.A to H.R. Gulati, Inspector who was examining the said consignment. At my instance, H.R. Gulati duly raised an objection and the exporter had to revise and raise the value five-fold. At this the representative of the firm became very annoyed and held out threats of retaliation on behalf of Sanjay Gandhi. M/s Maruti (P) Ltd., did try to materialise the threats by causing the disappearance of the consignment covered by shipping bill No. 6851 examined and handled by me by laying the entire blame on Customs thereby clearly implicating the deponent. Their claim, however, was rejected after a prolonged correspondence. This was a sort of clear-cut warning communicated to me that I would be taught a lesson for having acted in that manner towards the former Prime Minister's family.

I was posted in the Air France Warehouse from Junuary 1676 to May 16, 1976. On 22.4.1976, M.M. Puri, Supdt. direct-ed me to draw samples from the consignment of 20 packages covered vide shipping bill No. 1834 dated 21.4.1976 for Indira International for determining whether the garments were actually of 'mill-made' cloth as claimed or of 'power-loom' cloth. S.K. Kapoor, authorised representative of M/s Lee & Muirhead, who were handling the consignment, was asked to open the packages. The shipping bill aforesaid had already been examined on April 21, 1976 by M.S. Malik, Inspector, but the Superintendent doubting the declaration that the garments were made out of mill-made cloth, for draw-back purposes, had not allowed the consignment to be exported on that day, but had desired that the samples be shown to him the next day. Representative samples were drawn by me and presented to the Superintendent. The samples, in my opinion, were of 'power-loom' cloth and that exporter had mis-declared the goods for obtaining illegal benefit of draw-back which was at the rate of 3.5% on F.O.B. value on 'Mill-made' cotton gar-ments and 1.6% of F.O.B. value on 'power-loom' cotton gar-ments.

The Clearing Agents i.e. representatives of Lee & Muirhead were asked to produce definite proof by producing mill cutting of the cloth to substantiate the claim as was the prevalent practice. The Clearing Agents, Lee & Muirhead had no mill cuttings with them. They were asked to get in touch with the exporter for producing the same. S.K. Kapoor informed that the representative of the firm was waiting in the car outside the warehouse premises. Kapoor went out to contact the repre-sentative and came back after a few minutes to inform that mill cuttings were not available. Kapoor and his other collea-gues particularly Harish, in a threatening tone declared that the consignment belonged to the mother-in-law of Sanjay Gandhi. The representatives of the Clearing Agents namely Lee & Muirhead including S.M. Kapoor and Harish held the Superintendent in awe by describing the might of Sanjay Gandhi, who according to them, was already enraged due to the hold-up of the consignment and the Superintendent suc-cumbed to their threats and ordered me to reseal the consignment as if the same was correct according to the declaration given in the concerning documents. I, too, was over-awed and had to reseal the consignment, which should have been otherwise seized and proceeded against for the said mis-declaration.

I continued to remain in the Air France Warehouse till May 16, 1976 during which period Indira International continued to export consignments of made-up fabrics but none of the consignments was deliberately presented on the day when I was on duty during day time for fear of losing the illegal gain which Indira International were earning by misdeclaring the power-loom garments as mill-made cotton garments.

I was transferred from Air France Warehouse to Air India Warehouse on May 17, 1976 and continued to work in the said warehouse till June 1, 1976 when at about 16.00 hours R. Tyagi, Sub Inspector Incharge, Palam Airport Police Post was accompained by another person in mufti whose name I came to know as Santosh Rai, A.S.P , Dhaula Kuan, approached me on the pretext that their Supt. of Police, Gurcharan Singh wanted to export some goods through Palam Airport and was requiring my guidance in the matter of observance of various formalities connected with the export of the consignment. I explained to the aforesaid two officers that it would be better if some Senior Officer of the Export Section of the Air Cargo Unit should be consulted in that regard. But at the instance of the aforesaid two officers and on their implorings, I agreed and accompained the said two officers to the Palam Airport Police Post. However, on reaching the Police Post I did not find the Supdt. of Police as was claimed by the two officials.

The said two officials thereafter asked me to accompany them to Delhi Cantt. Police Station where the Supdt. of Police had gone because of urgent business according to them. I told the said officials that my work in the warehouse was pending and that I was required to go back to attend to my duties specially when I had not taken the permission of my senior officer to leave the place of my posting and duty. However, due to the persistent demands and requests by the aforesaid two officials, I was coerced to go to Delhi Cantt Police Station, but I did not find the Supdt. of Police even there. I was left over to the custody of Prithvi Raj Bhatia, SHO Delhi Cantt. Police Station and the two officials left the Police Station after giving the order that I should be kept in the Police Station

for the night. I demanded to know the reasons for my detention but instead of telling me anything I was abused and
slapped. My request to allow me to telephone to my senior
officers and to inform my family to arrange for my bail was
curtly turned down accompanied by hurling of filthy abuses.

When I requested Prithvi Raj Bhatia to allow me to communicate with my family, M.S. Malik, Inspector of Central
Excise who was posted in the Lufthansa Warehouse Custom
Palam Airport, Near Delhi, was also brought to the Police
Station. In the night I and Malik aforesaid were lodged in the
Police lock-up of Delhi Cantt. Police Station along with other
criminals. I was not allowed food, drinking water and was not
even allowed to answer the call of nature. My requests for
the aforesaid amenities were replied to by abuses and threats
of violence.

On the next day I was taken out of the Police Lock-up of
Delhi Cantt. Police Station and hand-cuffed. I protested to the
S.H.O. that I was an educated person, a law-abiding citizen
and was a Graduate and confirmed Goverment employee
paying Income-tax. I also told him that I had not committed any crime. This protest of mine was answered by abuses
and manhandling. I was taken to Parliament Police Station
in hand-cuffs by bus in which my friends were also travelling.
When they enquired of the reason of my arrest, the Police
constable escorting me told them that they were not aware
about the reason of the arrest. The Police constable however,
admitted that I was arrested under the orders of Supdt. of
Police, South, New Delhi.

On arrival at the Parliament Police Station, I was again
kept in the Police Lock-up. My relatives and the persons who
had come to make arrangements for my bail appeared before
Harit, S.D.M. Delhi Cantt. when the papers regarding my
arrest were presented to him. The Magistrate did not say anything except returning the papers to Prithvi Raj, S.H.O. Delhi
Cantt. after writing something. I was never produced before
him. Although some false entries were made in the record of
the Police Lock-up indicating that I was taken out of the
Police Lock-up for the purpose of production before the Magistrate whereas I was, in fact not produced. The bail application was not entertained, when presented by the counsel on my
behalf.

I was taken back to Tihar Jail New Delhi in the prison van in the evening of June 2, 1976. On arrival in Tihar Jail, I was placed in a barrack along with other 150 detenus and criminals though the space in the said barrack was scheduled to accommodate only 60 inmates. I was subjected to inhumane treatment in the jail by denying me the facilities of soap, water for drinking and bathing. One day, a snake came out in the barrack keeping me and others in tension and in terror.

On June 3, 1976, I was served with an order signed by Virendra Singh, A.D.M., South, under Section 3(i) of the MISA ordering my detention. I was also served with a declaration by Virendra Singh that my detention was made for effectively dealing with Emergency. I was shocked to know that I had been detained under the MISA, because I had not committed any act in my life which could justify the detention. I was a disciplined Government servant and was faithful to the Government establishment by law. I had never committed any act which could disrupt the maintenance of supply of essential commodities and further that I had no affiliation directly or indirectly with any political party or with any other parties which were banned by the Government. The declaration under section 16 A of the MISA was malafide issued to find an excuse not to furnish the grounds of detention to me because there were in fact no grounds on the basis of which my detention was made. The A.D.M. issued the order of detention and the declaration in the colourable exercise of powers conferred on him.

I learnt from Prithvi Raj Bhatia, S.H.O., Delhi Cantt Police Station on June 3, 1976 when he came to serve on me orders of detention and declaration under MISA simultaneously in Tihar Jail that I was arrested under Section 108-151 of the Cr. P.C. allegedly for raising slogans protesting against the Emergency and plotting to over-throw the Indira Government outside Lufthansa Warehouse on June 11, 1976 at about 16.30 hours. I reminded the S.H.O. Delhi Cantt. Police Station Prithvi Raj that I was brought from Air India Warehouse at about 16.00 hours on the pretext of assisting and providing guidance to the Supdt. of Police and it was illegal on his part to have concocted the false case against me.

Justice Shah	: *Anybody could be whisked away and put behind bars. . . .*
Mrs. Ghosh	: *Sir. . . we even went to the residence of N.K. Singh. In those days he was more powerful than the Minister. His wife saw us and said:*
	Dont disturb him, he is going to see a Cricket match.
Mrs. Poornima Chatterjee	: *While they were searching my one room house for 5 hours . . . my two little children had to stand out in the open.*
Justice Shah	: (*greatly moved*) *Man's inhumanity to man knows no limits . . . particularly officials . . . . . . What sin had your husband committed . . . It is shocking that things like this can happen.*
	Why did you sleep over this . . . . . . ?
Director CBI D. Sen	: *No Sir . . . . . (not understanding the purport of the remark).*
Counsel Khandalawala	: *I am getting tired of examining you , . . but I hope you are not .*
	(*scratching his head*)
Justice Shah	: *I am sure it is mutual*
Counsel Khandalawala	: *You raided Mookerjee's house and what did you find . . . . . . ? I will read it for you . . . . . . This is what your officer has to say . . . standard of living is moderate and we found an almirah . . . a frig, record player . . . radio and 2 kilograms of milk.*
D. Sen	: *My officers are very dedicated . . .*
Counsel Khandalawala	: *Another report says . . . he has 6000 rupees in the National and Grindlays Bank and accepts liquor at parties . . . But your FIR says the officer is living beyond his means . . . . . Malik . . . your report goes on to say has 9 children of which 6 are school-going . . . Well 9 children can be asset or a liability . . .*
D. Sen	: *No . . . .*

Counsel Khandalawala	:	*You have been saying No. . . . your own officer Mookerjee reported to you that the standard of living of the Inspectors was miserable . . . and it was agonizing to search their house !*
D. Sen	:	*No . . . he never told me . . . .*
Counsel Khandalawala	:	*Yet . . . you had a report on Bhatnagar indicating that he does not enjoy a good reputation . . . but you did not look into it any further . . . Why the double standard . . . ?*
D. Sen	:	*No . . . Not double standard . . . but different considerations . . ,*
Counsel Khandalawala	:	*A Vendetta against those two and no vendetta against these two . . .*
Justice Shah	:	*My understanding must be very thin . . . If a man is under MISA . . . it doesn't hurt him to have his house searched !*
Counsel Khandalawala	:	*This is one of the most sordid cases that I have come across . . .*
D. Sen	:	*Sir, there was reasonable suspicion.*
Justice Shah	:	*What is reasonable about it . . . You became a tool of Bhinder . . .*
D. Sen	:	*Bhinder was very emphatic.*
Justice Shah	:	*Some can be more emphatic than Bhinder . . . You were the senior most police official in the country and should have shown greater care . . . Why were you so enthusiastic to be a tool in the hands of Bhinder?*

XVI—STATE TRADING CORPORATION

In March-April, 1975 there was a spate of questions in Parliament on Maruti Pvt. Ltd. One of the questions related to alleged import of machinery by Maruti Pvt. Ltd. who were not permitted any such import under the terms of the licence granted to them. The four officials R. Krishnaswamy, Dy. Secy. in the Ministry of Heavy Industry, A.S. Rajan, Development officer, DGTD, L.R. Cavle, Chief Marketing Manager, PEC, and P.S. Bhatnagar, Deputy Marketing Manager, PEC, were, in the normal discharge of their duty, collecting information to prepare a reply to the Parliament question which had been listed for reply in Parliament on April 16, 1975. In the process of gathering this information these officials contacted Maruti Pvt. Ltd. and also M/s Batliboi Company, one of the associates of the Project Equipment Corporation. On April 15, 1975 R.K. Dhawan, Indira Gandhi's Private Secretary, contacted A.S. Rajan and P.S. Bhatnagar on telephone and forbade them from collecting any further information on Maruti Pvt. Ltd. Dhawan also talked to T.A. Pai, the then Minister for Heavy Industry and complained against the officers who were collecting the aforesaid information. Pai was personally called by Indira Gandhi at her residence and according to him she was completely upset and furious. She talked to him about the alleged harassment of the Manager of Batliboi Company by officials of his Ministry. In the presence of T.A. Pai, Indira Gandhi called Dhawan and told him to ask D. Sen, Director CBI to start CBI enquiries against the concerned officials. Indira Gandhi also called D.P. Chattopadhyaya, the then Minister of Commerce at her residence on the evening of April 15, 1975 and directed him that immediate enquiries should be started against Bhatnagar because he had caused harassment to certain parties.

On the same evening Director CBI D. Sen called his Dy Director, Intelligence Cell, Y. Rajpal and ordered him to verify information against Krishnaswamy, Rajan and Bhatnagar. Y. Rajpal was informed that all these officials were corrupt and were having assets disproportionate to the known sources of their income. He was directed to collect information against them immediately and furnish a report within 5 days. Accordingly, on April 16,1975 Rajpal directed his subordinate officers to collect the requisite information and also to mount surveillance against these three officials. However, before any worthwhile verification could be done, the Director CBI asked Rajpal to send whatever information was available against all these officers on April 16, 1975 itself and the files were accordingly sent to him. Rajpal had not recommended any action against any of these officials since the verification had just been started. Acting in great haste, Director CBI ordered registration of cases against Bhatnagar and Rajan on April 16, 1975 itself. The cases were formally registered against these two officers under Prevention of Corruption Act for the offence of disproportionate assets on April 17, 1975 and their premises were searched on April 18, 1975.

The STC authorities had swung into action on April 15, 1975 evening itself in pursuance of a note sent by D.P. Chattopadhyaya, to the effect that P.S. Bhatnagar had kept representatives of a firm waiting for an undue long time and coerced them to part with certain information. The then Chairman STC, Parekh called the Chief Personnel Officer, of STC, B.C. Malhotra, to his office at about 8 P.M. and ordered him to issue suspension orders in respect of Bhatnagar and also to deliver the orders personally to Bhatnagar at his residence the same evening. N.K. Singh, Special Asstt. to the Minister was present in the room when Parekh gave these orders to Malhotra. The instructions were dutifully complied with and Bhatnagar received this suspension order at 10.30 P.M. on April 15, 1975 itself.

Cavle, the other STC official involved in collection of information concerning the Parliament question, was on casual leave on April 15, 1975. But on that day at about 7.30 P.M. he was rung up by N.K. Singh, Special Assistant to the then Minister of Commerce, who wanted to know what had transpired in his office regarding the Parliament question pertaining to M/s. Maruti Pvt. Ltd. Cavle informed him that Bhatnagar was working under his instructions. When he reached office on the morning of April 16, 1975 he was served with orders transferring him from Delhi to Madras. These orders had been issued under instructions from the Chairman, STC. The transfer orders first received by Cavle were dated April 16, 1975 but subsequently this order was withdrawn and a fresh order issued to him which was anti-dated April 15, 1975, the content of the order being the same.

Cavle did not accept the transfer order meekly and protested strongly to the Chairman STC and others. In this connection he met P.J. Fernandes, the then Director General, Bureau of Public Enterprises and narrated his woeful tale to him. Fernandes took up the case with Parekh who expressed his helplessness because he was acting under Superior instructions. When Cavle met Parekh he was told that in order to avoid further complications and possible harassment he should accept the transfer and go to Madras. Apparently Cavle did not listen to the advice of the Chairman and came to grief.

The CBI started their "Verification" on him on April 21, 1975 and he was placed under surveillance. The enquiries did not reveal any incriminating material which could justify registration of a case against him but on April 27, 1975 the Director ordered registration of a preliminary enquiry. The Director CBI ordered that the copies of the registration report of the preliminary enquiry should not be sent to the usual recipients. The Intelligence cell of CBI was also directed to collect further information "so that the preliminary enquiry could be converted into a regular case." When the Intelligence cell failed to collect any worthwhile material which could warrant the registration of a regular case and the search of the premises of Cavle, the Joint Director, CBI A.B. Choudhry pressurised and coerced the Superintendent of Police, K. Vijayan to record a note on May 1, 1975 suggesting search of the premises of the suspect. The officer was intimidated with dire consequences and pressurised to write down a note suggesting search in the matter on the basis of which a regular case was registered against Cavle and his premises searched on May 3, 1975.

The harassment of Cavle did not stop with this. The Chairman STC asked him to resign from his job informing him that if he continued in the STC he would get into more trouble and harassment would increase. On June 15, 1975 under pressure from the Chairman, Cavle submitted his resignation which was promptly accepted. His efforts to secure a job for himself and his wife in other Companies were frustrated and he had to remain unemployed for a long time because of the stigma of a CBI case against him and because of the scare that he was a victim of Sanjay Gandhi. Even when the CBI case was finally closed against him, the STC did not take him back.

The fourth victim in the case involving the aforesaid Parliament question on Maruti, R. Krishnaswamy, could not escape punishment at the hands of the CBI even though the enquiries conducted by the Intelligence Cell revealed that the officer enjoyed a good reputation, came from a well off family and that his standard of living was moderate. The reports submitted by the junior officers of the Intelligence Cell and the notes recorded by the Dy. Director Y. Rajpal time and again, clearly brought out these facts in favour of the officer. But the Director CBI did not appear to be satisfied and directed that more information should be collected against the officer. From the facts available on the file till April 27, 1975 there was not enough material to warrant any action against Krishnaswamy, but Director CBI desired that a preliminary enquiry may be registered.

Copies of the registration report were ordered not to be sent to the usual addresses in order to maintain secrecy. The Joint Director A.B. Choudhry also indicated on April 27, 1975 that "after more information is available 4-5 days after registration of the preliminary enquiry, the case will be converted into a regular case." This took place on May 3, 1975 when Krishnaswamy's residence and office premises were searched by the CBI. The Additional Secretary of the Ministry was merely informed about the search at about 8.15 A.M. while actually the search party had reached Krishnaswamy's house at 7.30 A.M. The harassment to this officer continued unabated and he was asked to proceed on leave "in his own interest." He proceeded on four months' leave from August 18, 1975 and had to extend his leave on half pay, and in Feb. 1976 he was reverted to his parent cadre of Railways.

The CBI tried every method at their disposal and put a tooth comb through most of the files which the officer had dealt with in the Ministry in order to find some material in which to justify their action but nothing incriminating could come out. The CBI was instrumental in registration of a case against Krishnaswamy under Excise Act for alleged possession of liquor over the permissible limit, which the CBI had discovered during his house search. However, the Court did not find Krishnaswamy guilty of any violation and acquitted him on March 4, 1977. The officer's wife was also harassed on false allegation of some alleged exchange violations. The officer's 70 year-old father was put to harassment and his locker was searched in Madras.

Krishnaswamy, Cavle, Rajan and Bhatnagar were harassed and criminal cases were instituted against them, apparently, because they were instrumental in collecting information, though legitimately and in the normal discharge of their official duty, for preparing a reply to the Parliament question under reference.

The allegations of possession of disproportionate assets on the basis of which CBI registered cases against these four officials and searched their premises, could not ultimately be proved and were dropped.

Former Minister : *Power in this country has been used to*
T.A. Pai *create tears in the people's eyes instead of*
wiping them . . . My own Secretary to the
Government of India . . . Mantosh Sondhi
was in Moscow and his wife was being
detained here in Delhi . . . If that is her
concept of honesty . . . then I am glad I am
dishonest!

Counsel : *Did you feel humiliated . . . ? Why did you*
not resign . . . ?

T.A. Pai : *I never felt humiliated . . . I felt it was un-*
reasonable . . . Unfortunately I had never
seen her losing her temper before . . . She
was so angry . . .

Counsel : *It is impossible for a man to get in a word*
Khandalawala *to a angry lady . . . !*

Lt. Governor : *Not a fly could move without the PM's*
Krishan Chand *knowledge !*

Counsel for : *My Lord in America . . .*
Pranab Mookerjee

Justice Shah : *America is far away . . . I am only concern-*
ed with this country . . .

Rajan : *Sir . . . for the first time in many years . . .*
the truth is being established . . . that is
my own feeling.

Counsel : *This was according to you . . . A MAMOLI*
Khandalawala *matter . . .*

R.K. Dhawan : *A Private Secretary should not surprised at*
the actions of the PM . . .
(*dressed in a greyish pin-striped suit with*
the looks of Saville Row . . . and well grea-
sed hair)

Counsel : *My Lord . . . Dhawan the loyal servant of*
Khandalawala *the former Prime Minister . . .*

R. K. Dhawan : *Every Minister and Officer who tells a lie*
gets better treatment . . . Mr. Pai has come
and deposed before you and in those days
when he had a problem he would say "come
and have breakfast with me" What has
happened to these Ministers.

Justice Shah : *Well . . . you must be very important.*
(*laughter*)

XVII—BHIM SEN SACHAR AND OTHERS

The late Bhim Sen Sachar, aged 82, veteran freedom fighter and ex-Governor Andhra Pradesh, Orissa, ex-High Comm. of India in Sri Lanka and ex-Chief Minister Punjab, and Sewak Ram, Chairman Delhi Branch of the Servants of the People Society, Vishnu Dutt, Executive Secretary Citizens for Democracy, K. K. Sinha, Advocate Supreme Court, S. D. Sharma, of Indian Service Mission, J. K. Sharma, Head of the Philosophy Deptt. Hans Raj College, Delhi University, Krishan Lal Vaid, Sarvodaya Worker, and J. R. Sahni, of Adhyatama Sadhna Kendra all around or above sixty, had jointly addressed an open letter dated July 23, 1975 to Indira Gandhi, the then Prime Minister of India. Cyclostyled copies of this letter were also sent to distinguished persons in the field of politics, culture, religion and also to the Press. Some important paras from this letter are reproduced below :

We are amongst the very humble of your fellow countrymen, just ordinary citizens interested chiefly in constructive work, none of us belonging to any political party. We have no political axe to grind nor are we interested in any political office of power. Our chief interest is in upholding the freedom and dignity of the individual.

We regard Pandit Jawaharlal Nehru as one of the principal architects of Indian democracy. He used to say "No one, however great he may be, should be above criticism." It was he who had said about the freedom of the press :

"To my mind, the freedom of the press is not just a slogan from the larger point of view but it is an essential attribute of the democratic process. I have no doubt that even if the Government dislikes the liberties taken by the press and considers them dangerous, it is wrong to interfere with the freedom of the Press. By imposing restrictions you do not change anything you merely suppress the public manifestation of certain things, thereby causing the idea and thought underlying them to spread further. Therefore, I would rather have a completely free Press with all the dangers involved in the wrong use of that freedom than a suppressed or regulated Press.

"It was he who gave the memorable slogan when the British came down heavily upon us in the freedom struggle : 'Freedom is in peril, defend it with all your might'. We sorrowfully remember him for, had he been alive today, we have no doubt that he would have given the slogan : 'Democracy is in peril; defend it with all your might'.

"We do not, we repeat, challenge your right to arm yourself with additional powers even when ample powers are with you already for dealing with offenders against law; what, however, we fail to appreciate is the denial of normal opportunities to the people—to all the people—to discuss openly the merits and demerits of government measures. Our democracy in not yet out of the woods and many are bound to feel puzzled over what meets their eye.

". . . It would be an outrage on Parliamentary democracy if even our Parliament's proceedings cannot be published without precensorship . . .

". . . We hope with all our heart that the arrested Members of Parliament will not be deprived of the opportunity to have their say in the current session of Parliament. Was it really necessary to withhold from the public even the names of the political leaders and workers you have arrested and to deny facilities to their near and dear ones to meet them and arrange their legal defence, if any such defence is at all possible in the midst of present ordinances . . .

"Apart from your political supporters, the common people of Delhi now talk in hushed tones as they do in communist societies; they do not discuss politics in the coffee house or at the bus stands and look over their shoulders before expressing any opinion. An atmosphere of fear and political repression prevails and politically conscious citizens differing from your view-point prefer to observe a discreet silence, with some of them afraid of the mid-night knock on their door.

"Must the monster of fear devour us again, the monster for the annihilation of which our beloved leader Pandit Jawaharlal Nehru had sacrificed his all—his riches, his comforts, his parents and even the dearest deity of his heart. He held fear to be enemy No. 1 of India's destiny. It is well to seek fresh inspiration from his memorable words :

" 'The greatest gift for an individual or a Nation so we had been told in our ancient books, was *Abhaya* (fearlessness). Not merely bodily courage but the absence of fear from the mind.' Janaka and Yajnavalka had said, at the dawn of our history, that it was the function of the leaders of a people to make them fearless. But the dominant impulse in India under British rule was that of fear—pervasive, oppressing, strangling fear; fear of the army, the police, the widespread secret service, fear of law meant to suppress. It was against this all pervading fear that Gandhi's quiet and determined voice was raised :

'Be not afraid'."

The present situation looks every citizen in the face enquiringly and the old surviving freedom fighters in particular. We must respond to the call. Accordingly we propose, with effect from 9th August, 1975 and regardless of consequences to ourselves, to advocate openly the right of public speech and public association and freedom of the Press, for discussing the merits and demerits of the Government arming itself with extraordinary powers. The intention is not to embarrass authority . . . . Our self suffering will just be an humble offering at the feet of the Motherland, in the breaking of whose chains we had been previleged to play our small part inspired by the mighty lead of the Father of the Nation.

This letter was received in the Prime Minister's Secretariat and is available in their file. According to the statement of Sushil Kumar, the then District Magistrate, Delhi, he was called to the then Prime Minister's house by R.K. Dhawan, Addl. Private Secretary to the Prime Minister. Sushil Kumar has stated :

I received a telephonic call from Shri R.K. Dhawan, Addl. Private Secretary to the then P.M. to come over to PM's House. When I reached there, I found Shri Dhawan alone in his office. Immediately thereafter, Shri P.S. Bhinder, DIG (R) joined us. Shri Dhawan told us that the P.M. had directed that Shri Bhim Sen Sachar and seven others who had apparently addressed some communication to the P.M. be detained under MISA. I also recollect Shri Sanjay Gandhi walking in when Shri Dhawan repeated to Shri Gandhi what he had been telling us.

I must confess that I felt a little shaken because when I was working as a junior officer in Andhra Pradesh Shri Bhim Sen Sachar was the Governor and had visited Adilabad District where I was an SDM and had been personally very kind to me. Having had an opportunity of knowing him a little and realising that he must be in his early seventies, I found myself in a very painful situation. I immediately enquired from Shri Dhawan whether he had communicated the direction of the Prime Minister to the Lt. Governor, because I must have clearance from the L.G. before any action can be taken.

He said that he will inform the L.G. I also told Shri Dhawan that a formal request with material for detention will have to be made to the concerned detaining authority to enable further action being taken in this behalf. Therefore, I went to Raj Niwas and informed the L.G. of the decision communicated by Shri R.K. Dhawan, when L.G. told me that he had also been informed by Shri Dhawan and that the concerned ADM may be asked to take further necessary action. I communicated the decision of the Lt. Governor to the concerned ADM. Thereafter the case was dealt with by the detaining authority.

Bhim Sen Sachar was detained under MISA by the order of Meenakshi Datta Ghosh, ADM (New Delhi) passed on July 25, 1975 on the following grounds :

Bhim Sen Sachar has, since the imposition of the emergency proclaimed by the President under Article 352 of the Constitution of India on 25.6.75, been advocating on a number of occasions that during the

period of emergency the people should have the right
of public speech and public association and freedom
of Press, with a view to propagating that the Government during the present emergency has indulged in
arbitrary pressure against prominent political figures
and political parties; and Shri Bhim Sen Sachar along
with others gave wide publicity of his intention to
discuss in public the merits and demerits of the
Government arming itself with extraordinary powers.

Vishnu Dutt, Sewak Ram, J.R. Sahni, K.K. Sinha and S.D.
Sharma were detained under section 3(1)(a) (ii) of MISA
under the orders of P. Ghosh, the then ADM (South) passed
on July 25, 1975 on exactly the same grounds as were given
by ADM New Delhi in respect of detention of Bhim Sen
Sachar.

It will be seen from the above that these ADMs had not,
while referring to the prejudicial activities of these persons,
given any details of time, date and place in respect of such
activities. Enquiries made with the Special Branch, have confirmed that none of the above detenues was noticed for any
adverse activities, political or otherwise, before their detention.

Both P. Ghosh and Meenakshi Datta Ghosh have stated
that these detentions were ordered "under the specific directions of the DM who stated that it was the wish of the Prime
Minister and that the grounds would be furnished by the SP/
CID (SB)." They admitted to have learnt at the same time
that "these persons had written an open letter to the then
Prime Minister and that was the cause of their detention."
They also stated that "the grounds were subsequently furnished
after the detention orders were issued but were pre-dated."
Rajindra Mohan, the then SP (South), has confirmed in his
statement that "the warrants had been received from the ADM
(South) direct and were served upon the subjects and the
grounds of detention were sent to the ADM later on."

J.K. Sharma was detained under section 3 (1) (a) (ii) of
MISA under the orders of S.L. Arora ADM (North) passed
on July 25, 1975 on the following grounds:

Shri J.K. Sharma along with others is reported to have

decided to advocate, propagate and fight for the right of public speech, public association and freedom of press, so that the public could have an opportunity to discuss the merits and demerits of the government arming itself with extraordinary powers.

J. K. Sharma is also reported to be secretly mobilising public opinion in his favour and inciting the public to violate the law and bring down the legally constituted government by resorting to force and violence.

Parkash Singh, the then SP (North) has stated that P. S. Bhinder, DIG (R), had ordered him on telephone about the detention of J. K. Sharma under MISA and the grounds of detention were also dictated on telephone by DIG(R) who informed the SP that the decision to detain Sharma had already been taken and the DM was instructed to issue warrants.

Krishan Lal Vaid was detained under section 3 (1) (a) (ii) of MISA under the orders of Ashok Pradhan, the then ADM (Central) on the following grounds :

That Krishan Lal Vaid is an active leader of Congress (O). In recent months he has been advocating the cause of Lok Sangharsh Samiti and Janta Morcha in the rural areas of Delhi especially Najafgarh and the villages around.

That on February 19, 1975 he organised a meeting in Najafgarh Main Bazar where he advocated launching of Bihar type Andolan and called upon the people to join the proposed rally to be held at Delhi on March 6, 1975 under the leadership of J. P. Narayan.

That Krishan Lal Vaid, since the imposition of the emergency proclaimed by the President under Article 352 of the Constitution of India on June 25, 1975 has been advocating on a number of occasions that during the period of emergency the people should have the right of public speech and public association and freedom of press, with a view to propagating that the Govt. during the present emergency has indulged in arbitrary repression against prominent political parties.

These detention orders were executed on 25th/26th July, 1975 and all of them, except Krishan Lal Vaid were transferred to Central Jail Ambala on the July 26, 1975. A Secret Note dated July 26, 1975 giving "the names of 8 persons to be sent to Haryana" was sent by K. S. Bajwa, the then SP/CID (SB) to the Chief Secretary, Delhi Administration. This list included all the detenues of the present case except Krishan Lal Vaid. J. K. Kohli, the then Chief Secretary recorded the following endorsement in the margin of this secret note and sent the same to the Special Secretary (Home).

The name of Rup Narain was also later included. For n. a. please. Chief Secretary Haryana has agreed.

Sd/-J. K. Kohli

26.7.55

It is not understood how the SP/CID (SB) could write to the Chief Secretary Delhi Administration for the transfer of the detenus from Tihar Jail to Ambala Jail and the same was approved and orders issued the same day. It is significant to note that a copy of this Secret Note was also marked to P.S. Bhinder, DIG (R) Delhi "for information".

Transfer to Ambala meant added hardships to the detenus in the sense that their family members could not avail of the facilities of weekly interviews without incurring sizeable expenditure and undergoing strains of journey.

Lalita Sachar wife of Bhim Sen Sachar filed a writ petition in the High Court of Delhi on August 6, 1975 challenging the detention of her husband. It is seen from the files that the case was admitted after hearing the Counsel on August 19, 1975. The Court felt that the question of the competence of the Court as to whether the detaining authorities had adequate materials to pass orders of detention is a substantial question which needs investigation and September1 1, 975 was fixed for arguments.

While the strategy to deal with this writ petition was being finalised in the Ministry of Home Affairs in consultation with the Law Ministry the detention order in respect of Bhim Sen Sachar was revoked by Lt. Governor on August 31, 1975 i.e. one day before the date fixed for hearing in the High Court.

(Extracts from Cross-Examination)

Sevak Ram	:	*My Lord . . . this was a shameful period in India's history . . . striking terror and causing fear in the citizen's heart . . .*
J.K. Sharma	:	*My brother-in-law was dying and wanted to see me . . . In those days a dying man could not seek solace from his last wish . . . Every Congress worker was a full fledged BHARAT SARKAR. After all we were human beings and like all human beings should have been treated with care . . .*
Delhi Additional District Magistrate Ghosh	:	*I was called by Navin Chawla and told they were anti-social elements . . . fabricate the grounds and arrest them . . .*
Justice Shah	:	*Did you apply your mind as to satisfaction . . . ?*
ADM Ghosh	:	*No . . . (without the slightest hesitation)*
Justice Shah	:	*They were done at the behest of the Police...! This is a complete perversion of the Act . . . putting people behind bars . . .*
ADM Ashok Pradhan	:	*Some adjustment had to be made . . .*
Justice Shah	:	*(disturbed) Arrested at all cost . . . whether authorised by law or not . . . !*
ADM Arora	:	*DM issued the instruction . . .*
Justice Shah	:	*You had not independently applied your mind . . . you did not perform your duty that the statute bestows on you . . .*
Counsel Khandalawala	:	*You were very nice to them . . .*
R.K. Dhawan	:	*That is my nature . . .*
Counsel Khandalawala	:	*I am trying to understand you . . .*
R.K. Dhawan	:	*Why bring Sanjay . . . ?*
Khandalawala	:	*One lie is saved by another lie . . . You really want me to believe . . . if you tell one lie and then you tell two lies . . . the proposition becomes stronger . . .*
R.K. Dhawan	:	*I was a pretty small fry . . .*
Justice Shah	:	*Why involve you . . . a pretty small fry they could easily say . . . the PM . . .*
R.K. Dhawan	:	*They had no guts . . .*
Khandalawala	:	*My Lord Dhawan was only the Chota Prime Minister.*

XVIII—CHADHA PRABATHKAR AND MARUTI

Harihar Lal, Director of Inspection (Investigation) Income Tax, (hereinafter referred as "the D.I. (Inv.)") authorised search and seizure operations under section 132 (1) of the Income-Tax Act 1961, on August 12,1975 in respect of Prabhatkar, an ex-M.P. (CPI) and General Secretary of the All India Bank Employees' Union (hereinafter referred to as AIBEA). On the same day Harihar Lal telephoned the then Commissioner of Income Tax, Bombay City-1, Bombay, from New Delhi and conveyed to him that action under Section 132 should be undertaken in the case of D.P. Chadha, President of the AIBEA who resides in Bombay. The information as noted down by the Commissioner of Income Tax, Bombay City-1, was :

> Shri Chadha was drawing a salary over Rs. 2,000/-P.M.; he had purchased a flat in Punjab National Bank Housing Society near Lallubhai Park (at Andheri); and he may not be an income tax assessee.

The D.I. (Inv.) also specified that the search should commence at 10.00 A.M. on August 13, 1975. Thereafter, D.I. (Inv.) spoke to V.R. Vaidya, Deputy Director at Bombay and directed him to advance the time of the search to 8.00 A.M. on August 13, 1975.

The search operations were accordingly carried out on the next day *i.e.* August 13, 1975 at the residential permises of D.P. Chadha at 9, Punjab National Bank Housing Society, near Lallubhai Park, Andheri, Bombay. Beyond the information recorded by the Commissioner of Income Tax, Bombay on the basis of telephonic message he received from Harihar Lal D.I. (Inv.) there is nothing on record to show the specific nature of information leading to search.

Regarding Prabhatkar, Harihar Lal, D.I. (Inv.) called V.S.
Wahi, Assistant Director (Intelligence) on August 12, 1975 to
his room and told him that he had received information of tax
evasion about Prabhatkar, General Secretary of All India
Bank Employees' Association. Wahi, Assistant Director recorded a note on August 12, 1975 stating that information from
a very reliable "source" was received to the effect that :

By virtue of his position Shri Prabhatkar received
remuneration of Rs. 2,000/- p.m.

He stayed in a house rent of which was borne by the
Union.

The Union has provided him with a motor vehicle.

In 1973 he received gifts totalling up to Rs. 1 lakh at
the time of his daughter's marriage.

Parts of the above noted amount had been invested
and deposited in a Bank account.

He had been receiving various other pecuniary benefits
and had amassed wealth much beyond his known
sources of income.

He had a standard of living much above that warranted by his known sources of income.

Wahi, Assistant Director has stated that the reliable source
referred to by him in his note dated August 12, 1975 was the
then D.I. (Inv.), (Harihar Lal) himself. In this connection,
Harihar Lal, in his written statement dated September 9, 1977
has stated as under :

I hereby state that the said information had been
given to me personally by D. Sen, the then Director
of Central Bureau of Intelligence, in his office where I
had met him at his request. The information received
by me from D. Sen regarding Prabhatkar was passed
on by me personally to one of the Asstt. Directors
of Intelligence in the Intelligence Unit at Mayur
Bhawan for recording it. Ordinarily, the information
would have been passed on by me to the concerned
Commissioner of Income Tax for necessary action
but as it appeared that Shri Prabhatkar was not

being assessed to Income tax (his name did not figure in our PAN Directories) and it was not known in what Commissioner's jurisdiction he would be assessable, I authorised search operations in his case, on the basis of the information received from Shri D. Sen. The information received by me from Shri D. Sen regarding D. P. Chadha was passed on by me personally on the telephone (STD Line) to the concerned CIT viz. Shri O.V. Kuruvilla, the then CIT Bombay City-1.

It is seen from a scrutiny of the CBI's file No. INF/97/75-IC in this regard that proceedings in this case commenced with a note dated July 21, 1975 recorded by D. Sen which reads as under :

Secret

The following two gentlemen are office bearers in various Bank Unions :

Shri Prabhatkar
Shri Chadha.

It is said that they extort money for donations for the Union from persons who are sanctioned loans or given overdrafts, etc. by the Banks. They are also said to be misusing Union funds and living in good style. Will you please make immediate enquiries about them confidentially and let me have a report soon.

Sd/- (D. SEN)
21.7.75

Enquires in this regard were made by the officers of the CBI and their reports on the file clearly indicate that there was no evidence to substantiate the allegation that Prabhatkar or Chadha was extorting money for donations for the Union from persons who were sanctioned loans or given overdrafts by the Banks. In the case of D.P. Chadha the report of the Bombay Branch of the CBI states inter-alia as under :

Secret enquiries revealed that he is not fond of high living and furniture in his flat is reported to be of moderate value. The enquiries have further revealed that he is not living beyond his means and is reported to be a sincere and non-controversial figure.

This report was received at the New Delhi Office of the CBI on August 9, 1975 i.e. 4 days before the search. Inspite of this search and seizure operations were undertaken at the residential premises of D.P. Chadha. It is further seen from the CBI file that the then Director CBI had recorded a secret note dated August 16, 1975 on the file. Only an office copy of this note is on record. It is not clear for whom the original note was intended and to whom it had been sent. The note reads as under :

Secret

Central Bureau of Investigation

I had given the following information to Shri Harihar Lal, Director of Inspection (Investigation) about Shri Prabhatkar and Shri S.P. Chadha :

Shri Prabhatkar :

He lives at 10/9 East Patel Nagar, New Delhi. The rent of this house, which belongs to Jaipur Golden Transport Co., is being paid by All India Bank Employees Association of which Shri Prabhatkar is the General Secretary. This association seems to have been formed under the aegis of Jan Sangh.

Shri Prabhatkar has an income, including the salary which he receives from the Bank Employees Association, of about Rs. 2,000/- per month but he is not paying a single pie as income tax.

Shri Prabhatkar lives in good style and had spent a lot of money on the marriage of his daughter in 1973 and that at the time of marriage a number of cash gifts were received from the various of All India Bank Employees Association.

Shri S.P. Chadha :

He is the Honorary President of All India Bank Employees Association.

He is working in the Fort Branch of Punjab National Bank in Bombay but spends most of his time in doing Association work.

He owns a flat in Andheri and has a fixed deposit. He is, however, paying income tax.

On the basis of the above information the houses of Shri Prabhatkar and S.P. Chadha were searched by Shri Harihar Lal. A copy of his report giving the result of these searches is enclosed.

Sd/

(D. Sen)

Director. C.B.I.

16.8.75

The statement that the association is formed under the aegis of the Jan Sangh is surprising in the context of the note dated July 4, 1975 recorded by the DIG at pp. 5-7 of the note sheet, wherein, at page 6 the DIG clearly indicated that the Association is not a Jan Sangh sponsored organisation but affiliated to AITUC, a CPI sponsored organisation, especially because the file had been submitted to the Director, CBI on August 5, 1975. It is further seen from the file of the CBI that copies of reports of Harihar Lal D.I. (INV.) to S.R. Mehta, the then Chairman, CBDT and to C.C. Ganapati, the then member of CBDT are also endorsed to the Director, CBI who is hardly concerned with Income Tax evasion in individual cases.

There is nothing on the "Satisfaction file" of the Directorate relating to Prabhatkar to say whether any inquiries were conducted by the then D.I. (Inv.) to verify the allegation/information alleged to have been conveyed to him by D. Sen, Director, CBI before authorising searches. This is particularly significant as the allegations were such as could have been verified without resort to the provision of search and seizure.

It should, however, be pointed out that Prabhatkar had not then filed returns of income in relation to his "honorarium" from the AIBEA, or returns of Gift covering gifts said to have been made by him to his son and daughter. Here again, the income tax department could have required him to file the returns by issue of appropriate notices under the relevant enactments.

It will be relevant to point out that in both the case of Prabhatkar, General Secretary and D.P. Chadha, President of the AIBEA the search operations were conducted on the same day *i.e.* August 13, 1975 at New Delhi, Bombay and Calcutta and further that the time of commencement of the search operations at Bombay was advanced, to bring it close to the time of the search operations at Delhi. Further in both the cases the information regarding the concealment of income had been received from the Director, CBI on the same day.

During this period the AIBEA had stoutly opposed the proposed increase in working hours in the Bank and the Bonus ordinance, whereby the Banking industry was taken out of the purview of the Bonus Act. Besides, the worker directors on the boards of most of the Nationalised banks were vigorously opposing certain credit policies and proposals of those Banks. It is alleged that the searches at AIBEA leaders' residence and the publicity given to it through a press release seven weeks later is a "motivated campaign of calumny and character assassination of the leadership of AIBEA with a view to disrupting" the organisation.

Another aspect of this case is that the *only* "incriminating document" found and seized by the Income Tax authorities during the search of D.P. Chadha's residential premises was a paper attacking political interference in regard to appointments in Nationalised Banks, with special reference to interference by Sanjay Gandhi. The paper also alleged that Maruti Ltd. had been given "unduly excessive" credit limits by the Central Bank of India and the Punjab National Bank; total credits according to the paper, amount to rupees one hundred and ten lakhs.

Director CBI	:	*Whether I was a tool . . . I cannot say . . .*
D. Sen		
Counsel	:	*You are not a Constable . . . you were a Director . . .*
D. Sen	:	*I don't understand the question . . .*
Counsel	:	*Your intelligence only goes that far . . . but you have to be intelligent enough as to i.ari. eetzl*
Justice Shah	:	*You were concerned only with public servants . . .*
D. Sen	:	*NO . . . I did not know . . .*
Justice Shah	:	*Sanjay Gandhi and Y. P. Kapoor also wanted these matters to be looked into. . . ?* *You know Chadha was a Director of a bank objecting to loans to Maruti . . .*
D. Sen	:	*If I knew it I would not have proceeded . . .*
Counsel	:	*Yet their houses were raided . . .*
D. Sen	:	*Harihar Lal got the houses searched on his own . . .* *I did not tell him . . .*
Counsel	:	*What was the need to say "Jan Sangh". . .*
D. Sen	:	*It is not this . . . It is simple . . .* *(looking like a fuddy-duddy with a chaotic memory)*
R.K. Dhawan	:	*I do not remember . . .*
Counsel	:	*Isn't it true that Sanjay Gandhi asked you to get their houses raided. . .*
R.K. Dhawan	:	*This is totally false and completely incorrect.*
Justice Shah	:	*Who asked you to look into this matter ?*
D. Sen	:	*Sir, Mr. Dhawan. . .*

XIX—JUSTICES AGGARWAL AND LALIT

Justice R.N. Aggarwal who belonged to the Delhi Higher Judicial Service, was appointed as Additional Judge of the Delhi High Court for a period of two years on March 7, 1972. On the completion of this period, Justice Aggarwal was reappointed as Additional Judge for a further period of two years with effect from March 7, 1974. Subsequently, the Chief Justice of the Delhi High Court recommended that he should be made a permanent Judge in the vacancy caused due to the retirement of Justice Jagjit Singh on August 13, 1975. This recommendation was turned down by the Central Government with the result that Justice R.N. Aggarwal had to revert as District and Sessions Judge, Delhi. It is alleged that the refusal on the part of the Central Government to make Justice R.N. Aggarwal a permanent Judge was an act of political vendetta. He was, it is said, was one of the two Judges constituting the MISA Bench of the Delhi High Court and his Bench had delivered a judgement unfavourable to the Government in Kuldip Nayar's case. When the question of his confirmation came up, the fact of the judgement referred to above came to be mentioned in the relevant file.

Justice U.R. Lalit was appointed an Additional Judge of the Bombay High Court for two years with effect from January 17, 1974. Since the period of his appointment was to expire or January 16, 1976, the Chief Justice of the Bombay High Court had recommended that Justice U.R. Lalit should be appointed as Additional Judge for a further term of two years. The Governor and the Chief Minister of Maharashtra had endorsed this proposal. Justice Lalit was to be appointed as Additional Judge against the post he was already holding. The file was put up to the Chief Justice of India and he agreed to the proposal on November 25, 1975.

Despite all these recommendations, Justice Lalit was not given an extension by Indira Gandhi, the then Prime Minister of India with the result that he ceased to function as Additional Judge of the Bombay High Court with effect from January 17, 1976. The file on the subject does not mention any reason by the then Prime Minister for the refusal to reappoint Justice Lalit.

It was pointed out by the Joint Secretary in the note recorded by him in the relevant file: "There has been only one case in which it was proposed not to make him either permanent Judge or extend the term of additional judgeship." The same note also reproduced the observations made by K.N. Wanchoo, the then Chief Justice of India, in his minute of June 29, 1967 which runs as follows :

when a Member of the Bar is appointed Additional Judge, it must be with a view to make him permanent in due course. If that is not possible, Additional Judgeship should not be offered to a Member of the Bar.

172   *(Extracts from Cross-Examination)*

Justice Shah : *Some note was placed before you regarding Justice Aggarwal . . . and you put your own note stating that the allegation made was not correct.*

Former Law Minister H.R. Gokhale : *I had meanwhile collected the facts and handed the file personally to the Prime Minister.*

Justice Shah : *Have you any reason to believe that some sort of allegations were being trumped up against Mr. Justice Aggarwal as a matter of punishment for deciding against the government in the Kuldip Nayar case?*

H. R. Gokhale : *I had reason to think that allegations were false and perhaps somebody had made a deliberate attempt "to get this allegation."*

Secretary to the Government of India, S. L. Khurana : *After the arguments, perhaps it was considered as unusual that the Court had given the judgement when the order of detention had been revoked.*

Justice Shah : *When you argue a case before the court, when you find that the decision is likely to go against you, you say we are withdrawing from the proceedings of the court. The effect of your order was to render the court functus officio.*

S. L. Khurana : *(looking at the file) It is clear that the report was called for much earlier . . .*

Justice Shah : *The report was received on the 13th "when the file was already under submission" and it was sent up on the 14th . . .*

K. L. Khurana : *. . . I did not go into any of these things . . .*

Counsel Khandalawala : *Her cryptic answer is "It was not intended to confirm Justice Aggarwal.' Who did she consult? . . . It is a piece of affrontery. . . because she deeply resented the independence of Justice Aggarwal.*
Is it not paradoxical that though she did not appoint him as a Judge. . . he was considered fit to be a Sessions Judge.

Justice Shah : *They don't deal with MISA cases.*

Counsel Khandalawala : *. . . And there the cat comes out of the bag.*

XX—KISHORE KUMAR

The Ministry of Information and Broadcasting in January, 1976 started negotiations with representatives of the Film Industry in order to get their cooperation for participation in the programmes of AIR/TV and films and songs etc. in praise of the 20 point programme. "G.P. Sippy, Sriram Vohra and Nazir Hussain of the film industry called on the Secretary on 29.4.1976 when JS (I), Director (Films) and myself were also present . . . Sippy, Sriram Vohra and Nazir Hussain mentioned that most of the cinema artistes . . . would readily cooperate but there may be some people who may not be willing to do so."

In this connection, the name of Kishore Kumar was mentioned. It was stated that Kishore Kumar was not cooperating in this venture. Secretary desired that we should immediately ban all records of Kishore Kumar on TV and Radio for a period of three months. We should contact various gramophone companies such as Columbia and HMV etc. and request them to freeze all records of Kishore Kumar's songs and no record of his song should be sold. It should be found out how BBC was playing Kishore Kumar's songs, under what contract and what can be done to stop this.

The list of films which are now under production where Kishore Kumar is the play-back singer should be obtained from the Chairman, CBFC and steps should be taken not to release any raw stock of films etc. It should also be examined whether such films could be refused censor certificate.

(Note of C.B. Jain, Jt. Secretary on file dated May 1, 1976)

Shortly, before this, the Joint Secretary (Broadcasting) and Director of Films had been sent to Bombay to negotiate with the film world. "In this context, JS (B) mentioned how non-cooperative Kishore Kumar was. He did not condescend to meet any one of them and was persuaded to speak to them over the telephone. I said that all the songs of Kishore Kumar should be banned from AIR and Doordarshan and that all the films in which he was the play-back singer should be listed out so that suitable action can be taken against these films. Besides, the representatives of HMV and other gramophone record companies should be sent for and, in consultation with the Ministry of Education, sale of Kishore Kumar's records and discs should be frozen. Measures against Kishore Kumar as mentioned above had tangible effect on the film producers."

(Note of S.M.H. Burney, Secretary on file dated April 30, 1976 was seen by V.C. Shukla and approved by him on May 11, 1976.)

Accordingly in compliance with Burney's instructions, DG AIR issued orders on May 4, 1976 stating inter-alia "It has been decided to black-list Kishore Kumar, film play-back singer. Songs sung by him—solo or duet etc. should not be broadcast henceforth in any of the services of AIR including Vividh Bharati/Commercial Broadcasting Service." The D.G., Doordarshan ordered on May 5, 1976 with immediate effect that :

The films or film excerpts in which Kishore Kumar personally appears *should not be shown over TV.*

If there is a film or a film excerpt in which Kishore Kumar's voice is present for play-back singing, his name *should not appear in any title or in any other form over TV.*

If any gramophone records of Kishore Kumar are available with any TV Centre, they should henceforth not, repeat not, be broadcast, and taken over by the head of office and kept in his or her personal custody.

On May 7, 1976 DG AIR further clarified his orders as follows :

Spots/Sponsored Programmes which include Kishore Kumar's voice but do not name him *should continue to be broadcast* till the present contract expires. Spots/Sponsored programmes which use his voice but also name him should be reported back to Directorate. No Spots/Sponsored programmes which use Kishore Kumar's voice are to be accepted in future.

Further in compliance of the Secretary's instructions D. K. Sen Gupta, DDG (Commercial) AIR and G. H. Vyas, Station Director, Bombay, met the representatives of HMV and Polydor respectively. During the discussions with HMV, HMV Managing Director expressed that "the HMV had from 1100-1500 catalogues which contained songs, 2 out of 5 of which had Kishore Kumar's voice with other artists. In such a circumstance it would be difficult for him to refuse taking these records for print or not to put them in circulation." (Note of D. K. Sen Gupta, DDG (Commercial) AIR on file dated June 4, 1976.)

Similarly, G. H. Vyas discussed two points with Polydor "(i) suspension of the sale of gramophone records containing songs rendered by Kishore Kumar and (ii) suspension of pressing of new songs by Kishore Kumar". As Polydor had contracts with the Producers, Polydor had suggested that this matter will have to be tackled at the Producers' level. He also informed that as a sequel to the action to black-list Kishore Kumar from the broadcast of All India Radio, there has been some slow-down of the booking of this Artist by the Producers for their new films." (Note of G. H. Vyas, Station Director, AIR on file dated May 28, 1976.)

Regarding films under production "The CBFC was informally consulted about the films under production in which Kishore Kumar is a play-back singer. Since the CBFC replied that there was no picture at that moment under production in which Kishore Kumar is to be play-back singer, the question of issuing necessary instructions to FFC for stopping of the release of raw stock for such pictures did not arise." (Note of R. D. Joshi, Under Secretary on file dated July 5, 1976.)

It is apparent that the pressure was successful and that Kishore Kumar had succumbed by letter dated June 14, 1976 received by C. B. Jain, Joint Secretary. "In this letter, Kishore

Kumar has said that he has decided to extend his full cooperation. He has proposed to do a programme for Bombay TV
and has said that he would be in a position to do the recording
in about a fortnight's time . . . . One alternative could be
that we wait till Kishore Kumar actually does a programme
for TV and then remove the ban. That would, however, appear
to be crude. In view of the undertaking given by Kishore
Kumar in writing to cooperate, we may lift the ban with
immediate effect and watch the degree of cooperation that he
extends. Needless to say, it is always open to us to re-impose
the ban whenever we feel that such cooperation is not forth
coming (Note of C. B. Jain, Joint Secretary on file dated June
16, 1976.)

This was agreed to by Burney and accordingly the ban
was lifted.

XXI—BARODA RAYON CORPORATION

On April 21, 1976 Harihar Lal, Director of Inspection (Investigation) (hereinafter referred to as "the D.I.") called S. N. Shende, Deputy Director (Intelligence) (hereinafter referred to as "the D.D.I.") around 11.00 A.M. and told him that a major all India search in the cases of Baroda Rayon Corporation and its directors and important executives was required to be carried out within a short period of time and that it should be organised within a period of a week or so. From the statements recorded by Shende and the Assistant Directors (Intelligence) concerned, it is seen that none of them knew about the proposed action under section 132 in the case of Baroda Rayon Corporation before Harihar Lal's conversation with Shende in the fore-noon of April 21, 1976. Nor had they gathered any worthwhile intelligence regarding evasion of taxes by Baroda Rayon Corporation or any of its Directors or employees till then.

On going back to his room Shende collected some information and informed the D.I. that it would be necessary to conduct survey at places like Surat and Baroda. Thereafter with the approval of the D.I., the D.D.I. sent two Assistant Directors (Rangabhashyam and Mathur) by plane to Bombay and further to Surat mainly with a view to assessing the manpower requirements. After the Assistant Directors left the office, the D.D.I. was called by the D.I. at about 4.45 in the afternoon and told that the search and seizure operations should be advanced from April 27, 1976 as originally planned to April 24, 1976 and further that the residential premises of V. K. Shah, the Managing Director of the Company and Fateh Singh Gaekward, who was the Chairman of the Company not be searched. When the D.D.I. specifically desired to know the reasons for the latter direction, he was merely informed that the residential premises of the persons referred to above should not be searched under any circumstances. The last minute change in decision not to search the two residential premises was conveyed by the DDI to V. Mathur one of the Assistant Directors, at his residence.

The note dated April 22,1976 recorded by the D.D.I., on the basis of which the D.I. authorised on the same day the search and seizure operations refers to a "source" which had made various allegations as put down in the D.D.I's note. In his statement Shende has stated that the "source" referred to in his note dated April 22, 1976 was the then D.I. (Investigation).

Search operations in the case commenced on April 24, 1976 at the Company's factory premises near Surat and the residential premises of some of its executives. However, as April 24, 1976 happened to be a Saturday and the office premises of the Company at Bombay happened to be closed on that day they were sealed and the actual search commenced only on April 26, 1976. It is seen from a statement furnished by S. Talwar, Assistant Director that as late as on April 23, 1976, the officers-in-charge of the search and seizure operations did not even have the correct address of the head office of the Company at Bombay.

The actual search of the head office at Bombay therefore commenced on Monday April 26, 1976 and covered a period of two days namely Monday April 26, and Tuesday April 27, 1976. In course of the search operation on April 27, 1976 S. Talwar, Assistant Director went upto C.S. Parida who was one of the authorised officers for the search operation and told him that they were to search for certain documents and papers regarding donations collected by Vinay K. Shah, Managing Director of the Company. Talwar added that this was the direction of the D.I. Accordingly Parida and Talwar went to the Personal Secretary of V.K. Shah and asked him to produce the file regarding donations collected by Shah. After consulting Shah, the Secretary produced certain files from a cupboard. Parida has stated that he remembers having seen in those files names of various Companies and persons etc. from whom money was collected as donations for the Congress Party.

This statement of Parida is corroborated by the statement

of V.R. Vaidya, Deputy Director at Bombay. It would
appear at this stage S. Talwar telephoned or otherwise contacted Harihar Lal who was then camping in Bombay. There
upon Harihar Lal directed Vaidya to personally go to the
office premises of Baroda Rayon Corporation at Bombay to
supervise the search of V.K. Shah's chamber. He was specifically asked to ensure that Shah's brief-case was searched.
Accordingly Vaidya went to the premises and helped the
authorised officers in conducting the search of Shah's cabin
and his brief-case. During this Parida and Talwar brought
to Vaidya's notice the papers indicating (substantial amounts
against the names of some individuals and industrial business
concerns). In this connection Vaidya says as under:

> These papers were shown to V.K. Shah who admitted
> that these amounts represent donations received
> from the businessmen and industries for the Congress
> Party and certain payments made to some individuals
> who were influential persons in Gujarat at the relevant
> time. Shri Shah informed me that this was "explosive
> material.

As per the specific directions of the D.I. (Investigation)
the existence of these papers was immediately brought to
his notice. They were then taken informally from the premises
of Baroda Rayon Corporation to the Income-tax office and
shown to the D.I. who kept them and asked Vaidya to see
him after about an hour. Subsequently Vaidya was asked
to seize these papers but to make a separate Panchnama of
such papers "which were not relevant to the assessment of
Baroda Rayon Corporation". On his return to B. R. C. office,
Vaidya advised the authorised officer, Parida accordingly.
Parida however objected to a separate Panchnama in respect
to a few items only, of a continuous search and seizure operation but his objection was over-ruled in view of the specific
orders of the D.I. The papers seized under the separate Panchnama along with one folder seized under the general Panchnama were taken to the D.I. The D.I. returned one of the four
items covered by the separate Panchnama (being a file containing three hundred and fifty one receipts of the Souvenir
Committee of the All India Congress Committee in favour of
Baroda Rayon Corporation for a total sum of about Rupees
three and a half lahks) and took possession of the other three

items as well as one of the items under the general Panchnama.

The seized items which the D. I. took possession of were
brought by him to Delhi on or about April 28, 1976. He had,
on that occasion, requested S. N. Shende to come to the
airport to meet him as he was carrying some important papers.
These seized papers so brought by Harihar Lal from Bombay
were handed over by him to S. R. Mehta the then Chairman
Central Board of Direct Taxes. One of the three items covered
by the separate Panchnama was returned by the D. I. to the
D. D. I. and the item covered by the general Panchnama was
handed over by the D. I. to his D. D. I. at New Delhi, on
April 7, 1977.

This leaves two items covered by the separate Panchnama in regard to four items seized from the cabin of
V.K. Shah. These two items have not yet been returned by the
D. I./the then Chairman CBDT to the Income tax officer
having jurisdiction over the concerned assessees, to whom they
should have been sent within a period of 15 days from the
date of seizure, in accordance with the provisions of sub-
section (9A) of Section 132 of the Income-tax Act, 1961.

Chairman CBDT	:	*No . . . Sir . . . I only suggested it to*
S.R. Mehta		*him . . .*
Justice Shah	:	*What is the difference between a direction and a suggestion . . .?*
S.R. Mehta	:	*I did not ask Harihar Lal . . .*
Justice Shah	:	*Did you go to the PM's house to see R.K. Dhawan on April 29 . . .?*
S.R. Mehta	:	*If the records say that . . . I may have gone but it was not to see Dhawan.*
Justice Shah	:	*Did you go on the afternoon of April 30 . . .?*
S.R. Mehta	:	*Documents came to me on the 29th . . .*
Justice Shah	:	*What gave them the impression . . . you wanted to see R.K. Dhawan . . .?*
Director of Investigation Harihar Lal	:	*It was a clear direction not a suggestion . . . I could not ask the Chairman . . . it is not customary . . .*
Counsel Khandalawala	:	*The section of the Income Tax Act was clear . . .*
Harihar Lal	:	*But . . . I always believed that truth will ultimately be found . . . I did not like the idea of a rebuke from him . . .*
Counsel Khandalawala	:	*I can understand that . . . but it appears that the raids took place because of an ulterior motive . . . I mean some officers are strong and powerful . . . others are also well connected at high level . . .*
Harihar Lal	:	*S.R. Mehta was one of them . . .*
Counsel Khandalawala	:	*He used you and your organisation. . .*
S.R. Mehta	:	*It was not illegal . . .?*
Justice Shah	:	*It was improper . . .*
Harihar Lal	:	*Yes . . . may be . . . .*
S.R. Mehta	:	*You are one of the strict disciplinarians . . .If I asked you to jump in a well. . . will you?*
Justice Shah	:	*There are degrees . . .*
Harihar Lal	:	*No . . .*
Counsel Khandalawala	:	*So . . . what you are saying is that Pranab Mukherjee told you that there was concealment of income in Gwalior Rayon . . · What suits you is*

	correct and what is inconvenient is incorrect . . .
Justice Shah	: A Minister need not have expertise in any subject . . . This was an extraordinary raid and therefore extraordinary methods were adopted . . .
Counsel Lekhi	: No wonder you were awarded the PADMA BHUSHAN in 1976 . . .

XXII—THE BAJAJ GROUP

The search and seizure operation in the Bajaj Group of cases was conducted on May 18, 1976 after H. Lal the then Director of Inspection (Investigation) (hereinafter referred to as DI) had collected "reliable information" regarding tax evasion by this group. The process of collecting information was initiated after S.R. Mehta had given to the DI the name of this case. The relevant portions of the DI's statement dated September 9, 1977 are as under :

> . . . as these assessees had, according to information which had come to his (S.R. Mehta) knowledge amassed huge wealth by indulging in tax evasion on a large scale, I should gather intelligence regarding their concealed incomes and wealth and take necessary action against them by way of authorising and organising search operations . . . . These cases were the Scindia Group of Gwalior and Bombay, the Modi Group of Modinagar, the Jaipuria Group of Kanpur and Gaziabad, the Baroda Rayon Corporation of Surat and Bombay, the Bajaj Mukund Group of Bombay and the Mahindra and Mahindra Group of Bombay and other places.

No record of the information passed on by S.R. Mehta was kept by the DI as seen from his statement dated September 21, 1977.

> . . . The said "information" was of a general nature and not specific or detailed and S.R. Mehta mentioned it to me orally and did not give it to me in writing. I did not maintain any record of what S.R. Mehta had stated to me regarding the cases under reference . . . I received some information about the case men-

tioned to me by S.R. Mehta, from certain informants, personally. I did not record their names and addresses as they had specifically requested that their identities should be kept secret and not brought on record and made it clear that they were not interested in claiming any reward for the information given by them.

Details about this group were collected for the first time by S. Talwar, Assistant Director of Inspection (Intelligence) in March 1976 and were handed over to the DI, as seen from the statement of Talwar dated August 17, 1977.

> I had gone to Bombay in the third week of March for doing reconnoitry work in the case of M/S Auto Pins. Before leaving for Bombay I was called by D.I. (Inv.) and asked by him to collect information regarding Mukand Group ... The perusal of records of Mukand Iron & Steel Limited showed that Jeevan Ltd. was also connected with them as well as the Bajaj Group. Besides going through the assessment records I also tried to gather whatever possible information from local enquiries ... On my return from Bombay, in the month of March itself, ... I mentioned to D.I. (Inv.) that Mukand Group was closely connected with the Bajaj Group and whatever little local enquiries I made at Bombay suggested that Bajaj Group had a clean reputation. D.I. (Inv.) asked me to hand over the files to S.N. Shende, DDI and thereafter nothing further regarding this group was mentioned to me and I got the impression that the matter was closed.

No action was taken in the matter till the DI called a meeting of S.N. Shende, Deputy Director of Inspection (Intelligence) (hereinafter referred to as DDI) and the ADSI then working at Mayur Bhavan, New Delhi sometime in early May 1976 and told them that he had with him some information regarding evasion of tax by this group and a search should be conducted very early. The details of the meeting in the words of S.N. Shende, are as under :

> The meeting which the DI had in early May 1976 was mainly with a view to inform me and the ADsI present that it had been decided to carry out search

and seizure operations jointly in the Bajaj, Mukand and Jeevan groups, as they were inter-connected, within a very short time and to direct us to take all necessary consequential action.

V.S. Wahi, V. Mathur, S. Talwar, K. Rangabhashyam and R.R. Gupta, ADsI have also given statements to this effect.

For organising the raids under Section 132(1) the D.D.I. (Int.) and the ADsI were sent out to various places in the country "to carry out reconnoitry work and to gather all intelligence they possibly could" (V. Mathur's statement dated August 26, 1977). The officers collected the addresses and details of places, later on covered under the section 132(1), as per Annexure to the satisfaction notes of the D.I. (Inv.), mainly from telephone/trade directories. Apart from seeing these places to prepare road maps for the guidance of Authorised Officers and to determine the manpower requirement for each of the places, no intelligence could be gathered within this short period. This is clear from K. Rangabhasyam's statement dated October 22, 1977 :

. . . I was later asked by S.N. Shende to 'recky' the places at Madras, Bangalore, Hyderabad and Wardha. I flew on May 10, 1976 and reached Madras at about 10 A.M. and completed the work at Madras by the same night. I left for Bangalore on May 11, 1976 morning and completed the work there by the evening and left for Hyderabad on the same day. I did "recky" at Hyderabad on 12th throughout the day and left for Wardha by 10 P.M. train. Reached Wardha on 13th morning and completed 'Recky' by the afternoon and left for Nagpur by the afternoon train. I left Nagpur for Delhi on the evening flight. Early morning on 14th I met the then DDI and orally informed him about the places 'reckied'. There was no written report regarding the work done by me. I did not collect any information during the trip except for the fact that I located various places which may be searched in the above group of cases.

The statements of other ADsI corroborate this.

After the officers returned, various organisational chores were assigned to them. V.S. Wahi was asked to write a note regarding the intelligence gathered in the Bajaj groups of cases. S. Talwar was asked to write similar notes in the Mukand and Jeevan groups of cases. The notes which were corrected by the higher authorities including the D.I., contain vague allegations of evasion of tax. There is no supporting material or specific information on record to substantiate these allegations. They were purportedly based on "confidential and knowledgeable sources" and discussion between the officers.

Wahi, who recorded the first note in the Bajaj Group of cases, has this to say about his source :

> The confidential and knowledgeable sources mention-
> ed by me in this note are no one else than the Director
> of Inspection (Inv.), New Delhi.

S. Talwar, who recorded a similar note in the Mukund and Jeevan Groups of cases says :

> The confidential and knowledgeable sources mention-
> ed by me in this note mostly refer to the information
> received from D.I. (Inv.) and some other collected
> from the local enquiries. As far as I know there was no
> informant in this case as nobody came to me to give
> any information.

However, in his authorisation dated May 14, 1976 in the Bajaj Group, Lal says :

> I have perused the foregoing notes of the ADI (Int.)
> V.S. Wahi and the DDI (Int.) S.N. Shende and dis-
> cussed with them the information contained therein.

> After careful consideration of the said information
> from various aspects, I have reasons to believe that the
> assessees including directors of the assessees' companies,
> connected concerns, related persons and also associates
> (referred to hereinafter as the assessees of the Bajaj
> Group) would be having in their possession books of
> accounts and other documents reflecting their un-
> accounted transactions of incomes, which they would
> not produce before the Income Tax Authorities in

response to statutory summons/notices u/s 131/142 of the Income Tax Act.

Further, I have reasons to believe that the Bajaj Group of assessees would be in possession of money, jewellery and other valuable assets representing their unaccounted incomes which they have not or would not disclose for the purposes of the Income Tax Act.

I am, therefore, issuing authorisations u/s 132(1) of the Income Tax Act for search and seizure operation in respect of the Bajaj Group of assessees (vide the persons/premises located in the Annexure hereto).

A similar note has been recorded by the DI in the Mukand and Jeevan Group of cases. The only significant feature there is that neither the DDI (Int.) nor the DI refers to the Jeevan Group of cases, which is disposed of in one small paragraph, more as an afterthought by S. Talwar.

Search and seizure operations in these groups of cases were commenced on May 18, 1976. It is seen that certain blank warrants of authorisation had been issued in these cases and that some of such blank warrants had actually been used for searches in Delhi.

In his report dated May 25, 1976 to S.R. Mehta, the DI mentions that one hundred and fourteen premises situated in twelve cities or towns were covered by the search and seizure operations which were still continuing at that time; apart from survey operations at nine business premises in six cities or towns. However, the annexures to the Satisfaction notes refer only to twenty nine premises or persons in the case of the Bajaj Group and twenty five premises or persons in the case of the Mukand and Jeevan Groups.

On May 26, 1976 when the search operation had not yet concluded, the DI sent to the Director of Information, Government of India, "Samachar" and the "Economic Times" an "Information Note", which said, inter-alia, that :

The total value of the seizures aforesaid consisting of unaccounted cash and jewellery, and unaccounted or unexplained promissory notes and fixed deposits, amounts in the aggregate to about Rs. 52.50 lakhs.

The value of the seized valuable assets is likely to increase further when the authorised officers open and examine the contents of 44 bank lockers which were detected and sealed during the course of the searches.

It is not clear how, at that stage, the DI could state so categorically that the valuables seized were "unaccounted".

The investigation carried out in the Directorate at Delhi as well as by the concerned Income Tax Officer at Surat pursuant to the search and seizure operations has not revealed any concealment based on seized material. No concealed profit has been estimated in the order under Sub-section 5 of Section 132 of the Income Tax Act, 1961.

It has further been noticed that in this case certain blank warrants of authorisation for search had been issued by the DI on April 22, 1976.

XXIII—THE VISHWA YUVAK KENDRA

From the affidavits filed by Ramkrishna Bajaj, the Managing Trustee of the International Youth Centre and P.T. Kuriakose, the Director of the International Youth Centre, the Vishwa Yuvak Kendra (International Youth Centre) is a multi-purpose youth centre set up by the Indian Youth Centres Trust. It is housed in its own building which is located in the Diplomatic Enclave, Chanakyapuri, New Delhi. In 1959, the Executive Committee of the Indian Assembly of Youth decided to establish an International Youth Centre with a view to providing training in youth work to workers of youth organisations. The Centre was also to serve as an international meeting place for young people from all over the world.

The Ministry of Education, Government of India, provided a grant of six hundred thousand rupees towards the cost of the building and the Ministry of Works, Housing & Supply supported the proposal by allotting a two acre plot of land in the Diplomatic Enclave, New Delhi. Internationally, the project was supported by the UNESCO which included it in the International Gift Coupon Schemes. The Konrad Adenauer Foundation of West Germany also extended some financial help to this institution.

Encouraged by this wide ranging support, a trust was set up in 1961 with Ramkrishna Bajaj as the Managing Trustee. The Trust has the overall responsibility regarding the management of the Kendra. The Managing Trustee acts on behalf of the Trust. The Director of the Kendra is responsible for the day-to-day management of the Kendra including detailed planning and implementation of the various programmes.

As early as May 22, 1973, V.C. Shukla, the then Minister of State for Defence Production, is alleged to have informed

Ramkrishna Bajaj, the Managing Trustee of the Kendra, that Indira Gandhi, the then Prime Minister of India, had desired that the composition of the Board of Trustees of the Indian Youth Centres Trust should be changed. When R.K. Bajaj conveyed this proposal to the Board of Trustees, a discussion was held and the Board of Trustees decided not to accept the proposal.

During the Emergency, the Delhi Administration requisitioned the building of the Vishwa Yuvak Kendra under Section 23 of the Defence and Internal Security of India Act on August 30, 1975. Bajaj complained about it not only to Brahmananda Reddy, the then Minister for Home Affairs, but also to Indira Gandhi, the then Prime Minister of India. He sent a written complaint addressed to the Prime Minister of India on September 13, 1975.

After the Delhi Administration had requisitioned the building of the Vishwa Yuvak Kendra, Krishan Chand, the then Lt. Governor of Delhi, had told Ramkrishna Bajaj in November 1975 that the derequisitioning of the building could be done fast if the latter could agree to reconstitute the Board of Trustees. A hint was also thrown that Ambika Soni could be considered as one of the possible members of the Board. When Bajaj showed reluctance to consider the name of Ambika Soni since it would have gone against the non-political character of the Board of Trustees, Krishan Chand advised Bajaj to discuss possible new names with him and Shriman Narain so that a list could be submitted to the Prime Minister.

V.C. Shukla pressurised R.K. Bajaj to hand over the management of the Trust to the former who would run the Kendra building in consultation with Sanjay Gandhi. On January 29, 1976, R.K. Bajaj was advised by Mohamed Yunus, the then Special Envoy to the Prime Minister to cooperate with the Government and abide by the advice given by V.C. Shukla. Yunus told Bajaj that during the emergency the Government had enough powers and if the trustees did not cooperate, the Government could put the trustees behind the bars.

R.K. Bajaj thereupon called a meeting of the Board of Trustees in Bombay on the same day (i.e. January 29, 1976) which was attended by the following trustees :

Naval Tata
S.P. Godrej
V.V. John
R.K. Bajaj

In the meeting, the suggestion of Naval Tata that all the trustees should resign as a protest against the manner in which the Trust was treated by the Government, was not accepted by the Trustees.

Naval Tata informed the Trustees attending this meeting that he had contacted Sanjay Gandhi on phone and the latter had told him that he was interested in the building earlier but was no more interested in it since the building had been allotted to the Delhi Tourism Development Corporation. When Bajaj talked to V.C. Shukla and conveyed to him the gist of the conversation between Sanjay Gandhi and Naval Tata, Shukla expressed surprise at this and remarked that Sanjay Gandhi might have casually mentioned it without actually meaning it.

On February 17, 1976, Krishan Chand, the then Lt. Governor of Delhi, advised Bajaj that the latter and Sanjay Gandhi should agree on a solution as to how the Kendra should be run.

R.K. Bajaj again met the Lt. Governor on April 10, 1976 and informed him that the Trustees wanted the Kendra to remain a non-political institution and they might agree to the addition of some persons to the Board provided their joining the Trust would not go against the non-political character of the Trust. On this, the Lt. Governor asked him whether the Trustees would be willing to accept the advice of the Prime Minister. Bajaj promised that he would immediately convene a meeting to discuss this suggestion.

Accordingly, a meeting of the Board of Trustees was held on April 29, 1976, and the Trustees decided to seek the advice of the Prime Minister and in pursuance thereof Bajaj addressed a letter to Indira Gandhi, the then Prime Minister of India, on May 1, 1976. The relevant extract from this letter is reproduced below :

Futher to my letter of 10th January to you, I have had
occasion to meet the Lt. Governor, Delhi. In the light
of the discussions I had with him, the Trustees of the
Kendra, in their meeting yesterday, reviewed the situation and decided to seek your advice in regard to the
activities of the Kendra and the future of the Trust,
including the composition of its Board of Trustees,
in order to make it more broad-based and to enable
it to fulfil its objects more effectively. The Trustees
have also decided to abide by your advice.

On behalf of the Trust, I am therefore writing to request you kindly to spare some time to look into the
matter and let us have your valuable advice and guidance. If you so desire, I will be happy to call on you
to clarify any further points.

Bajaj has further mentioned in his affidavit that when
he along with S.P. Godrej and P.T. Kuriakose met the Lt.
Governor on May 3, 1976, and informed him of the decision of
the trustees, the Lt. Governor expressed his satisfaction and stated that "he was happy that a sorry chapter was coming to an
end. As a government servant, he only carried out orders but
he stated that when the building was requisitioned he realised
that it was all politics, but he could do nothing about it. He
stated that he tried to do what he could viz. not to allot the
building to anyone who could use it and therefore would not
vacate when some settlement was made. He said that the
whole thing was engineered by V.C. Shukla, who seemed to
have the inkling that the Prime Minister had some reservation
about me and harping on it, had poisoned her mind further."

The affidavit filed by V.V. John, who is also a trustee
and who attended the meeting of the Board of Trustees on
January 29, 1976 corroborates the allegation. V.V. John
has stated in his affidavit that "Ramkrishna Bajaj told us that
he had had talks with V.C. Shukla, the then Minister and
Mohamed Yunus in order to persuade the Government to
derequisition the said building. Ramkrishna Bajaj told us that
he was advised by Shukla that all the Trustees should resign
and leave the matter in the hands of Sanjay Gandhi. Bajaj
further informed us that he was advised by Yunus not to an-
tagonise the Government and to accept Shukla's advice. We

were informed by Bajaj that Yunus had warned him that if the Trustees offered any resistance, they could be put behind the bars." V.V. John has stated that "Mr. Naval Tata who was in the chair in the meeting held on January 29, 1976 strongly expressed himself against the highhanded way in which the Government had dealt with the Trust. Naval Tata was of the view that all the Trustees should resign. Tata informed us that he had a talk with Yashpal Kapur and Sanjay Gandhi with regard to the derequisitioning of the Vishwa Yuvak Kendra building. Naval Tata told us that Sanjay Gandhi told him that although at an earlier stage he was interested in the Kendra building and the same was offered to him, however, he was now no longer interested in the said building since the Government had handed over the same to Delhi Tourism Development Corporation."

He further stated :

...that I told the Chairman, Naval Tata that I was not prepared to resign, I further told the Trustees present in the meeting that I could not abdicate the trust reposed in me particularly in the circumstances in which we have been landed by the Government.

...That I told the Trustees that I had no intention to resign making it easy for any outsider to step in. I further said that the threat of detention in jail could have no effect on me and that people much better than us had already been sent to jail.

...Tata left before the meeting was concluded since he had another engagement elsewhere. Naval Tata said before he left that he was sending in his resignation from the Trust. The other Trustees present including me decided not to resign from the membership of the Board of Trustees.

Chief Secretary of :	*Sir every time I talked to the Lt. Governor. .*
Delhi J.K. Kohli	*he would ask me to talk to Navin Chawla. . .*
Justice Shah :	*Wetted the Order. . .What does it mean. . .*
	You only acted mechanically. . .
J.K. Kohli :	*I put up the proposal to the Lt. Governor. . .*
Justice Shah :	*Did you discuss with the Lt. Governor whether it could be done lawfully. . .You are a senior officer and the illegality of the action will be considered by you. . .Why did you show such apathy ? You were transfered as Jt. Secretary to the PM. . .*
J.K. Kohli :	*Yes. . .*
Justice Shah :	*What office did Navin Chawla hold. . .?*
J.K. Kohli :	*Secretary. . .to the Lt Governor.*
Justice Shah :	*WHY was it that you were directed to take orders from Navin Chawla. . .?*
J.K. Kohli :	*Well Sir. . .he was in. . .*
Justice Shah :	*Why Navin Chawla. . .What was the source of his authority. . .?*
J.K. Kohli :	*Sanjay Gandhi . . . Krishan Chand was the Lieutenant. . .and Navin Chawla was the Governor. . .*
Lt. Governor of :	*Those were different times My Lord. . .I*
Delhi Krishan	*can't put my hands in my pocket before my*
Chand	*father. . .You are showing respect to him. . . Sir. . .but my son puts his hands all over. . .*
Counsel :	*The building was objectionable but not its*
Khandalawala	*activities.*
Shashi Bhushan :	*It was reported in Time Magazine.*
Counsel :	*The Time Magazine hasn't taken the pres-*
Khandalawala	*tige of a Scripture . . . By the way you know Sanjay Gandhi?*
Former Minister :	*Yes.*
of Information and	
Broadcasting	
V.C. Shukla	
Counsel :	*A friend of yours?*
Khandalawala	
V.C. Shukla :	*No . . . no friend of mine . . .*
Khandalawala :	*This must be incorrect . . . or was it a voyage of discovery . . ?*

XXIV—MANGAL BIHARI AND OTHERS

Harideo Joshi, the former Chief Minister of Rajasthan, recorded the following note on August 20, 1975.

R.K. Dhawan, Private Secretary to the Prime Minister rang me up to convey the following :

> S.N. Sharma, Advocate, 74-Sarojini Marg, Jaipur is reported to have burnt records relating to his and his wife's activities as followers of Anand Marg. R.N. Gaur, Addl. S.P., inspite of being informed about the burning of records did not reach in time and allowed the records to be burnt. It was desired that S.N. Sharma should be detained under MISA.

> His wife Chandra Sharma, Lecturer in Maharani's College, Jaipur, should be removed from service.

> An enquiry should be conducted immediately in the conduct of Gaur.

> It was also desired that Mangal Bihari IAS should also be relieved from service.

> Please take necessary action.

Sd/- Harideo Joshi
20/8/75
Chief Minister, Rajasthan

On receipt of the above note from the Chief Minister, the Chief Secretary, Rajasthan, initiated the following action :

> A top secret d.o. letter No. 5993/CS/1 dated August 20, 1975 was addressed to District Magistrate, Jaipur,

desiring that S.N. Sharma should be detained under MISA on the grounds mentiond in para 1 of the Chief Minister's note reproduced above. A top secret note was sent to the Education Commissioner to the effect that the University may be asked to terminate the services of Chandravati Sharma as on the basis of information received, the Goverment was satisfied that she is an active follower of Anand Marg and her continuance in service is not desirable in the interest of the University and in public interest. A top secret d.o. letter dated August 20, 1975 was addressed to Inspector General of Police, Rajasthan, for initiating enquiry into the conduct of Gaur, Addl. Seperintendent of Police, Jaipur. Mangal Bihari, IAS, the then Member Board of Revenue, Rajasthan, was told on August 20, 1975 to apply for leave. A note of the Chief Secretary dated September 2, 1975 says that Mangal Bihari was given leave for one month after talking to Secretary, Department of Personnel & A.R., Government of India, and Behl, Joint Secretary in Prime Minister's Secretariat.

(Chief Secretary's note dated September' 2 1975 and August 25, 1977)

In pursuance of the Chief Secretary's d.o. letter dated August 20, 1975 mentioned above, the District Magistrate, Jaipur, detained S.N. Sharma under MISA on August 20, 1975 and the detention order was duly confirmed by the State Government with the approval of the Chief Minister subsequently.

In so far as R.K. Dhawan's telephonic instructions to Harideo Joshi, the former Chief Minister of Rajasthan regarding termination of services of Chandravati Sharma are concerned, it is seen from the record that on receipt of the top secret note of the Chief Secretary the Education Commissioner sent the following instructions to Joint Director (Women) Jaipur-Ajmer Range, in a letter dated August 23, 1975 :

On the basis of information received the Government is satisfied that Chandra Sharma w/o S.N. Sharma, Advocate, 74, Sarojini Marg, Jaipur, who is working as Assistant Teacher, in Maharaja Girls' Higher Secondary School, Jaipur, is actively associated with an organisation declared illegal and her continuance in service is not desirable in public interest.

You are, therefore, requested to terminate her services forthwith, under intimation to the undersigned.

The Joint Director (Women) Education Department, Jaipur accordingly passed orders dated August 23, 1975 terminating the services of Chandravati Sharma with immediate effect and informed all concerned including the Education Commissioner. The State Government's record shows that Chandravati Sharma met the Education Commissioner on more than one occasion after the termination of her services and tried to impress upon him verbally as well as through written representation that she has been made a victim of personal animosity between her husband S.N. Sharma and their landlord B.B. Gupta. She produced a letter from B.B. Gupta, the landlord, to her husband in support of her contention. The Education Commissioner also brought this matter to the notice of the Chief Secretary. Chief Secretary's letter of September 16, 1975 to Director CBI is noteworthy and is reproduced below :

As for the action taken against S.N. Sharma and Chandravati Sharma it is presumed that it was based upon additional information besides information furnished by Dr. (Miss) Pushpa Khanna.

Since R.N. Gaur the Addl SP of Police had visited the building where the records of the association of S.N. Sharma and his wife were alleged to have been burnt, the Commission has recorded his statement, the operative portion of which is reproduced below :

On July 6, 1975 I visited C-74, Sarojini Marg, Jaipur on the instructions of Superintendent of Police, Jaipur to contact Dr. Miss Pushpa Khanna at about 9.15 P.M. Dr. Miss Pushpa Khanna handed over some loose pages from a diary—most of the pages were blank. Six pages only contain some spiritual material. These pages contained no evidence of burning by way of smoke marks or burnt edges. Dr. Pushpa Khanna did not show me the place where burning took place, nor could she produce her servant before me on my specific request.

In the case of Mangal Bihari, a complaint has been received by the Commission from him stating that he had been posted as Chairman, Rajasthan State Electricity Board, since September 1974 and would have normally held this post for a tenure of three years. On June 30, 1975 he was, however, suddenly transferred out as Member of the Board of Revenue, Ajmer. Mangal Bihari has attributed his sudden transfer to the following events which are reproduced below verbatim from his complaint :

> As Chairman Rajasthan State Road Transport Corporation I refused the use of Corporation buses for being taken to Delhi in the big rally organised by the Congress Party against J.P.'s movement in March, '75.

> As Chairman, R.S.E.B. I refused to exempt from electricity charges an exhibition organised by Mrs. Yash Pal Kapoor inspite of much pressure on me from all quarters in this regard.

> As Chairman Rajasthan State Electricity Board I refused to allow "free" use of 100 trucks and 10,000 workers for participating in the rally organised by the Congress Party on June 20, '75 in Delhi to exhibit the so-called "peoples' solidarity" for the former Prime Minister after the Allahabad Judgment. I was verbally instructed by the Political bosses in the State to allow these workers to go without taking leave and not to charge anything for the trucks.

> As Chairman Rajasthan State Electricity Board I ordered that full charges at normal private rates be recovered for the 58 trucks which were requisitioned for the rally in spite of tremendous political pressure on me to the contrary. After the rally, the organiser of the rally in Rajasthan is believed to have complained to Yash Pal Kapoor and Sanjay Gandhi about my non-cooperative attitude in these matters.

Shri Mangal Bihari was, consequently allowed to resume duty w.e.f. December 15, 1976. He had to remain on leave/ Await Posting Orders from August 8, 1975 to December 15, 1976 i.e. from the date R.K. Dhawan rang up the ex-Chief Minister of Rajasthan.

Chief Secretary of Rajasthan Mohan Mookerjee	:	*Sir .. it was the Prime Minister's satisfaction . . .*
Justice Shah	:	*You are under so many assumptions . . .*
Mangal Bihari	:	*Sir in those days . . . R.K. Dhawan cleared everyone . . . I went to the Prime Minister's house . . . on June 26 . . . I really do not wish to quote it . . .*
		Here silence is golden . . .
		We made mistakes . . . a lot of them . . . for many years . . .
Justice Shah	:	*He had a cavalier attitude . . .*
Mangal Bihari	:	*I saw R.K. Dhawan dealing with two three cases . . .*
		They even tried to touch his feet . . . There was also a poor woman and he just ignored her . . . Sir . . . They never forgave me for the orders that I gave that industrial rates be charged for the . . . Mela that Mrs Yashpal Kapoor had arranged . . . They said it was of National importance . . . though when I went over it was a four month mela of gambling and money-making . . .
Secretary to the Government of India, Khurana	:	*I tried to do all I could for him . . . I even talked to Om Mehta . . .*
R. K. Dhawan	:	*Everyone is telling lies . . . . .*
Former Chief Minister of Rajasthan H. D. Joshi	:	*I phoned up Dhawan again . . .*
R. K. Dhawan	:	*He never phoned me . . .*
Mangal Bihari	:	*In the PM's house he told me . . . "Are you Mangal Bihari and you distributed sweets on the day of the judgement of the Prime Minister?"*
R. K. Dhawan	:	*I never met him.*
Mangal Bihari	:	*The second time I met him he was in a staff car and all he said was "Don't worry everything will be alright."*

4 Vidya Charan Shukla . . . And the Wisdom of the Hind

News media owners pride themselves in their motto, *"All the News that is fit to print"*. What is not printed presumably is neither News nor a Fit. What happens when you get one should make an interesting story. Will that get printed? Well it may not be News, but then won't that be News fit to print. No, not exactly since news, is what you want to print, and what you want makes it fit.

Vidya Charan Shukla had no Wants, nor did he have any Fits but he sure knew what newspaper owners want and what makes them get a Fit. Having known that, all he wanted was to be in the news—not a terribly uncommon affliction. The simplest solution is to own a newspaper, or be wealthy or be very handsome, but not too poor, another good way is to be in a position of power and yet another, and the best, is to have all this and then be the MIB—the Minister of Information and Broadcasting.

What happens then is not only News, but every word uttered becomes News fit to print. Whether these are the foibles of only Newspaper owners or Editors too is a different matter, but the fact remains that in a business virtually in a state of plethora only six die-hard journalists had the nerve to print what most definitely gave others the fit.

Preventing unfavourable news and views which expressed dissent may be very laudable ideas, depending on what one is fighting for. Censorship is even better, then you don't have a problem of determining what India is all about. But what about the infamous doctrine of the Code of Ethics? Was it the idea of government to make the press colourless, tasteless and odourless?

V.C. Shukla always felt the press was neither fish nor fowl in the first place, and under the circumstances this is no . . . story. Then he asked them to bend and instead they crawled, but this does not make good Copy . . .

‘Wisdom of the Hind’, famous words uttered by Ambassa- dor Gujral recently at the confessional of the Commission tells a different story and possibly Vidya Charan Shukla realises it, but does former Minister of Information and Broadcasting Inder Kumar Gujral? But then that is not news nor is it fit to print.

XXV—NEWS MEDIA

On the declaration of the Emergency on June 26, 1975 the news in all its forms whether through newspaper reports, or AIR broadcasts, or TV programme, or Films Division documentaries, was sought to be put under the general control of the Government in the following manner:

> Unfavourable news and views which expressed dissent with the Government viewpoint were suppressed. As early as June 30, 1975, V.C. Shukla directed that "Censor Officers should be stationed at newspaper offices in each major centre of publication begining with Delhi." Similarly Indira Gandhi at her high level meeting held in July, 1975, said "A vigilant eye should be kept on some language magazines and periodicals . . ." She also said, "Foreign correspondents refusing to furnish undertakings and submit writings for pre-censorship should be deported."

To suppress dissent, censorship was imposed in the country under rule 48 of the DISIR. Soon after statutory orders based on rule 48 were issued. The manner in which censorship was imposed has been discussed and detailed at the appropriate place in this paper.

The other side of the Government policy was to play up news favourable to the Government often without giving the opposing view point. Indira Gandhi said at her high level meeting of August 12, 1975, that "most of the newspapers make dull reading these days. Ways and means should be devised to provide them necessary material so as to make them interesting and entertaining for the readers". "In view of the restraints

Government departments and agencies should provide sufficient materials to the newspapers." "Publicity of positive aspects
of the Emergency and economic programme should be arranged in friendly foreign newspapers."

The Government was not merely content with censoring
news or supplying information and material to the media but
it also decided "if necessary, editorials should be got written
and published, if newspapers appeared with blank editorials".
Similarly, the Chief Censor ordered that "there has been a
'bundh' in Ahmedabad organised by the ruling party (Janta
Front). If the agencies and the correspondent's copies say
'bundh' was a flop, it may be allowed". On August 8, 1975,
Vidya Charan Shukla ordered that "we have to prepare interesting material and photographs giving accurate information about
conditions in the country", "prepare a list of influential and
important media in the western world which could be used for
highlighting facts about India". This was in response to a
decision taken at Indira Gandhi's meeting of August 7, 1975
where the possibility of "inducing established foreign writers
to write the facts about India" was discussed.

One of the most important aspects of news and media management as the Emergency continued was the building up of
the image of Indira Gandhi as the sole and infallible leader
of the Congress Party and the country. To parallel this simultaneously a campaign was launched to build up Sanjay Gandhi
as a leader in his own right.

Early in July, 1975 PIO, Baji was directed by V.C. Shukla
to contact Editors of various newspapers in Delhi and ensure
that they accord prominent publicity both "news-wise and
photo publicity-wise" to the statements and activities of the
Prime Minister. Baji was cautioned by the Minister that what
he was stating should not go on record.

Similarly, to give the impression that Indira Gandhi was
the undisputed leader of the Congress Party and that under
her leadership there were no factions in the Congress, the Censor issued instructions to all his regional and branch offices
that "if any story including comments gives the impression
of instability to a Ministry of revolt by a group or faction it
will have to be killed", "the guiding test in allowing a story is

to ensure that there is no group politics instability in the Party".
(Chief Censor telex dated January 8, 1977) V.C. Shukla at his
meeting on June 29, 1975 "referred to the over-emphasis on
the personality of Ministers in the media coverage, particularly,
AIR, on TV and Radio. This must be avoided and he said
that with the exception of the Prime Minister there should be
no undue stress on Ministers in the news coverage".

As regards Sanjay Gandhi, publicity was given to him
extensively both over AIR and Doordarshan. Doodarshan
spent Rs. 8,33,000 on publicity of Sanjay Gandhi's Five Point
Programme and over 265 items were telecast on Sanjay Gandhi
from January 1, 1977 to January 18, 1977. AIR was also told
to give adequate coverage to Sanjay Gandhi. "AIR was asked
to describe Sanjay Gandhi as Youth Leader, but subsequently,
we were asked to drop the words 'Youth Leader' in order to
convey the impression that he was a national figure and not a
mere Youth Leader. Between the above mentioned period 192
news items were broadcast about Sanjay Gandhi from AIR
Delhi alone." said S.C. Bhatt DNS in AIR.

In fact, the entire attitude of Indira Gandhi and Shukla
towards media can be seen by their speeches at the AIR
Station Directors' Conference on September 9, 1975. "I find
that he had said something about credibility of Radio. And
this question had arisen even before Emergency. Quite hones-
tly I do not know what it means. Who has credibility? The
newspapers who have day in and day out filled their pages with
falsehood? Now if you say that the people keep on believing
these things, well, all I can say is that they are free to do so,
*but it is not going to help them much in getting information or
having any knowledge of what is happening in the country*",
said Indira Gandhi.

"Amongst the truth we pick and choose, we only emphasise
such things which we considered in our judgement best for
helping and abetting the developmental process of the country
in the direction that we have set for it and certain other set of
facts which may not be helpful in that direction, we ignore
those facts." "Credibility does not consist in balancing facts"
said V.C. Shukla.

On September 12, 1975, S.M.H. Burney held a meeting in his
room to discuss measures to improve television programmes in

the light of P.M.'s address to Station Directors/Directors of TV Centres. In this meeting he drew attention to PM's observation relating to AIR and TV being under the Government and said "it should now be clear to everyone concerned that, being a Government department, there was no question of AIR or Television adopting an attitude of neutrality or to be concerned about their credibility".

Censorship : Censorship was imposed because "we are facing an entirely new situation similar to the Chilean one. We believe in freedom of the Press but a section of the Press had been behaving irresponsibly". (Indira Gandhi's note on a letter dated July 9, 1975 written to her by Saroj Mukerjee, M.P.) "The decision to regulate newspapers was an unpalatable one, but the recklessness with which some of them were publishing malicious and wholly fabricated reports . . . left little option". (Indira Gandhi's letter dated July 9, 1975 written to J.N. Sahani)

The Emergency was imposed on June 26, 1975, but at that time the Government was not ready with the censorship apparatus. The Government, therefore, in order to prevent the newspapers from publishing their editions resorted to the simple expedient of cutting off electricity connections of all newspaper offices situated on Bahadur Shah Zafar Marg from June 26, 1975 to June 29, 1975. For three days all newspaper offices remained without electricity and, therefore, could not bring out their daily editions. During these three days the Government succeeded in setting up the censorship apparatus and appointed the PIO, Baji, as the Chief Censor till such time as H.J. D'Penha could be appointed as Chief Censor.

Similarly, P.N. Behl, Joint Secretary, in the Prime Minister's Secretariat, was sent to the News Services Division of All India Radio to direct the news operations. Behl functioned in the AIR till such time as Vidya Charan Shukla took over as I&B Minister and the Censorship Organisation started functioning.

Pre-censorship was enforced under rule 48 of DISIR on June 26, 1975 and these rules were amplified in Statutory Order 275 (E) of the same date. Between June 26 and August 12, 1975, the Home Ministry issued a series of statutory orders and GSRs under relevant rules of DISIR. The result of the issue of these orders and rules led to wider expansion of the scope of Press Censorship and concentration of powers in the Central Government and the Chief Censor.

Rule 48 of the DISIR gave powers to the Central/State Governments to impose censorship for the purposes of securing the defence of India, Civil defence, the public safety, the maintenance of public order and the efficient conduct of military operations. Subsequently, the scope of rule 48 was expanded to include President's Rule in Tamil Nadu, President's Rule in Gujarat and Family Planning. In the case of Family Planning the Law Ministry had advised that "before the subject of Family Planning and other matters incidental to it . . . be prohibited from publication without pre-censorship, it is necessary to examine whether the subject would be germane (to rule 48 of DISIR)". "In that view of the matter the proposed amendment to the censorship order dated June 26, 1975 would not appear to be permissible". In spite of this clear advice given by the Ministry of Law, the Secretary, I&B S.M.H. Burney ordered "we must continue killing all such Family Planning news/stories/periodicals etc. regardless of advice given by the Ministry of Law".

H.J. D'Penha and K.N. Prasad got guidelines approved for the benefit of the Censor Officers from Vidya Charan Shukla. One of these guidelines advised censor officers that "nothing should be permitted to be printed which is likely to convey the impression of a protest or disapproval of Governmental measures. The practice of leaving the editorial column either blank or filling it with quotations should not be permitted". It may be noted that these instructions are beyond the scope of the DISIR. The general guidelines to the Press which were issued by the Government on June 27, 1975 included a provision for avoiding stories and to keep in mind" any attempt at denigrating the Institution of the Prime Minister". It may be noted that the Appeal Court (Division Bench consisting of D.P. Madan and M.H. Kania JJ) held that "the guidelines issued under Clause (3) of the Censorship Order do not have statutory authority". The Court also laid down certain important principles which the Censor must also bear in mind. The Press is not only an instrument of disseminating information but it is also a powerful medium of moulding public opinion by propaganda and in this the press has an important role to play. It was not the function of the Censor acting under the Censorship Order to make all newspapers and periodicals trim their sails to one wind or to tow along in a single file or to speak in chorus with one voice.

Commenting on the Chief Censor's guidelines the judgement states that "public criticism which is the lifeline of democracy is sought to be cut by these guidelines . . . to permit such guidelines to operate even for a moment more will be destructive of our cherished democratic social order . . . the Chief Censor has been more loyal to the king than the king himself and has outwitted the people in their attempt to maintain even the basic form of democracy in this country". (C. Vaidya Editor *Bhumiputra* Baroda v/s Shri D'Penha, Chief Censor.)

On July 5, 1975 at V.C. Shukla's Coordination Committee meeting he desired that "the opinion of the Law Ministry in writing should be obtained . . . if proceedings and judgement of courts are censored" whether this amounts to contempt of Court. The advice of the Law Ministry was sought and it advised that "great caution should be exercised in censoring the judgement of the court . . . He also stressed that only that part of the judgement which has a definite bearing on the relatable heads should be subject to censor and not the entire judgement". At a meeting held in Shukla's room on May 31, 1976 the Law Secretary felt that "it would not be advisable to defy the orders of the court". However, in spite of the advice of the Ministry of Law, newspapers' reports on court proceedings were censored. Instances will be given below under the specific cases which are being discussed.

A few illustrative examples of the type of news management which the Censorship authorities were carrying out are given from the log books which were maintained by them :

No story is to be cleared pertaining to Parliament business or Supreme Court appeal filed by Prime Minister. No reference to the case (July 12, 1975).

As per instructions . . . only the date fixed for hearing of PM's appeal is to be given. Lawyers' names may be given . . . no names of judges are to be given (July 14, 1975)

Reports on proceedings in the Verghese v/s Birla case should be reduced to the minimum and should

be very brief. The arguments need not be mentioned. If they are allowed, should not be more than
a para or two. (July 22, 1975)

There has been a 'bundh' in Ahmedabad, organised
by the ruling party (Janta Front). If the agencies and
the correspondent's copies say that the 'bundh was a
flop' it may be allowed, provided the description of
the 'bundh' does not go against Censor Instructions.

Any statement made by the Chief Minister, Gujarat,
criticising any action taken by the Centre should be
spiked, but if his statement is innocuous it may be
allowed. In case of any doubt please ring up Addl.
Chief Censor, U.C. Tiwari. (July 26, 1975)

No reports, comments (including editorial), articles,
statement or news on bonus to employees shall be
allowed until further instructions from us. (September 4, 1975)

(i)   No adverse criticism of the Ordinance on
        Bonus by Trade Unions in Public Sector Orga-
        nisations is to be allowed ;

(ii)   editorial comments on bonus are permissible ;

(iii)   these comments should be within the official ex-
        planation on the bonus issue and should not
        support an agitational approach ; and

(iv)   that these comments are subject to pre-
        censorship.

        Teleprinter message to all the State Censors has
        been sent on the above lines, with the following
        additions :

        words like 'shock', 'deplore' or 'ill-advice' should
        be altered to 'disappointed' or 'surprise'. (Sep-
        tember 26, 1975)

Please ensure that Allahabad High Court judgement
today upholding MISA detenues right to move High
Court under article 226 is not published in the State.
Instruct your Censor in Allahabad to kill story.
(October 30, 75)

As required, the official version of JP's release, with

instructions not to give prominence to the news and not to use photographs, was communicated to agencies and local papers . . . . (November 13, 1975)

Any message on JP should be cleared from Prasad (phone residence-279377 ; office-384597) CC and JCCP should be first consulted before reference.

KMLP (Gujarat) has been dissolved. There is likelihood of some members issuing statements withdrawing support to the Janta Front Government in Gujarat. Such statements *should be allowed.* Statements pledging support to the Janta Front Govt. by some of the members *should be spiked* (Instruction CC). (February 11, 1975)

All the statements made by Janta Front Leaders alleging that Centre or Congress was out to topple their Ministry or that the Janta Front would take to agitation etc. should not be allowed. The statement of KMLP leaders dissolving their party, in support of the Janta Front are also not to be allowed. Anything which is unhelpful to the present plan of the Centre should be killed. (February 15, 1976)

Political overtones in stories emanating from Paunar should be disallowed. (Instruction from OSD) (March 2, 1976)

As desired by JCC (P) all the local dailies and news agencies were informed that Tulmohan Ram's case should be sent to us for pre-censorship. All references to L.N. Mishra, Chattopadhyaya and N.K. Singh are to be deleted. (March 5, 1976)

I have requested Samachar (Lazarus) not to circulate any story, comment etc. regarding the reported factionalism in the Kerala Youth Congress in connection with the visit of Ambika Soni, M.P., Youth Congress President, to Trivandrum on the 17 April, 1976 . . . . (April 19, 1976)

About mid-day today the office of 'Veekshanam' daily (Cochin) was searched by the police for reasons not known. This daily newspaper is run by the Kerala Pradesh Congress Committee. Some of the newspapers which referred a story on this to me were advised not to carry anything for the time being . . .

This development assumes more importance in view of the widening rift within the Congress party in the State. The section which is rallying behind the PCC President, who published the daily is very sore about the police search. The police portfolio is held by the Congress Minister, Karunakaran, who is identified with the rival section in the party.

This incident is likely to precipitate further. (April 22 1976)

State Censors have been advised not to permit any comments references about the transfer of High Court Judges. (June 1, 1976).

The above quotations are taken from the Log Book, wherein oral instructions given to Newspapers have been kept for record. These instructions were obviously incorrect because the censors themselves have noted on April 2, 1976 regarding Family Planning that although this is not covered by SO 275 (E) and as such although State Censors cannot give the aforesaid advice in writing they should do so orally. Similarly, the Chief Censor sent a telex message to all State Censors which read as follows :

Since all instructions on censorship are secret and meant only for use, these are not supposed to be communicated. You are expected to advice the Editors orally about the course of action and not communicate my instructions.

The censorship provisions were utilised to shut down a number of newpapers/magazines or to enforce such a rigid pre-censorship on them that they were unable to bring out their editions in time. Given below are a few illustrated cases :

Opinion : This magazine carried an article which was supposed to be part of a written proposition filed by N.A. Palkhiwala in the supreme Court regarding the life-long immunity which was proposed to be granted to the Prime Minister and some others. This was held to be objectionable by the censor "as this has a bearing on the office of the President and Prime Minister, it would appear to be actionable". "Gorwala was asked to give us certified copies of the court proceedings but he declined to let the censors see them". On this the Chief Censor, Bombay recommended, "it would appear that denial of the present press for printing his publication would be a fit response".

On February 6, 1976 Debendra Satpathi M.P., sent a copy of the *Opinion* to V.C. Shukla. On this, instructions were issued by the Chief Censor that action should be taken for forfeiture of the press.

On February 17, 1976, the *Opinion* published an issue devoted wholly to a judgement of the Bombay Hight Court regarding press censorship. The Chief Censor ordered the forfeiture of the press.

On May 1, 1976, O.S.D. K.N. Prasad noted : "I am indeed surprised that we should have tolerated this journal *Opinion* for all these months. It should have been placed under pre-censorship in addition to the other steps that have been taken to deal with the specific offences. It is our failure to deal with such journals that bring discredit to the Organisation of the Censor".

On May 3, 1976, the Chief Censor ordered that action should immediately be a taken to prosecute Gorwala within 48 hours. Gorwala was asked to deposit a security of Rs. 25,000/-. On this he went to the High Court on a writ and obtained a stay order. He was also fined Rs. 100/- after being prosecuted under the Registration of Books Act. Eventually *Opinion* was banned on July 2, 1976 but Gorwala continued getting it cyclostyled or typed and getting it distributed through the mails. This too was finally stopped when the Chief Censor requested PMG, Bombay that "the question of discontinuance of concessional mailing facilities given to the said weekly may be considered".

Sadhana : This magazine published by S.M. Joshi was constantly publishing articles allegedly against the Goverment. Between June, 1975 and October, 1975, 11 issues of this magazine were forfeited to the Government and the publisher was made to give a security of Rs. 1000/- which was forfeited. Consequently, the Government of Maharashtra ordered the closure of this magazine. The MHA referred the case to the Law Ministry. The Law Ministry made a thorough examination of rule 47 of DISIR and opined that "conferment of powers in relation of this rule is limited to the particular pre-judicial report."

The Law Ministry also advised that "there is no provision in the PPOMA empowering the Government to impose an order on the *Sadhana* press prohibiting publication of *Sadhana* weekly on the ground of persistent violation of censorship orders. Actually none of the rules of the DISIR appears to confer such powers on the Government". Subsequently, the Law Ministry re-examined the matter and the same officer the late P.V. Swarlu, (JS & LA) who had given the earlier opinion, now gave a completely opposite opinion. Subsequently *Sadhana* was banned from publication on July 2, 1976.

Mainstream : *Mainstream* had been under watch since May, 1967. The Chief Censor noted the satirical tone of *Mainstream* articles regarding Sanjay Gandhi and his Four Point Programme. However, the Censor was of the view that action should not be taken against *Mainstream* because it was supporting the Government's economic policy, and not because criticism of Sanjay Gandhi was not covered under the DIR.

In this note, dated December 9, 1976 to Minister, the Chief Censor examines two editorials which appeared in the *Mainstream* on November 27, 1976 and December 4, 1976. Though one of the editorials deals with the AICC Session at Gauhati and the emergence of Sanjay Gandhi and though the subjects were outside the scope of rule 48, according to the Chief Censor, "I had spoken to the Editor on 2nd December about his editorial on Gauhati Session", "both the editorials are highly critical of the functioning of the Centre and the tenor leaves much to be desired". "Since dictating this note at a discussion with MIB, pre-censorship orders have been served on *Mainstream* ".

Himmat : *Himmat* published by Raj Mohan Gandhi was frequently publishing articles not to the liking of the authorities. In October, 1975. *Himmat* was put under pre-censorship and the Censor Officers were told that there is "no need to give any reasons to the Editor of *Himmat* as pre-censorship is still mandatory". Subsequently in May, 1976, the Chief Censor ordered "tell him to impose a security of Rs. 20,000/-''. This order was issued about an article which was "held objectionable for the reasons that it was not submitted for pre-censorship".

On June 7, 1976 on the complaint from the DPIO, Bombay, it was noted that he (Raj Mohan Gandhi) is "careful to avoid violation in the strictest sense. The writings in the *Himmat* have to be checked and I think total censorship is the only solution" (Censor noting dated June 25, 1976). In August, 1976 *Himmat* published an article which interalia stated that Indira Gandhi's statement in Colombo that censorship in the Press has been relaxed is wrong and he cited numerous instances of censorship. This was again noted adversely by the Censor. Subsequently, MHA received a secret report asking for action against '*Himmat*'.

The main charge against it was that it has "vehemently opposed press censorship and the steps being taken to effectively implement the Family Planning Programme". On this K.N. Prasad has asked the Chief Censor "I do not know how this journal . . . (has) not received attention of the State Censor. It is a pity that the journals should have been allowed to violate censorship orders with impunity". Subsequently with the announcement of the Election the whole case died away.

Seminar : "No 203 issue of *Seminar* of July 1976 carried articles referring to the relevance of the Emergency . . . the articles are undoubtedly loaded and technically fall within the scope of the censorship order . . . There are two ways of looking at this issue. The fact a journal has written in this vein is a reflection of the liberalism of censorship and to that extent enhances the Government credibility. But there is a danger that others may take the cue" (H.J. D'Penha, Chief Censor's note dated July 7, 1976 on file). "I have given serious consideration to the views of CC above. But in view of para 3 of his note we are left with no alternative except to impose pre-censorship on this publication . . . we may also take action against the printer and publisher". (Orders of Vidya Charan Shukla, dated July 14, 1976)

The *Seminar* refused to obey the pre-censorship order and preferred to stop publication. The articles in the *Seminar* which were supposed to be violative of censorship were "restrained" and "they attempt to build up a case in true academic style". As the Chief Censor himself admits these articles are serious articles which give both sides of the picture regarding the Emergency.

Bhoomiputra : At his meeting of July 17, 1975 Vidya Charan Shukla directed that "OSD might speak to the Chief Secretary of the State concerned, convey our view that action should be taken against the publication. "The nature of the action . . . would be . . .

> forfeiture of the offending issue
>
> forfeiture of security deposit
>
> forfeiture of the press
>
> prosecution of the Editor under DISIR"

All this action was taken against the *Bhoomiputra's* and when the paper went on a writ petition to the Gujarat High Court and won its case the High Court insisted that its judgement be published without censorship, the Chief Censor instructed "All papers in your region should be advised not to publish" *Bhoomiputra* case judgement delivered by the Gujarat High Court at Ahmedabad.

The Law Ministry had pointed out beforehand to the Chief Censor, possible deficiences in the Censor's Order to the *Bhoomiputra.* Inspite of this when the High Court quashed the Censor orders H.J. D'Penha discussed the possible bias of one of the judges of the case Justice Sheth with V.P. Raman Addl. Solicitor General. The matter was not pursued further because of the Law Secy. P.G. Gokhale who advised "The allegation of bias of one of the judges would require an affidavit to that effect, for a mere allegation would not be enough". (d.o. letter to D'Penha dated Feburary 13, 1976)

Tughlak : *Tughlak* is a Tamil fortnightly edited by Cho Ramaswami. In its July 15, 1975 issue it published a "cleverly done satire on the Prime Minister and the Proclamation of Emergency and the action taken thereafter". In the Coordination meeting dated July 17, 1975, MIB desired that "action should be taken against the publication". He also specified the nature of action to be taken such as forfeiture of the offending issue, forfeiture of security deposit, forfeiture of the press and prosecution of the Editor/Printer under DISIR "depending on the merits of the case".

Commenting on a letter to the Prime Minister by Vayalar Ravi, MP pointing out the "personal attack on the Prime Minister" in the July 15, 1975 issue of the *Tughlak*, Sharada Prasad, Information Adviser to the PM observed, "I hope something has been done to defuse Cho", On July 25, 1975 in the Coordination meeting "MIB directed that the next issue of the Madras fortnightly *Tughlak* should be examined by the local Censor, and if it contained any objectionable matter, it should be withheld from distribution. If the journal after the imposition of the Censorship still violates the guidelines, the State Government should be asked in writing to ban the publication and seal the press". On July 25, 1975, the journal was asked to submit to pre-censorship, and the editor suspended its publication.

It resumed publication from October 1, 1975 (CC's note). On May 12, 1976 Cho Ramaswami sent a telegram to Indira Gandhi complaining of censorship harassment. The matter was referred to the DCC, Madras who opined that "such persistent and insidious attacks, though seemingly on another political leader, would impair the credibility of the action taken by the Government of India."

Positive Publicity, Slanting of News : The office of the Chief Censor, PIB, AIR and other media were utilised for slanting of news in favour of the Government. All these were utilised at the instance of Indira Gandhi. For example, at the high level meeting held on August 12, 1975 Indira Gandhi said "favourable speeches of Members of Parliament should be published through Radio, TV, Newspapers", "publicity of positive aspects of the Emergency and economic programme should be arranged in friendly foreign newspapers" and "in view of the restraints Govt. department and agencies should provide sufficient materials to the newspapers".

When the Lok Sangharsh Samiti launched a country-wide satyagraha on November 14, 1975, K.N. Prasad issued instructions on the file to the media units which said that "steps should be taken to defuse the situation, particularly in Kerala, Karnataka, Bihar and Rajasthan. The media units should be instructed to strenghten public opinion against this agitation iu a discreet and cautious manner". Subsequently, at a meeting held in Prasad's room on December 10, 1975 which was attended by representatives of the Home Ministry, C.V.

Narsimhan and of the Intelligence Bureau Narain Rao, along-
with other officers of the I&B Ministry it was decided that
all media units should project that the centre must not be
weakened in any manner and all the actions and policies of the
Government are formulated in the larger national interest."
"It should also be made clear to the general public that there
was no question of going back to old days of licence and
irresponsibility. . .permissiveness. . .in public life would never
be allowed again".

The Lok Sangharsh Samiti agitation which was laying
stress on the effort to build Indira Gandhi's personality cult
was to be "vigorously countered by quotations from Prime
Minister's own speeches and interviews, where she had em-
phasised that all decisions were taken collectively". The themes
for the campaign however were to "centre round the new ideas
propounded by the Prime Minister in her recent speeches".
Subsequently the Intelligence Bureau sent to K.N. Prasad
statements "where the L.S.S. agitation continues in a steady
shape, where students have come to notice participating in
the agitation and where extensive leaflettering has been resorted to".

Again when President's rule was imposed in Tamil Nadu,
C.V. Narsimhan Joint Secretary MHA wrote to K.N. Prasad
"regarding Censoring arrangements in the present situation in
Tamil Nadu". His enclosed note interalia suggested that
"There are 42 publications in Tamil Nadu including the language dailies and weeklies. 26 have taken a pro DMK/anti-emer-
gency stand, 3 are neutral and 13 are pro-emergency and positively supporting the Prime Minister. All the 26 papers which
have shown a pronounced pro-DMK stand should be put on
the pre-censorship list immediately." "Publicity should also
be given to such other aspects. . .which would indicate the
neglect of the State's real needs. . .attributable to the total
lack of public purpose or national good in the motivations of
the ruling party in the State".

Accordingly on February 2, 1976 Prasad issued necessary
instructions to the PIO and Chief Censor.

The way the office of the Chief Censor was used for slanting news in favour of the Government can be seen from the
following examples quoted below from the Log Book :

CC desires that some one should be sent immediately to Barua's residence (23, Tughlak Road) to get from Pitambar, his PA, a copy of the statement about asking Congress (O) Members believing in the Congress ideology to join the Congress.

After the receipt of the statement it should be given to PTI and UNI with the request that it should be given full coverage. (October 11, 1975)

Though there is no pre-censorship on the judgement of the Supreme Court it is essential to ensure that the five separate judgements are correctly reported in proper perspective. Arguments should not be torn out of context. Similarly, the headlines and the news should clearly indicate that the appeal of the Prime Minister has been upheld, that the cross appeal by Raj Narain has been dismissed and that the order of disqualification of the Prime Minister has also been set aside, and her election to the Lok Sabha upheld. Particular care should be taken to alert the language papers informally. (Chief Censor's message to State Censors dated November 7, 1975)

I.O. C.S. Savoor said that the Press has been told 'unofficially' that the news agencies owe Rs. 70 lakhs to the Government (paid as loans) and owe Rs. 15 lakhs to P & T. Government is taking steps to recover the amount and P&T also has taken some steps. Savoor said if any news agency or newspaper files a story on the above lines it should be allowed for publication *and should not be cut.*

I had today earlier sent to you a message regarding Shri JP's letter to the Prime Minister about PM's contribution for purchase of dialysis machine. I had stated that this letter should not repeat not be published in the papers of your area. Samachar is likely to issue a story giving JP's letter along with a statement of a Congress leader. There is no restriction on the Samachar story and the newspapers should be allowed to publish Samachar story. (June 16 1976).

Subsequently OSD rang up to say that the statement of the Congress leader (General Secy. of AICC) is not likely to come today. I have informed Chandran of Samachar not to do a story until the statement is issued and clearance obtained from Sharda Prasad. (Remarks of U.C. Tiwari, dated June 6, 1976).

Padmanabhan (Madras) rang up to say that a story about resignation of Thiru Nedumaran, one of the General Secretaries of TNCC has appeared in *Makkal Kural*, an independent tamil daily. This has been killed locally and wanted it to be killed at Delhi also, however instructions were left with the Samachar that it should not be circulated. (April 23, 1976.)

Regarding Mir Mushtak Ahmed's statement on Turkman Gate, Navin Chawla was contacted. He said that the Lt. Governor was interested in publicising the statement as widely as possible and the reference to the Imam in the statement was deliberately made... (April 24, 1976.)

Matrubhoomi and *Indian Express* rang up wanting to know if the story on the 'Kerala Congress' faction leaders meeting P.M. should be referred to us. Since Kerala Congress is a separate party I told him no need arose, only advise them to make it clear it had nothing to do with the Indian National Congress ... later CC rang up, the story was read out to him and as suggested by him Samachar was asked to confine itself to talk with the P.M. only and leave out discussion with the Ministry of Home Affairs etc. They agreed. (January 8, 1977.)

As desired by CC, Samachar (Kasbekar) was informed not to use item regarding M.P. Congress leaders meeting P.M. or any other leader in Delhi. He also requested to inform Bhopal correspondent not to use such story. (January 10, 1977.)

It was not only the office of the Chief Censor but also the PIB which was indulging in this type of slanting of news. A few examples given below make it clear:

Letter from C. Raghavan Editor-in-Chief PTI to V.C. Shukla, dated August 26, 1975. "On Thursday, August 21st, our correspondent in London... filed a cable to us .... the cable was apparently received in India on

22nd morning about 4 A.M. It was, however, delivered to us on our telex only about 1400 hrs. or so on
August 22. However, on August 21, about 11 A.M. or
so I was rung up by the Censor's office (U.C. Tiwari)
who said that the ITV interview of Sasthi Brata was
'not to go'. Since we had not received the cable I was
mystified and did not know what it was all about.
However, I left instructions that any such news items
should be referred to me. The cable that was received
at 1400 hours on August 22 was sent to me and only
two other persons in my office were aware of its existence or had even seen the cable . . . . I learnt by the
evening of the the 22nd that the text of the cable sent
to us (and which we have not submitted and hence
not officially in Govt.'s possession) was in the hands
of some M.P.'s who had drafted a statement incorporating chunks from the cable . . . . Editors of two
newspapers . . . . were also furnished copies of the
cable addressed to us." On this letter the PIO Baji
endorsed a note to V.C. Shukla saying "I had informed MIB on the morning of August 21 that on my responsibility I was holding back the cable and not
releasing it to PTI. The idea of getting some MPs to
issue a statement was discussed with OSD and Sharada
Prasad and it was issued on August 22, 1975 (Censor
Office Log Book)

PIB was also utilised to issue handouts on the alleged misdeeds of R.N. Goenka, even though these cases were sub-
judice in Courts. These handouts were brought out on July 24,
1976 and July 26, 1976. On August 9, 1976 another release on
the Indian Express was got ready on which K.N. Prasad made
a note to the Minister "MIB may like to see. This is the third
instalment. Instructions have been given to PIO and Samachar to treat this release in the same manner as the earlier
two were treated". It may be noted that Government at that
time was having problems with the publication of news in the
Indian Express group of papers which is owned by Goenka.

Two newspapers *Milap* and *India Weekly* were given
advertising support because "we feel it is essential for our
purpose that the journal should be kept going for at least two
years . . . we are suggesting to the journal that it should start

a regular column to refute propaganda and criticism in Britain. *India Weekly* needs at least two pages of advertisement . . .with the help of I&B we shall try to get them these advertisements", (H.Y. Sharada Prasad) to which Indira Gandhi gave her assent.

In following up action on Indira Gandhi's suggestion in her inaugural address to the State Information Ministers' Conference S.M.H. Burney at his meeting on April 19, 1976 directed that a group be formed" "to devise suitable machinery for monitoring false propaganda and recommend means to channelise them for effective countering". This was a secret body consisting of the PIO, Chief Censor and Director, Research and Reference Division. In countering the propaganda this group asked the media units to note the following:

> There should be no mention of any clandestine literature of propaganda . . . . But (for example), in dealing with the subject of declining prices it should be emphasised that apart from the good monsoon a variety of measures adopted by the Govt. have been responsible for the fall in prices. (Minutes of the Group meeting dated May 22, 1976).

The meetings of this group were followed up closley and and action was taken by the media units concerned. This group was particularly concerned with countering claims made by clandestine opposition literature which was under circulation underground and in trying to show that the RSS was a Hindu communal organisation. The DAVP brought out some booklets on the banned organisations and some others justifying the emergency. In this connection, Sethi the then Director of Advertising and Visual Publicity wrote to Ayub Syed, Editor of *Current* Bombay on October 27, 1975, commending his booklet 'June 26' and seeking his permission to print a large number of copies under the auspices of DAVP. Subsequently the DAVP printed this booklet. However, it was brought out without DAVP by-line. Besides this the DAVP also brought out the following four booklets without its by-line and distributed them:

RSS IN ITS OWN MIRROR—by K.N. Seth.

RSS—A SECRET PARA-MILITARY ORGANISA-TION—by Subhadra Joshi, M.P.

FOUR FACES OF SUBVERSION—by Trevor Drieberg. This booklet was against RSS, Anand Marg, Jamiat-e-Islami-a Hind and Naxalites.

NAXALVAD YA NA AKALVAD—Hind booklet by Bishan Kapoor.

DAVP also distributed these booklets.

The DAVP was also to bring out a pamphlet called "Rule of Violence". Most of the material for this pamphlet consisted of out-of-context statements of J.P. Narayan, Morarji Desai and similar out-of-context photographs all juxtaposed to project the idea that the opposition parties were fomenting violence. This pamphlet was not published at the instance of K.N. Prasad on account of the state of health of Jayaprakash Narayan.

All India Radio was also given instructions to give news which was favourable to the Implementation Committee of the Congress Party which was set up to monitor the 20 Point Programme. The actual directive reads as follows :

> Sustained publicity should be given to the work of the Implementation Committee formed by the Congress Party to assess and monitor the execution of the new economic programme by the Prime Minister (directive given by Shukla in the Coordination Meeting held on July 17, 1975).

Some examples from AIR's news bulletins which slanted the news in favour of Indira Gandhi and the then ruling party are given below :

> Acharya Vinoba Bhave today called off the proposed agitation on the issue of banning cow-slaughter and expressed his thanks to the Prime Minister Indira Gandhi. He declared at Paunar Ashram today that by and large the problem of banning cow slaughter has been solved. Acharya Vinoba Bhave said the credit goes to God; Rukmani his mother; Mahatma Gandhi and the Prime Minister. The first three are in heaven; Indiraji is on earth. Thanks to Indiraji. (AIR English News Bulletin of September 8, 1976).

> The dominant impression the convention gave was one of youth's near worship of Sanjay Gandhi. His charismatic personality inspires unbounded enthusiasm

in the youth of the country. Mr. Gandhi received a thundering ovation repeatedly. (Sub. National Convention of Youth Congress by S.P.K. Gupta of Samachar in 'Spotlight' an AIR programme dated November 20, 1976).

It is very significant that Indira Gandhi's regime has brought the people of the country nearer to each other and has created a new sense of integration (National Integration by D.R. Goyal, Editor *Secular Democracy* on 'Spotlight' dated July 2, 1976).

Similarly, NSD (News Service Division) was utilised for broadcasting inspired news, denigrating Congress leaders like Siddhartha Shankar Ray, and Nandini Satpathy when they fell from favour with the ruling coterie. Between November 28, 1976 and December 16, 1976, AIR broadcast 20 stories which were condemnatory of Nandini Satpathy, and which stated that Indira Gandhi's intervention was required in Orissa affairs. When President's rule was imposed in Orissa "six MP's from Orissa have welcomed the imposition of President's rule in the State. . .(and) thanked the Prime Minister on behalf of the people of Orissa." (AIR News Bulletin December 16, 1976-2100 hrs).

In a Coordination Meeting dated February 20, 1976 it was directed that "counter propaganda against DMK should concentrate on subjects, like institutional corruption in DMK rule, party interference in the management of Trade Unions, Cooperatives, Educational Institutions and Temples".

The slant against the Opposition was so obvious that in December, 1976 the AIR bulletins devoted 2207 lines to pronouncements by the spokesmen of the Ruling Party as against 34 lines to the Opposition. In December, 1974 the same figures were 571 and 522 respectively.

Image Building : The third main aspect of news media management was the building up of the image of Indira Gandhi as the supreme and beloved leader of the country; of Sanjay Gandhi as an up and coming leader in his own right and as a corollary to build up the Congress and the Youth Congress. The following will illustrate how this was done by the various media organisations of the Government :

With a view to building up the image of Indira Gandhi two multi media campaigns namely, 'A Decade of Achievement' and 'A Year of Fulfilment' were organised. The former was organised when Indira Gandhi completed 10 years in power as Prime Minister. A meeting was held on December 11, 1975 in the room of K.N. Prasad where H.Y. Sharada Prasad, Information Adviser to the Prime Minister, and L. Dayal, then Joint Secretary and other media heads were present. The object of this campaign was to "project in a systematic and concentrated manner, that while the nation is on the march since Independence, the last one decade (1966-75) has been a period of all round progress". (Extracts from the copy of extracts of meeting placed in file No. F. 5/1 (xx)/76-OSD).

In this meeting it was also decided that the Directorate of Field Publicity would screen extensively the seven films on the then Prime Minister which were available, besides selecting more films for the campaign in semi-urban areas. Films Division was asked to recast the film on 'Decade of Achievement' as the one prepared by them earlier was not approved by the OSD and the I.A to P.M. The Films Division also prepared another film 'A Day with the Prime Minister'. The Directorate of Field Publicity was also asked to obtain in sufficient numbers tapes of the then M.P's broadcast of November 11, 1975 from the DG, AIR. The DG, AIR was asked to prepare a tape containing extracts from important broadcasts of Indira Gandhi in the last 10 years. The units of the DFP were asked to play these tapes in rural and semi-urban areas.

All India Radio was asked to select carefully about 2000 quotations from the speeches of Indira Gandhi and to put out daily 5 to 10 of these quotations, by each Radio Station as a message for the nation but without bringing in the name of the Prime Minister. The Publications Division was asked to make special efforts to boost the sale of books on the Prime Minister. DPD was also asked to publish informative and interesting sketches with photographs of Indira Gandhi in the various journals and periodicals of the Publications

Division within the first quarter of the year 1976. Besides this other media like TV and Song and Drama Division and PIB and DAVP were also asked to organise special programmes for the 'Decade of Achievement'.

All media units were asked to organise special programmes on January 24, 1976 as on that day Indira Gandhi completed a decade as Prime Minister. The Ministry of Education was requested to advise all Primary and Secondary Schools to adopt the three songs selected by the Ministry of I&B. They were informed that one of these songs could be sung in chorus at the assembly time before the commencement of the classes.

The file contains a cyclostyled copy of CCC/6457 dated December 31, 1975 of All India Congress Committee (Central Campaign Committee) addressed to all the Presidents of PCCs and DCCs and the leaders of the Congress Legislative Parties, in which the details of programme for celebrating "the dynamic decade" are given.

The campaign 'A Year of Fulfilment' was organised from June 25, 1976. The launching of the programme was proposed by OSD Prasad, in his note dated March 22, 1976 in file No. F. 5/1/(XVI)/76-OSD. The Secretary, Burney was not in favour of such a programme but Shukla approved the programme with the remarks "in such a campaign we do not play up the Emergency as such but the benefits of it. Therefore, I see nothing wrong in what is being planned. These are my standing instructions to play up the benefits of Emergency at every available opportunity".

The details of this campaign were finalised in the meeting held under the Chairmanship of K.N. Prasad on May 3, 1976 for his approval. He approved the same on June 7, 1976. The campaign was used to project the following :

20 Point Programme and its Achievements.

Economic gains.

Press response etc.

The DAVP brought out some advertisements on 'A Year of Fulfilment'. Out of these five samples were sent to the I.A. to PM on June 5, 1976. Out of these five samples three carried quotations of Indira Gandhi. To build up the image of Indira Gandhi, a documentary film called 'A Day with the Prime Minister' was made. She saw the film but was not satisfied with it. She desired that some changes be made as the ending was tame and the commentary lacked proper focus but before the changes were made she desired that "the film should also be shown to Sanjay Gandhi for his comments before proceeding further". (Sharada Prasad, I.A. to PM's note to S.M.H. (Burney) The film was eventually "reshot under OSD's supervision", and the total cost "including production, dubbing and preparation of 35 MM and 16 MM prints of this film comes to Rs. 9,94,993,10."

All through the Emergency period the speeches of Indira Gandhi. . . had naturally to be played up. In all, her pronouncements were carried on 171 occasions in the newsreels and Samachar darshan programmes during the Emergency. . .To a considerable extent coverage of the Prime Minister in office would be fully justified, but what is noteworthy about this coverage was that many of the utterances were at the familiar rallies outside her house and other devices to propagate the personality cult (Statement of S.C. Bhatt, DNS AIR).

The Films Division was also utilised for building up Indira Gandhi's image. Thus the Films Division while instructing its units to cover Mr. Gandhi's tour of the country told its units that "while covering her tours pl. focus your attention on the positive response and reaction shown by the people. . .their spontaneous joy, feelings and enthusiasm should be captured through the camera eye". This was apparently done to give an impression of enthusiastic and adulatory crowds.

The building up of the image of Sanjay Gandhi in the media including Doordarshan, began in a big way with the All India Congress Committee Session at Kamagatamaru Nagar, Chandigarh in the last week of December, 1975. There-

after his statements, speeches and visits to various parts of
the country were given wide publicity. Sanjay Gandhi visited
Calcutta on February 21, 1976. In this connection V.S. Tripathi, SA to Shukla forwarded the following note to DG, AIR
on February 7, 1976 "Shri Sanjay Gandhi will be visiting
Calcutta on February 20 and 21, 1976. It has been decided
that the fullest publicity should be given to his programme. The
video tapes of the day's programme of TV should be shown at
Calcutta and should also be flown by afternoon flight to Delhi.
Arrangements should also be made to show it on other TV Stations". Thereafter, Indira Gandhi's visits were also covered on
other TV Stations. The five point Programme of Sanjay Gandhi
was also covered on TV for which a total expenditure of
Rs. 8,33,055/- was incurred from June-July, 1975 to March
1977. Doordarshan carried 265 items on Sanjay Gandhi. Between January 18, 1977 and March 20, 1977 the Doordarshan
Kendras exposed 750 ft. of films on Sanjay Gandhi and used
127 ft. out of this.

During the period January 1, 1976 to January 18, 1977 All
India Radio carried 192 items about Sanjay Gandhi in the
main news bulletins/broadcast from Delhi alone as per the
statement of Director News Services, AIR. Extracts of various
news items on the activities of Sanjay Gandhi are given below :

Earlier on his arrival in Bhopal, Mr. Gandhi was
given a rousing welcome by a large crowd of men,
women and children. (AIR News : February 26, 1976-
2100 hrs).

Sanjay Gandhi was taken in a big procession to the
streets of Guntur to the Police Parade Ground. (AIR
News : March 21, 1976-0810 hours).

Hundreds of thousands of people lined up the roads
in Tirupati and Tirumalai to cheer Mr. Gandhi. (AIR
News : March 21, 1976-2100 hrs).

The Youth Congress leader Sanjay Gandhi had discussions with officials in Agra today on plans to
beautify and clean the historic city. "Earlier on arrival
in Agra Gandhi was given an affectionate welcome by
a big crowd. (May 2, 1976-2100 hours.)

On arrival at Bombay Airport Mr. Sanjay Gandhi was
accorded a big welcome. The Maharashtra Chief

Minister S.B. Chavan, his Cabinet colleagues. . .and many Congress and Youth Congress leaders received him at the Airport. He was profusely garlanded on behalf of several organisations. Several organisations gave a group welcome to Sanjay Gandhi all along the route from the Airport. (October 29, 1976-2100 hours).

Sanjay Gandhi is arriving in Lucknow tomorrow on a two day tour of Uttar Pradesh. . .He will address public meetings, inaugurate bridges and hospitals. (AIR News dated January 3, 1977 2100-hours).

Referring to the problems of Deoria District Sanjay Gandhi said that the State Government has chalked out a scheme for constructing 7000 tube wells in Gandak communal area. . .Sanjay Gandhi said the U.P. Govt. has decided to start youth camps for the educated unemployed. He said the youth attending these camps would get priority in Government jobs. (AIR News dated January 8, 1977-2100 hours).

The AIR correspondent says that lakhs of people turned up in Karnal to greet Sanjay Gandhi. The town wore a festive look. (AIR News : January 11, 1977-2100 hrs).

Mr. Sanjay Gandhi has been voted the Indian of the year 1976, in a poll conducted by the Bombay Journal *Illustrated Weekly of India*. . . the poll recorded Sanjay Gandhi's courage, fearlessness and dynamism as the qualities which appealed most to the readers. (AIR News: January 20, 1977-2100 hrs).

Films Division, New Delhi undertook the production of films to highlight the activities of Delhi Administration. These films had a very limited scope and showed Sanjay Gandhi very prominently. At meetings presided over by S.M.H. Burney on August 20, 1976, September 13, 1976, October 28, 1976 and December 3, 1976 it was decided to produce these films. At the instance of Navin Chawla, the Secretary to Lt. Governor, S.M.H. Burney directed the Films Division to obliquely project the image of Sanjay Gandhi in these films (Statement of K.K. Kapil, Jt. Chief Producer Films Division, New Delhi).

Films were accordingly produced on various subjects like, Trees, Time of Peace and Time for Learning. As regards the film 'Roots' which was regarding resettlement colonies, it was decided that "the Films Division should produce a documentary in colour. Navin Chawla agreed to give the script and the rough cuts would be shown to the Additional Secretary." "Rough cut of the film on Resettlement Colonies was shown to Navin Chawla on December 24, 1976 when some additions and changes were suggested by him. Additional shooting was done and the changes made and the revised rough cut shown again to Navin Chawla on February 2, 1977 and his approval obtained." (K.K. Kapil's letter dated February 7, 1977 to V. Gopalkrishnan, Director (IP) I&B Ministry).

That these films were meant to project the image of Sanjay Gandhi can be seen from extracts taken from the synopsis "a time for youth . . . a time for action . . . a time to think about the future . . . and under the dynamic leadership of the Youth Congress the people have arisen to the challenge". (Trees).

They felt harassed without a direct road to Narela. We did not know what to do. We went to Chowdhary Hira Singh, who took us to Sanjay Gandhi. He asked what has happened to your hands, you the young people of the village could yourselves make this 5 kilometer road and complete it by 2nd October, the birthday of Mahatma Gandhi.

The film 'Zoo Rail' was ready for release but "working of the Zoo Rail in Delhi has been temporarily stopped. Shri Navin Chawla, therefore, decided that the film may not be released till the Zoo Rail starts functioning again". (Letter dated March 7, 1977 from K.K. Kapil, Joint Chief Producer Films Division to Mushir Ahmed, Chief Producer). On April 1, 1977, Kapil wrote to Mushir Ahmed "the treatment given in the making of the film is not in accordance with the present policy of the Government. It shows Shri Mohamad Shafi Qureshi and Shri Sanjay Gandhi inaugurating the 'Zoo Rail' in Delhi".

In addition to the above film on Resettlement Colonies, we had earlier released the following films on developmental activities in Delhi :

'Youth in the forefront'—released on August 20, 1976 (Youth Congress Session in Delhi)

'Zoo Rail' has already been completed and will be released on some appropriate occasion.

'Narela Road' has already been agreed by Shri Navin Chawla and is to be released shortly. K.K. Kapil Joint Chief Producer, Films Division in his letter to Gopalkrishnan Director (IP) I&B Ministry dated February 7, 1977.

On the request of Navin Chawla it was decided to prepare the film coverage of Sanjay Gandhi, in this connection a Desk Officer, I&B Ministry put up the note on December 10, 1976 which reads "during the course of discussion regarding the roughcut of the film 'Road to Narela' Shri Navin Chawla, Secretary to Lt. Governor, Delhi has mentioned to Shri K.K. Kapil, Joint Chief Producer of Films Division, New Delhi that the coverages of the Prime Minister and Sanjay Gandhi should be kept intact in the Library and indexed properly so that if on some future date it is required it can be made available". The Desk Officer solicited orders on this. S.M.H. Burney ordered "Yes. But all these files, films etc. should be treated as Top Secret in all concerned offices". (Burney's order dated December 23, 1976 on file No. 112/92/76-F(P).)

Similarly, orders were issued by Burney on December 23, 1976 that "in the course of discussion yesterday Shri Sharada Prasad mentioned that there was a great demand from various sources for materials on Shri Sanjay Gandhi. It was suggested that R & RD may start collecting all the materials, press clippings, articles on him, speeches etc. and keep them in a secret folder . . . this task has already been taken in hand by the Chief Censor at my instance". This was also marked to SA to MIB.

To carry out Government policy effectively it became necessary to deal with such persons in the media who were not toeing the Government line. The following type of action was taken against such persons :

Arrest and detention under MISA, DISIR and other laws of the land.

At the Coordination meeting of the Minister on June 29, 1975 it was ordered that "whenever any newsman like an Editor/Journalist/Correspondent on the staff of any newspaper is to be arrested, the arrest should be made with the prior concurrence of MIB and request should be made to Chief Ministers of all States from Home Secretary immediately and confidentially. The Secretary contacted the Home Secretary on 28th afternoon to issue these instructions". The Home Ministry issued the following instructions : "Chief Ministers are requested that if it is considered necessary to arrest Editors of newspapers or Journalists they may before doing so consult the Minister of Information & Broadcasting, Shri Vidya Charan Shukla." (MHA wireless No. 7846/JS(SF)/75, dated June 28, 1975)

At the meeting held on July 11, 1975, Vidya Charan Shukla clarified that "while action against Journalists for the common Law offences need not be referred by State Govts. to MIB, any action proposed to be taken against a journal's Editor, private Correspondent etc. under the DIR for any infringement of their legal duties and responsibilities will require clearance of MIB".

In all, a total of 253 Journalists were detained in the country, 110 of them under MISA, 60 under the DIR and 83 for other reasons. In a number of cases accreditation of journalists whose reports were not to the liking of the Government, was cancelled.

At the time of proclamation of Emergency, four news agencies viz. Press Trust of India, United News of India, Hindustan Samachar and Samachar Bharati, were functioning in the country. But after the proclamation of Emergency, the Government of India wanted to restructure these agencies. In a meeting held in the room of the then Prime Minister on July 26, 1975, it was decided, "the organisation of news agencies needs restructuring. The advisability of constituting a public sector corporation with one agency each for Indian newspapers and journals and foreign journals should be considered".

In the working paper prepared by the Ministry, it was proposed that "a News Corporation of India may be set up by an Act of Parliament". However, K.N. Prasad recorded in a note on November 27, 1975 incorporating the views of the then Deputy Minister of I & B that "He (D.M.) feels that it would not be advisable to create a national news agency through an Act of Parliament. It is his fear that such a body would be subjected to scrutiny by some of the Parliamentary Committees and the Committee on Public Undertakings...D.M. feels that Members of Parliament will hold the Ministry of Information and Broadcasting accountable for its functioning and as a result, the working of this news agency would be subjected to Parliamentary scrutiny, which would not be conducive to its morale and efficiency.

"He suggests that the ideal solution would be to get PTI & UNI merged into an agency and to leave other news agencies to fend for themselves. He is confident that without Govt. support it would not be possible for the other news agencies to survive or compete with the restructured news agency.

According to him, the advantage would be dependent on the support of the Government but without making the Government accountable to Parliament for its functioning''.

A note for the Cabinet was prepared on December 13, 1975 in which it was proposed to establish by law an autonomous corporate body which would take over the aforesaid news agencies. It was interalia pointed out in the note that the ownership of PTI and UNI was mainly controlled by the four big newspaper groups and as such these two news agencies reflected the editorial policy of the controlling interests and were, therefore, unable to report objectively. Shortcomings in the areas of coverage of home news and foreign news, projection of country's image abroad were also mentioned.

The Cabinet considered the said note on the same day and "It was decided that certain other methods be tried initially, before the matter is taken up again''. L. Dayal the then Joint Secretary (I) in the Ministry of Information and Broadcasting has stated to the Commission "The Minister decided that the 'other methods' would mean that AIR would no longer subscribe to the news agencies, that no Government office would hire their teleprinters and that arrears of Government dues, if any, would be vigorously recovered''.

It is seen from Dayal's note dated December 20, 1975 in the file that in pursuance of this, the AIR discontinued the subscription to all the four news agencies.

It is also seen from the said note and from note dated December 24, 1975 that the Principal Information Officer was requested to get a list of teleprinters of the news agencies in use in various Ministries and Departments of Government through the Information Officer attached to these Ministries and Departments. It was decided that after this list was made available, the Secretary in the Ministry would get in touch with Secretaries of the Ministry and Departments concerned to persuade them to get the teleprinter service of the news agencies discontinued. Except for a few, the others were disconnected.

The position regarding loans given by the Govt. to the news agencies and their repayment position was taken up for review. L. Dayal recorded a note on December 20, 1975 in this regard and pointed out that "the following loans were sanctioned—

PTI—Rs. 55 lakhs, UNI—Rs. 4 lakhs, Samachar Bharati—Rs. 5 lakhs.

The entire amounts had been released in different instalments to PTI and UNI. The accounts show that they have not defaulted in payment. As regards PTI, an amount of about Rs. 4.59 lakhs would fall due for repayment on January 1, 1976. As for UNI, a sum of Rs. 40,000/- would fall due for repayment on the same date.

As regards, 'Samachar Bharati', out of Rs. 5 lakhs sanctioned, only Rs. 1.50 lakhs has been released so far. All the instalments due have been defaulted, amounting to Rs. 45,000/- excluding interest. It is suggested that

The sanction for the balance amount of Rs. 3.5 lakhs of loan may be withdrawn immediately.

Necessary legal action may be taken for the recovery of defaulted instalments amounting to Rs. 45,000/- along-with interest.

On December 13, 1975, the day the Cabinet decided to try 'other methods', "the Press was told unofficially that the news agencies owe Rs. 70 lakhs to the Government (paid as loans) and owe Rs. 15 lakhs to P & T. Government is taking steps to recover the amount. P & T also has taken some steps". (Entry dated December 13, 1975 in the log books of the Office of the Chief Censor). It may be noted that the Cabinet meeting was held on December 13, 1975 at 4.00 P.M. and entry in the log book was made some time after 7.30 P.M. the same day. It may futher be noted that L. Dayal in his above-cited note dated December 20, 1975 while giving the position of loans to news agencies, had said that the accounts showed that the PTI and UNI had not defaulted in repayment.

The pressures where also brought on the news agencies. N.R. Chandran formerly Manager PTI and now Manager of Samachar has stated to the Commission, "Among the methods used to pressurise PTI to accept merger was attachment of the PTI building in Parliament Street by the New Delhi Municipal Committee, posting of police to the building, cutting off electricity to the PTI building on two or three occasions, cutting off teleprinter lines arbitrarily and termination of AIR's agreements with PTI for supply of news. The merger was mooted soon after the declaration of emergency. The PTI Board and the General Manager resisted the merger move for some time but eventually had to fall in line as it became difficult for the agency to continue to function in the face of the various steps resorted to by Government". P.C. Gupta, the then Chairman of Press Trust of India has stated to the Commission "Samachar came into existence through undue pressure, arm twisting and thumb of the Ministry of Information and Broadcasting, against the wishes of the two major News Agencies. Its administration, planning and execution have been defective and undemocratic. Samachar during emergency has been giving coloured and politically motivated news."

This has been corroborated by C. Raghavan, ex-Editor in-chief, PTI, who has stated to the Commission

> The electricity for the building was also cut off—the reason given was some 'technical problem', even though in fact there was arrangement to obtain power from two different sources—but we managed to carry on a skeleton service with the help of a stand-by gene-rator.

> Mr. Chandran rang me up to inform that some of our teleprinter lines had been cut, even though we did not owe the P & T Department any dues, and that several Government Departments, subscribing to our service, had informed him that would have to discon-tinue as per instructions from the I & B Department. About the lines, he was advised to contact K.N. Prasad. Prasad when contacted would say everything would be alright if we only agreed to the merger.

> In between, the PIO, Dr. A.R. Baji, who tried to persuade Mr K.S. Ramachandran (the then General Manager of the PTI) to agree to the merger, warned him that otherwise he might be put under MISA

> Both the Minister and the officials called individual directors and applied considerable pressure against the stand of the Board and asking for support to the Government move. Acting under these pressures, the Board met on January 20, 1976 and agreed to the pro-posal for voluntary merger and suggested discussions amongst the four news agencies. . .

After the PTI Board passed a resolution "extending its whole-hearted support to the voluntary merger", they requested the Government to withdraw the discontinuance of news service of PTI by AIR, restore teleprinter connections which had been disconnected, release forthwith whatever money due to PTI in respect of All India Radio in terms of the Government proposal (P.C. Gupta, Chairman, PTI's letter dated January 20, 1976 addressed to K.N. Prasad). On this letter Prasad endorsed "Now we should take a view on all the above items".

The United News of India was also pressurised into agreeing for 'voluntary merger'. Ram S. Tarneja, the then Chairman of the UNI has stated to the Commission :

> The UNI had its Head Office at 9, Rafi Marg, New Delhi, which is an old building having limited space. As such UNI was actively pursuing the idea of getting suitable land allotted for its building. It was reliably learnt prior to the emergency that land for UNI building had been allotted and after some procedural formalities a letter of allotment would be issued by the Government. Despite all efforts made, no letter of allotment was issued by the Government.

> Indirectly this was another pressure tactic because UNI was badly in need of more spacious accommodation ... Soon thereafter, we learnt, that P & T Department had decided to discontinue the teleprinter lines of UNI and the apparent reason for the same was non-payment of the bills of the P & T Department by the UNI...Teleprinter lines could, however, be continued if, pending supply of news by one national news agency, UNI agreed to continue supply of its own news through the teleprinter channels to its subs-cribers, including AIR, on the understanding that with effect from February 1, 1976 the by-line of news supplied by UNI would be Samachar and not UNI. It was thus apparent that the real reason to cut tele-printer was not non-payment of dues by UNI but to enforce introduction of the by-line of Samachar. . . For obvious reasons under these compelling circumstances, UNI Board in the meeting on January 18, 1976 agreed to use the by-line of Samachar from February 1, 1976.

G.G. Mirchandani, the then Editor and General Manager of the UNI has stated to the Commission :

From the morning of December 15 (Monday) pressure suddenly mounted simultaneously on all the four news agencies from Posts and Telegraph offices throughout the country demanding immediate payment of varying amounts due to the department from the news agencies. This had never happened before during the long history of the news agencies. The Ministry of Information and Broadcasting at this stage owed about Rs. 13 lakhs to UNI on account of arrears of subscription from All India Radio. The amount due from UNI to the P&T Department was roughly Rs. 4.5 lakhs (less than a quarter's normal billing). Shukla refused point blank to release the amount of Rs. 13 lakhs due to UNI saying that this amount would be paid to the new news agencies formed after merger
. . . .

Pressure on UNI continued to mount and in early 1976, UNI and the three news agencies received more or less simultaneously communications from AIR saying that from April 1, 1976 AIR would not require their news services. . . . Eventually, V.C. Shukla succeeded. At a meeting of the UNI Board of Directors held early December, 1975, a resolution was passed in principle agreeing to the merger. Two more resolutions were passed later. The resolutions were drafted in the Ministry of Information and Broadcasting and passed on informally to the news agencies. . . . The de-facto merger took place from April 1, 1976. However at the insistence of the Minister of Information and Broadcasting, the managements of the news agencies had to agree to change the 'credit line' from UNI, PTI etc. to Samachar, from the midnight of January 31-February 1, 1976. This was done to give the outside world the impression that the merger had become effective from February 1, 1976.

Similar pressures were brought on the other two news agencies and they also passed the resolutions for voluntary merger.

The Ministry of Information and Broadcasting was actively associated with the further process of integration. On March

3, 1976. A.R. Baji sent a note to K.N. Prasad saying, "As desired, suggestions for the composition of the two committees on Administrative Integration and Professional Services, Samachar, are enclosed herewith."

On March 22, 1976 K.N. Prasad recorded a note on "Gist of discussion with G. Kasturi, Chairman of Samachar, held on that day." In his note Prasad had inter-alia recorded, "Shri Kasturi wanted to know my reaction to the advice given to him by Mohd. Yunus regarding the constitution of the three committees. I got the impression that he wanted these committees to be constituted after Samachar had done some spade work.

> I have advised Shri Kasturi to get these committees constituted as early as possible so that Samachar does not lose much time in getting on its feet.

In another note on 'Samachar' Prasad endorsed the following remarks on March 19, 1976:

> These have been cleared with Shri Mohd. Yunus and approved by MIB. A copy has been given to Shri Mohd. Yunus for further action at the next meeting of the Managing Committee of the 'Samachar'.

Prasad made similar endorsements on two other notes on some of the items which need urgent attention of Samachar. The endorsements are dated April 29, 1976 and one of them reads, "I have handed over this note to Shri Yunus for tomorrow's meeting of the 'Samachar'." Samachar was also forwarding the minutes of all its Managing Committee meetings to K.N. Prasad.

The Ministry of I&B also got rid of the persons who were opposed to the merger. G.G. Mirchandani, the then Editor and General Manager of the UNI has stated to the Commission :

> On February 14(Sunday) I was told by the Chairman of the UNI Board of Directors that I must retire from the company's service immediately. I realised that resistance was useless. I handed over retirement papers on February 17, 1976. . . . The Chairman of the UNI Board repeatedly expressed his regrets to me over the sudden end of my long service with UNI. . . . He told

me that V.C. Shukla had for a considerable time been insisting that I must go and that he had so far been resisting. Further resistance to Shukla's insistent demand was not easy.

This has been corroborated by Ram Tarneja, the then Chairman of UNI in his statement to the Commission. He has stated :

In so far as I can recollect now, from mid-September, 1975 onwards Mr. Shukla was keen to get me to agree that Mirchandani should not be continued as UNI's General Manager. I kept on telling him and persuading him that I did not agree with his views. This pressure continued for several months and Shukla kept on telling me himself and through his officials that I should take steps to retire Mr. Mirchandani. On or about February 14, 1976 Mr. Shukla was leaving India and told me on long distance telephone call that the ad-hoc arrangement of continuing UNI services under the by-line of Samachar was contingent on many factors that we must follow and Mirchandani's retirement was one of the most vital factors to which I should agree. I then had a prolonged talk with Mirchandani and he tendered his resignation on February 16, 1976.

In a Samachar Special Committee Meeting held on May 2, 1976 which was presided over by G. Kasturi and attended by Mohammad Yunus and Ram Tarneja, it was decided that "Mr. C. Raghavan be posted as Roving Correspondent at Bhubaneswar . . ." The transfer was to take place with immediate effect.

The key appointments were also made by the Ministry. W. Lazarus was appointed as Acting General Manager of Samachar at the instance of the Ministry. S.M.H. Burney, the then Secretary of the Ministry, submitted a note on February 15, 1976 to the Prime Minister, saying,

Minister of Information and Broadcasting had discussion with P.C. Gupta, Chairman, PTI and it was decided that since K.S. Ramachandran, the present General Manager, was to retire in April next, he

would proceed on leave and in his place, W. Lazarus
would be appointed as Acting Manager of PTI. He
would supersede C. Raghavan, who was suspected of
lobbying in a manner not conducive to the Samachar.
Lazarus took over charge as Acting General Manager
of PTI on February 13, 1976.

It may be clarified that Lazarus has not been appointed either as Executive Director or as General Manager
of the Samachar of which Kasturi is the Chairman. No
such appointment could have been made without
consulting him . . .

As desired, the above note is submitted to Prime
Minister for favour of information.

On February 18, 1976 Burney forwarded another note to
R.K. Dhawan, Addl. P.S. to the then Prime Minister in which
he had inter-alia recorded, "It is understood that Lazarus has
identified himself with the fostering of the image of national
leadership and the progressive policies and programmes of
Government. He is widely respected as a competent journalist
in the profession." It appears that Sanjay Gandhi was also
interested in the appointment of Lazarus as Chaman Lal
Bhardwaj has stated to the Commission, "I do not exactly
remember when I was asked about Lazarus. But it was during
one of the trips that Mr. Gandhi casually enquired from me as
to what kind of person was Mr. Lazarus . . . "

Raj K. Nigam, who was a Director in the Bureau of Public
Enterprises, was co-opted as a member of the Managing
Committee of Samachar in May 1976 at the instance of the
Ministry. In January 1977, he was co-opted as the Execu-
tive Member & Secretary of the Samachar. Nigam has stated :

I saw Sanjay Gandhi a couple of times on telephone
from PM's house. He mainly asked me about the economic situation in the country. Towards the end of
September or October, briefly Samachar also figured
in the talk and it was mentioned that it was not in a
satisfactory state of affairs. Editorial matter never
came up in the conversation, it was mainly management aspect of it. From memory I can say either it
was October or November. I was told by Minister for

Information and Broadcasting that I would be called for an interview with the Prime Minister which did take place in the Parliament House. She asked me about my academic career and about my writings on public sector. I was appointed subsequently to Samachar.

As regards employees of Samachar, Lazarus, Acting General Manager, Samachar, wrote to K.N. Prasad on July 28, 1976 in which he sent lists of the staff members of PTI, UNI, Samachar Bharati and Hindustan Samachar along with their permanent addresses. Accordingly, K.N. Prasad noted on this d.o. "Please open a file 'Verification of the antecedents' of the employees of the erstwhile four news agencies and put up." The lists were sent to the Intelligence Bureau of the Government of India for verification. This verification was to be made from the point of view of the association with the banned organisations. As these lists were not complete in certain respects, Lazarus was requested telephonically "to send ten copies of revised lists with all addresses completed and designation of PTI staff indicated."

When the term of the Managing Committee of Samachar was due to expire, K.N. Prasad noted on the file on January 1, 1977 that :

It is unfortunate that despite my advice to the Chairman, no effort was made to admit some selected members to this Society. As a result, the present membership consists of the 16 members of the Managing Committee. Left to themselves, all of them would like to offer themselves for re-election.

In the present situation, the correct strategy would be to get a smaller Managing Committee elected. This Committee would be free to admit some more suitable members and then enlarge itself. MIB may consider the following for re-election :

Shri G. Kasturi . . . Chairman
Shri Mohammed Yunus
Dr. Raj K. Nigam
Shri N. Rajan . . . Editor, *Hitavada*.

Shri Abid Ali Khan . . . Editor, *Siyasat* daily.

Dr. Ram S. Tarneja . . . *Times of India.*

The procedure for election will have to be settled in advance and our endeavour should be to get the above members re-elected by a consensus.

This note was put up to Shukla. After discussions with Shukla, Prasad noted in the file on January 24, 1977, "Discussed. MIB has talked to the concerned."

The Ministry was also keeping a close check on the editorial working of Samachar e.g. Burney inter-alia recorded a note in the file on July 20, 1976 "Another complaint has been made that the Indian Press did not cover at all the visit of D.K. Barooah, President, Indian National Congress, to Tanzania. This again is an instance of the failure of Samachar and responsibility has to be fixed as to how and why it happened. . . " The note was put to V.C. Shukla who said on August 6, 1976, "I will like to see the report." Lazarus, the General Manager, Samachar was asked to give a report in the matter and he reported that, "Regarding Congress President, we had no prior information about his visit and hence could not arrange local coverage in Tanzania. But Samachar did cover his activities there with the help of the External Affairs Ministry." On receipt of this report, Burney noted in the file on July 24, 1976, "In regard to the visit of the Congress President to Tanzania, I would suggest that G.M. should get in touch with the P.R.O. of AICC and follow an agreed procedure for coverage of the Congress President, internal and external visits adequately in future." This was seen by the Minister on August 6, 1976.

Samachar was also asked to play down the news about the then Opposition parties. The General Manager, Lazarus was keeping strict check on the News. C.P. Maniktala, Editor-in-Charge of the Foreign Wing of Samachar has stated to the Commission. "In the case of Pool Desk, messages going abroad were generally referred to the General Manager or the Editor, if these carried criticism of the Union Government. News emanating from Opposition parties was generally reported on a low key in our external cast because of the circumstances obtaining then."

P.S. Kasbekar, Editor (English Division) has stated, "The agency's services were utilised by the Government as no more than a channel for carrying its authorised versions of stories, but the Government ignored the fact that in the process the credibility of Samachar, so essential to a national news agency, was getting eroded step by step". This statement of Shri Kasbekar is borne out by various orders recorded in the log books of the Censor's Offices including the Teleprinter message dated May 5, 1976 from Jt. Chief Censor to all PIB offices/Censor Officers which reads "In reply to a question by Bibhuti Mishra, M.P., the Prime Minister said in Parliament to-day that there has been increased violence in the States and she said that the Governments were taking suitable action. The *Samachar* version of this supplementary question and answer has been approved. Kindly advise editors in your region to use only the Samachar version. No other version be allowed to be used."

The Teleprinter message dated June 16, 1976 from Jt. Chief Censor to all PIB Regional/Branch Offices, reads :

I had to-day earlier sent you a message regarding JP's letter to the Prime Minister about PM's contribution for purchase of a dialyser machine. I had stated that this letter should not repeat not be published in the Papers of your area. *Samachar* is likely to issue story giving JP's letter along with a statement of a Congress leader. There is no restriction on the *Samachar* story and the newspapers should be allowed to publish *Samachar* story.

On the copy of the said message U.C. Tiwari, Jt. Chief Censor has endorsed, "Subsequently OSD rang up to say that the statement of the Congress leader (Gen. Secy. of AICC) is not likely to come to-day. I have informed Chandran of Samachar not to do a story until the statement is issued & clearance obtained from Sharada Prasad." Log Book Entry dated December 10, 1976 reads :

M. Sundarrajan, DPIO rang up at 11 P.M. to say that Samachar had been given a story on the telephone exchange fire in Connaught Place. The locals were informed to carry the Samachar story and asked not to report any speculation about the cause of the fire.

The teleprinter message dated December 28, 1976 from the Chief Censor to Censor Officer, Bhopal reads, "Further to my message of this morning regarding the collapse of the T.V. tower at Raipur, the Minister of Information and Broadcasting has directed payment of Rs. 2500/- each to the family of the deceased person and Rs. 500/- each to the injured persons from his Discretionary Fund. Samachar has been asked to do a story and this story should be allowed to be published by the papers. Please inform everybody in your region to use the *Samachar* story on the subject." The Delhi English & Hindi dailies were also informed accordingly. Earlier a message was sent to Censor Officer, Bhopal and to dailies of Delhi not to allow/publish the news of the collapse of Raipur TV Tower.

Samachar also issued a number of stories based on the statements issued by several Congress MPs attacking Opposition parties, Jayaprakash Narayan, Jagjivan Ram and other parties. Most of these stories were done during the Lok Sabha Election campaigns. The statements received by the Samachar were typed on plain sheets of papers and were unsigned. The stories are available on the files of Samachar and are available with the Commission.

Another instance of the lopsided nature in which Samachar presented news can be seen by the "Election" survey it carried out in October, 1976. Kasbekar has said in his statement to the Commission :

> On the 27th of October 1976, or thereabouts a service message was addressed by the Acting General Manager to the various bureaus of Samachar in the country advising them to collect opinion on the subject and pass it on to Delhi . . . though the normal process for the issue of a survey was duly gone through . . . the election survey put out by Samachar suffered from being totally one-sided, to the almost complete exclusion of the opposite view point.

Again as Chaman Lal Bhardwaj, Special Correspondent of Samachar has stated to the Commission :

> In January 1976, a story was passed on to me to be creeded as it was under Bangalore date-line. This story

related to the meeting of the CPI at Bangalore. The
story was cleared with the people in charge in the office
and was sent on the creed machine to Bangalore
and the newspapers. The story was passed on by the
Intelligence Bureau to a Minister, who in turn gave
the story to Samachar. The Minister who passed on
the story was A.P. Sharma.

Regarding the build up of Sanjay Gandhi, the Samachar
assigned a special Correspondent for the sole purpose of covering his activities. As stated by C. Raghavan, Ex-Editor-in-
Chief of PTI :

> From the beginning, the stories in Samachar aimed
> at building up the personality of Sanjay Gandhi. Even
> before the formation of Samachar in 1975, the PIO,
> Baji had conveyed through Chandran, that PTI should
> assign Chaman Bhardawaj to cover Sanjay Gandhi
> at Chandigarh session of the Congress, where Sanjay
> Gandhi was launched on the political scene. . .

> A few days later, Chandran said he had been phoned
> up by Baji, who had said that the Minister had ordered
> that PTI should assign only Bhardwaj to cover the
> activities of Sanjay Gandhi and he should be asked to
> go along with Sanjay Gandhi everywhere. This was
> contrary to the PTI practice, who never assigned any-
> one to go along even with the P.M. within the
> country if any of the existing bureau staff could handle
> it. . . the PTI was (also) advised that the copy should
> not be edited or rewritten but issued as it was.

Chaman Bhardawaj in his statement to the Commission has
confirmed this, and has stated "After the formation of Samachar
I was deputed to cover solely the activities of Youth Congress
and Sanjay Gandhi. I used to travel with Sanjay Gandhi and
continued to cover his programmes till May 10, 1976".

Thus, from the above it is apparent that the erstwhile news
agencies decided to 'voluntarily merge' under pressure from
the Government and after the merger Samachar continued
functioning under Government pressure and control for par-
tisan ends.

XXVII—ALL INDIA RADIO

S.C. Bhat, Director NSD, AIR has stated that :

Two specific instances of aberrations during this period, were when Jagjivan Ram announced his decision to quit the Congress and the Government and when Indira Gandhi addressed her first election meeting in Delhi on February 5.

Jagjivan Ram's decision apparently came as a shock to the ruling party and the Minister himself was in frequent contact with me on that day (February 2). Although in the first bulletin broadcast by us after Jagjivan Ram announced his decision, we used the word "resignation," V. C. Shukla later directed us that we should describe it as "defection". He was annoyed that I tried to argue with him over the use of this word. Not only that, he directed us that full publicity should be given to the statements of Congress leaders condemning Jagjivan Ram's decision to leave the party, with the result that on that day and for two days thereafter, the bulletins became distorted although the important points made by Jagjivan Ram were also noticed.

The second occasion came when we did not describe the public meeting addressed by the then Prime Minister on February 5 at the Ramlila ground in Delhi as "mammoth". This was resented by the Minister and his displeasure was conveyed on phone to me the same night by the Secretary. My plea that we could not describe that meeting as 'mammoth,' without using a similar adjective for opposition meetings was not appreciated, and I had to ask the newsroom to revise the story using the word "mammoth" for the subsequent bulletins of that 'evening and repeat it next morning, which was very unusual. The next day, however, Jayaprakash Narayan's meeting at the same place was by all accounts twice or three times as big but we could not use any adjective. Later on at the daily meeting I raised this point, when the Secretary had to admit the validity of my contention and we were not compelled any further to use words like "mammoth" or "massive" for the meetings addressed by Indira Gandhi.

By around February 20, the Secretary was receiving complaints that coverage over the Radio was unnecessarily "fair" to the opposition and something should be done about it, because, as stated earlier, except for the two aberrations, during the period January 19 to February 20, our coverage on the whole was balanced and credible. After mentioning to me two or three times about the complaints received by him, the Secretary finally ordered me on February 24, that coverage should be done in a manner more favourable to the Congress and the ratio should be 2 :1. This was stepped up to a ratio of 3:1 in favour of the Congress Party, from March 3 onward. During the period March 8 to 11, the ratio was slightly more than 3:1 in favour of the Congress.

Even this was not found satisfactory by the ruling party because they discovered that the very limited coverage given to the Opposition was still effective; they complained that the points made by the Opposition leaders were presented in a "telling manner". Apparently for this reason on March 11, the Secretary told me at the morning meeting that from that day onward I should personally clear the major bulletins with him and the Additional Secretary. The division of labour was: the major morning and evening bulletins were to be cleared with the Secretary on telephone, and the afternoon and early evening bulletins with the Additional Secretary on telephone likewise.

The result was that the ratio rose during the period March 12 to 15 to the fantastic proportion of 8.5 : 1 and more or less the same ratio was obtained during the remaining four days. Not only that the Opposition points were now made in the most innocuous manner and names of only their top leaders were given in the bulletins, more to give assemblance of Opposition coverage than anything else.

At one stage during the pre-election period, it was realised by the ruling party that only their top leader was seen to be actively campaigning for the party. The Secretary, therefore, directed me to cover as many speeches of other leaders of the party, i.e. Union Ministers and State Chief Ministers, as possible. Since many of them were not active or unable to address any meeting, we were directed to obtain special interviews from them and thus give the Congress party campaign an appearance of a comprehensive and vigorous effort. Consequently, the number of Congress leaders others than Indira Gandhi covered in our bulletins went up from 17 during February 17-27, to 33 during March 8-11, and 58 during the period March 12-15, although for all intents and purposes many of these Congress leaders were conspicuous by their absence from the public scene.

Ban on References to Certain Names

From the very beginning, certain names were anathema to the Minister of Information and Broadcasting and the senior officers working under his directions, and they wanted us not to carry in AIR bulletins any reference to these opposition leaders or any speeches or statements by them. In the initial stages this applied to leaders like H.N. Bahuguna and. Nandini Satpathy. When Vijaylakshmi Pandit came out openly against the Congress Party and the then Prime Minister, our report on her first statement had to be cleared with the Additional Secretary. A brief report was allowed to be broadcast. Later on, the Secretary and he asked me to give as little coverage to Vijaylakshmi Pandit as possible.

Gradually, the inclusion of names of leaders who were considered as second rankers like Ashok Mehta, L.K Advani, Piloo Mody, Madhu Limaye and others was frowned upon. On March 6, which was a holiday because of Holi, the Secretary spoke to me for half an hour on the telephone objecting to the inclusion of some of these names in that morning's bulletin. Subsequently, as the election campaign entered the most crucial final phase, we were allowed to carry the names of only a few opposition leaders namely Jayaprakash Narayan, Morarji Desai, Jagjivan Ram, Charan Singh, Atal Behari Vajpayee and Acharya Kripalani. Their speeches or statements were, of course, rendered as innocuous as possible.

Clash in Delhi (March 13, 1977) :

On March 13, 1977, there was clash in Delhi between follo-

wers of the Janata Party and the Congress Party in the Farash-
khana area of the Chandni Chowk constituency. The
Congress came out with its version of the incident not only
claiming that a Congress procession was attacked by the Janata
Party workers, but also that a Sub-Inspector of the Delhi Police
accompanying the procession was injured as a result of the
attack and later died. An AICC spokesman, D.R. Goel,
was quoted for this news. The Janata Party version of the
incident which was diametrically opposed to the Congress version was not allowed to be broadcast by AIR, while the Congress version had to be given at length in the 9.00 P.M. and other
bulletins of that day, and the next morning.

The Delhi Police had given their own version in which they
had not blamed either political Party for the incident and
also stated categorically that Sub-Inspector Pratap Singh who
was incharge of the escort party, died of "heart failure" on his
way to Hospital. When this was brought to the notice of the
Secretary, Ministry of I&B, with whom the bulletins were
being cleared by me personally, he instructed me not to use the
words "of heart failure" although I pointed out to him that
was the police version. After the broadcast of the bulletin, the
Police spokesman rang up the Newsroom to complain about
the significant omission. This was also brought to the notice
of the Secretary by me early next morning while I was getting
the morning bulletin of the 14th March cleared by him but he
advised me to ignore the Police protest.

This is only one of the many instances of playing up of
alleged violence by Opposition against the Congress Party and
its workers. I was told by the Secretary at one of the 11.00 A.M.
meetings to get as many stories of violence as possible from
different centres in the country, including one about the death
by boiling of a youngman in Punjab by the Akalis. We had to
ask our correspondents in Chandigarh and other places to get
reports or statements of such "violent" instances and play
them up as much as possible in the bulletins. It is in this context that the story of the alleged attempt on Sanjay Gandhi's
life has to be viewed.

Amethi Incident

AIR news bulletins were used for publicising prominently
the alleged attempt on Sanjay Gandhi's life to arouse sympathy

for him and the Congress Party. According to information conveyed to me, the Minister for Information and Broadcasting himself rang up the Director General, AIR, between and 1 and 2 A.M. on the morning of March 15 to give details of the alleged attack. In turn, DG instructed the Newsroom on telephone regarding the manner in which the news was to be treated, what was to be covered and what not and the need to elicit reactions from the top Congress leaders in Delhi as well as the State capitals.

The Night Editor-in-Charge, NSD, AIR, of March 14-15, 1977 in his service report, wrote as follows :

> DG rang up at 0210 hours to give a story on the attempt on Mr. Sanjay Gandhi's life as given to him by the MIB from Allahabad.
>
> DG said that this will be the lead story in all morning bulletins.
>
> DG said that the MIB desires that some reactions of important Congress leaders should be included in the morning bulletins.
>
> DG also informed that the reference about the return of fire by the Security Guard of Mr. Sanjay Gandhi, as given by Samachar need not be taken.
>
> Mr. Chhetry was contacted at about 0230 and sounded about the developments.
>
> Mr. Sharma was contacted in Patna at about 0245 hours and told that he should try to get the reaction from Mrs. Gandhi, if possible, or some other important leaders. Mr. Khade's phone in Bombay seems to be out of order. He can be contacted in the morning again for a reaction from Mr. Gokhale and Mr. Chavan. Our Chandigarh and Madras correspondents may also be contacted. Mr. Vivekanand Ray's phone also appears to be out of order.
>
> As desired by Mr. Chhetry, Mr. Trakroo should be informed early in the morning togather reactions from the Congress leaders present in Delhi.
> DNS should be informed as early as possible.
>
> Sd/- K. K. Agnihotri
> Nt. Editor-in-Charge

(Chhetry and Trakroo to whom reference has been made in the above report, are Senior Correspondents of the News Services Division, AIR, Sharma is Patna Correspondent, Khade is Bombay Correspondent and Vivekananda Ray, Calcutta Correspondent.)

I was contacted by the succeeding Morning Editor-in-Charge about 4.00 A.M. The attempts to get the reactions of various Congress leaders were intensified. The news of alleged attempt on Shri Sanjay Gandhi's life and the reactions were broadcast as follows in the morning news bulletins of March 15, 1977 :

A report from Amethi says a dastardly attempt was made last night on the life of Mr. Sanjay Gandhi. But he escaped unhurt. The incident occurred when Mr. Gandhi was travelling between Amethi and Gauriganj in Uttar Pradesh at 10.00 P.M. At a sharp curve, some men were sitting with their faces covered and they fired five shots at Mr. Gandhi's jeep. Three of the shots hit the jeep and one of them hit the back of the seat where Mr. Gandhi was sitting. Some of Mr. Gandhi's companions were slightly injured.

The District Magistrate of Sultanpur, in which Amethi is situated, informed the Uttar Pradesh Home Secretary about the incident and said that some of the bullets hit the seat and the body of the jeep. Mr. Sanjay Gandhi had a miraculous escape. The matter was reported to the police who are trying to apprehend the culprits.

Several prominent leaders and State Chief Ministers have condemned the incident. The Congress President Mr. Borooah who is now in Nowgong, Assam, described the attack on the life of Mr. Sanjay Gandhi as a ghastly incident. He said it is the result of the rancour, bitterness and character assassination indulged in by the opposition in their election campaign.

The Uttar Pradesh Chief Minister, Narayan Dutt Tiwari expressed shock at the attack and said the people of Amethi will give a fitting rebuff to the forces opposed to the democratic atmosphere prevailing in the country.

The Rajasthan Chief Minister, Mr. Hari Deo Joshi said in Kota that by this act, the opposition working in the name of democracy stands exposed.

The Chief Minister of Bihar, Dr. Jagannath Mishra said the opposition should ponder as to what the country's future will be if such forces are encouraged, particularly during elections.

The Assam Chief Minister, Mr. Sarat Chandra Sinha said in Gauhati that this incident shows the violence and hatred with which the opposition parties had launched their campaign against the Congress.

The Andhra Pradesh Chief Minister, Mr. Vengal Rao said the opposition parties are resorting to violence in a mood of desperation which poses a danger to democracy.

Condemning the attack, the External Affairs Minister Mr. Y. B. Chavan said at Thalatan in Satara district that such atmosphere of violence would vitiate the peaceful atmosphere so necessary for holding the election.

The Minister of Communications, Shankar Dayal Sharma described the incident as a desperate attempt by the combination of fascist forces to curb and intimidate the youth who are determined to build up a strong, vibrant and democratic socialist India.

The Minister of Information and Broadcasting, Vidya Charan Shukla, has strongly condemned the shameful attack on the life of Sanjay Gandhi. The attack very clearly shows that the forces of violence are guiding the election campaign and strategy of the Janata Party. Whenever they find defeat inevitable they resort to coercive and violent action. All sections of the people must join together to give a crushing defeat to these people who have always stood in the way of the amelioration of the weak and poor sections of our society, and posed a big threat to the unity of our nation.

The AICC General Secretary, Purabi Mukherjee, said in New Delhi that attempts to influence the people by terror and by using violent means is something that every sane person will condemn.

Minister Shukla figured more prominently then others because I was contacted at about 7.30 A.M. from Allahabad by his Special Assistant, who conveyed the Minister's order that his

message must not be edited. The Secretary of the Ministry
with whom the morning bulletin was personally cleared by me
directed me not to carry any opposition leader's statement
doubting the veracity of the alleged attack.

R AIPUR INCIDENT

There was an attack on Purshottam Kaushik, Janata
Party candidate in Raipur for the Lok Sabha election and a
CPI MLA, supporting him, allegedly by Congressmen on
March 18. Instructions of the Minister of Information and
Broadcasting were conveyed to me through DG, AIR and by
the Additional Secretary in the Ministry, during the early
hours of March 19, that there should be no mention of the
incident in AIR news bulletins broadcast from Delhi or in
the Regional bulletins broadcast from Bhopal. The Minister
was particular that we should take care that no bulletin
scheduled to be broadcast in the morning from any adjoining
area like Nagpur, which could be heard by the Raipur voters,
made any mention of the incident. No reference was thus
made in any AIR bulletins, broadcast either from Delhi or
any regional Station to the incident on March 19, the day of
polling in the Raipur Constituency.

G.L. VORA

G.L. Vora had been working as AIR-part-time Correspondent at Raipur from October 1, 1963 on a Staff Artist contract.
His performance was generally considered satisfactory and his
contract was renewed from time to time. On March 19, 1977,
the SA to MIB spoke to me to convey the desire of the MIB
that Vora's services should be terminated forthwith.
He mentioned that Vora had covered Vijayalakshmi Pandit's
election speech at Raipur, on March 17, for the regional
bulletin from Bhopal. I pointed out that the Regional
bulletin had covered her speech rather briefly giving it only
about a minute out of ten minutes on the basis of a Samachar
report, and not Vora's story since he had filed none. I was,
however, asked to carry out the orders and accordingly Vora
was telegraphically informed that his services were not required
any more.

XXVIII—TRANSLATORS AND THE CONGRESS MANIFESTO

G. Mookherjee, Translator has stated :

As far as I can remember, in the first week of Feb. 1977 the Senior Copy Writer Shri K.S. Srinivasan informed us, the Asstt. Editors, that Late N. Sethi (the then Director of DAVP) wanted to take us somewhere and that he wished to see us in his room after lunch. Accordingly when I went to Director's room I found that most of the Asstt. Editors, the Deputy Director (Admn) and some other staff members had already assembled there. We were told by late N. Sethi that, we were to be entrusted with an important job and to do that, we would be taken to a place outside our office (the duration, nature of job and destination were not disclosed to us). Late N. Sethi then reminded us that we were govt. servants and were under oath of Secrecy and that we were not to divulge the the above fact of carrying out that special job or the place of work to anyone.

On the same day around 2 P.M. the then Director took three of us viz., D.N. Swadia, J. Mangamma and myself in the staff car of the office to a building near Teen Murti. At first I had no idea that this building would be an office other than a govt. establishment but later on I was told that this was the office of the Viswa Yuvak Kendra. When we entered the building late Sethi introduced us two gentlemen who were already there, as "my officers". However, those two gentlemen were not introduced to us and as such their identity or any other particulars are not known to me.

In the meantime the other officers of DAVP also reached

that place. The following officers from DAVP were present
there viz., S.S. Sarna (Punjabi) D.N. Swadia (Gujarati) G.P.
Sohoni (Marathi) B.K. Saikia (Assamese) P.K. Tripathi
(Oriya) C.R. Mandal (Bengali) J. Mangamma (Telugu)
Kulundavellu (Tamil) and myself for Bengali.

All of us were taken to a large room where tables and
chairs were set for us to sit, some articles of stationery viz.
paper, pencils and erasers were provided and a cyclostyled
English text (17/18 pages) was handed over with instruction
to start translating it immediately in the concerned regional
languages. Scanning the text I found that it was the Congress
Manifesto and that it would take at least 6/7 hours to complete
the translation. I was told by one gentleman that the job to
had to be completed as quickly as possible so that it could
be released in time and that I could go home only after finish-
ing it. Sensing that there would be inordinate delay in
returning home I sought permission to inform my family. At
first gentleman seemed hesitant but then gave permission
but reminded me that I was not to mention anything about
the place of duty or nature of job.

When I rang up my husband, one gentleman was sitting
behind the reception desk with a pencil and pad before him
and one gentleman was standing behind me. When I finished
the phone call, the gentleman behind me asked me what
number did I dial. I asked why but he only repeated the
question. When I told him the number, the man behind the
desk looked at his pad and nodded. I wondered whether he
jotted down the number for verification. Incidentally late
Sethi rang up twice or thrice and asked for me to enquire
whether everything was going along fine. As a result my
identity was revealed to them.

Then I went back to that room and began translating the
English text. After sometime Iva Nag (Bengali News reader
of AIR) also joined me. She told me, 'I have been hauled
up from my residence'. Mandal could not translate and he
helped us by comparing the text. The translation was completed at about 9 P.M. During this period we were offered tea,
coffee, orange etc. After the completion of the job, we arranged the sheets and as I stood up to hand it over, one of the
gentlemen, who was hovering around all the time motioned

me back, came to us and collected all the materials including the original text. The sheets which were spoilt and thrown away were also collected. I asked casually for a copy of the manifesto but the gentleman expressed his horror and said I could see it when it is released. He enquired whether any of us had kept any paper with us. When we said 'No', he thanked us and said that we could leave and that they had arranged for taxis to take us home. This time no official car was made available to us. G.P. Sohoni, D.N. Swadia and myself left in a taxi. I did not pay any part of the share nor did I submit any bill for that. I was told Sohoni had paid the fare.

After a day or two I was called by S.S. Sarna (Campaign Officer) to his room where he handed over, most probably two sealed envelopes and requested me to translate the contents in sheets provided with it. I found that there were 3/4 scripts for posters and probably Cinema slides, all in the nature of Congress slogans. Again I had to do as I was told, and as my other colleagues had done. I did not claim nor did I receive any pecuniary benefit for doing those jobs.

After a few days (possibly following the day when a report was published in the press indicating a complaint lodged with the Election Commission that services of govt. officials were being utilised by the Congress Party for election purposes) I was informed by S.S. Sarna and Shri Kulundavellu that the SCW has asked the concerned Asstt. Editors to give a signed written statement denying any involvement with the translation of the Congress Manifesto. I refused to furnish any such statement on indirect verbal order. I therefore, requested for a written order to enable me to carry out that directive.

No such order was issued. Instead SCW called me to his room, showed a typed note issued and signed by late N. Sethi. In that, the then Director referred to the press reports about the involvment of some Asstt. Editors of DAVP with Congress Party's publicity campaign and requested SCW to verify the fact and let him know so that he could send a report to the Ministry. Then SCW handed over his note addressed to all the AEs concerned (in which he asked the AEs to state the actual position) and asked me to sign it.

I have now been shown pages 19 & 20 of File No. 20 (s)—
JSI-77. These are notes referred to by me and the note at
page 19 bears my initial.

Then he indicated that the Director wanted a written
statement from each AE denying any involvement with such
work. He wanted me to give this statement on a separate sheet
of paper. When I said that this would tantamount to
telling a blatant lie and might put me in an embarrassing
situation in future, he assured that he was there to safeguard
our interests and that this statement will be kept in his safe
custody. Considering the situation obtaining at that time I
thought my defiance could lead to anything, not only harrass-
ment but that I could also lose my job. Considering this and
this advice I submitted a noncommital denial note duly signed.
I have been shown a note at page 13 of the above noted file.
This is that statement and it bears my signature dated Feb.
24, 1977. The whole episode was revolting and I felt
that Sethi wanted to make his own stand clear at our cost.

In this connection I must mention that Srinivasan, while
conveying the directive, clearly and categorically advised me
that should it be required, in future, for me to state the actual
facts, I should not hesitate and must tell whatever I knew,
truthfully and correctly.

XXIX—"BOBBY"

M.P. Lele has stated :

As desired by D.G. a factual report with regard to the telecast of Feature Film 'BOBBY' on February 6,1977 is given as under :

On February 5, 1977 at about 8.30 P.M. I was informed by Duty Officer Saroj that I should attend to a telephone call from S.A. to MIB in Duty Room. SA to MIB said that the Ministry wants a change in the feature film to be telecast on February 6, 1977 i.e. a film called 'BHABHI' should be telecast instead of 'WAQT' as scheduled. The change should be publicized on Television. I submitted to him that this would not be advisable on following grounds:

We, have, already publicized the film 'WAQT' in our Transmission since Wednesday last and have also sent a Press Note.

It would be very difficult to locate a reasonable good print of film 'BHABHI' at Delhi at such a short notice. Even if it is available contractual formalities with the local distributor can also pose a problem. The Feature Films to be shown on TV are pre-screened and approved by a Central Committee at Bombay and a local committee at Delhi if necessary. A contract for 'WAQT' has already been signed with the Producer after screening and approval by the Committee. Secondly there is no time now to get the film 'BHABHI' screened and approved by even the local committee at Delhi.

SA to MIB said that since government wants telecast of the particular film, we should immediately take necessary steps to acquire the film print for telecast on 6th. He asked me that I should report about the progress of the matter to him within

an hour. I immediately instructed the film section to check-
up if the print of the film 'BHABHI' was available with any
of the local distributors. Shinde, CP (TV) who held the
current charge of Delhi TV those days, was present at the
TV Centre and I reported the matter to him. While we
were trying to get the print, I was told that ADG was
present in the News Room and I personally reported the
matter to him. ADG rang up SA to MIB. He suggested that
while there is no problem to start the transmission at 5 P.M. as
being desired instead of 5.30 P.M as announced earlier, it
would be very difficult to change the film for the reasons
already mentioned above. SA to MIB however, asserted that
film 'BHABHI' must be shown and Delhi TV should make all
our efforts to get the print for telecast.

Though it was obvious that the orders expected us to do an
impossible task, we had no option left but to continue efforts
to locate the film 'BHABHI'. It was known that the said film
was being exhibited by one of the local Cinema Houses-
EXCELSIOR. We tried to contact the manager of the Cinema
Houses on phone and to find out from him about the distributor of the picture in Delhi. Nobody lifted the phone,
contacts were made with one or two other sources also but
nothing could be known. There was thus no question of
making any publicity annoucement about the change in Sunday Feature Film.

It seems Shiv Sharma, SD was also contacted at home in
this regard. He rang me up to find out what progress was
there in the matter. At about 9.55 P.M. ADG left the Studio
premises and while I saw him off at the lift gate, Madhu
Malti, ASD informed me that SA to MIB was on telepe-
one line in the News Room and wanted to talk to me. I
attended to the call. SA to MIB told me that we should
immediately make an announcement on TV that tomorrow at
5 P.M. Raj Kapoor's popular feature film 'BOBBY' would be
telecast. I pointed out to him that so far we were talking
about 'BHABHI' and there seems to be a further change to
'BOBBY' of Raj Kapoor. He confirmed that 'BHABHI' was a
misunderstanding. The Minister wants 'BOBBY' of Raj
Kapoor to be shown on February 6, 1977 at 5 P.M. I told him
that it would be very risky to make any publicity announcement
without having the print in hand and be satisfied about its

quality. Moreover I expressed serious doubt about availability
of the print in Delhi and that there was no time to get it from
Bombay. SA to MIB said that he has already talked to Deputy
Secretary (Films) Ghosh and Khandpur, Controller of Films
Division and the availability of the print would be taken care
of. He also insisted that an announcement about the change
of the film be made after English News on TV i.e. 10 P.M. It
was already 9.55 P.M. and there was hardly anything that I
could do after SA to MIB had said that these were 'Minister's
orders.' I Informed. Shinde-CP (TV) and arranged for the
announcement

SA to MIB again gave a ring at 10.05 and said that since
the film has been announced, Delhi TV should see to it that
'BOBBY' is telecast on February 6, 1977 as announced. He also
instructed that we should send a press note to 'Samachar' for
Press Publicity, and PIO had already been instructed to ensure
that the papers carry it. We were also advised to request
Radio to make announcements for 'BOBBY' on Delhi Station,
as well as on the local Vividh Bharati channel. The Press
note was sent to Samachar at 10.45 P.M. but I withheld the
Radio announcement.

I received telephone calls from Shiv Sharma and ADG
since both of them had seen TV announcements at 10 P.M. I
explained to them the circumstances under which the orders
were received. ADG desired that we should put our best
efforts to obtain the print. Thereafter, myself and Shiv Sharma
both set ourselves to the impossible task of obtaining the print.

In consultation with Film Section at this Centre I contacted
a few film distributors in Delhi to enquire as to who holds
the exhibition rights of the said film in Delhi. I came to know
that Kothari Associates have the rights as well as one old
print. I rang up his residence and his son confirmed that a
very old print is available in his godown, which he said, could
be collected only next morning. We also tried to contact. V.S.
Shastry, DTC Bombay, since SA to MIB had mentioned his
name along with Khandpur, Controller of Films Division
to find out, if new print could be collected by them during the
night and air freighted by early morning flight to Delhi. I
could not get any of them on line. I also tried to get in touch
with R.K. Studio, Bombay. I was in constant touch with Shiv
Sharma on phone. At about 1.30 A.M. I left the office in sheer

disgust, though of course planning to resume efforts at 8 A.M. in the morning.

Sunday, February 6,1977 being a closed holiday for the local film market, I contacted a few more distributors at their residences to request them to help in the matter. I also visited the residence of Kothari. He was out of town. His son was not at home. I was advised to meet his partner Moolchandani, which I did and tried to persuade and request him to supply us the print. It was clear that for obvious business reasons the distributor was not prepared to give it for a TV showing. After spending a lot of time trying to pursuade him but in vain, I left his place at about 1.30 P.M. just to make some alternate arrangement for 5 P.M. telecast. I visited the residence of Shiv Sharma to exchange notes since he also was in constant touch with the concerned parties and was obliged to report the progress to SA to MIB at intervals. At about 2.30 P.M. he was informed by Moolchandani that the print is available at his godown and it was agreed that Shreedharan of Films Division would collect it and deliver it to TV.

Myself and Shiv Sharma came to TV Centre to preview the print since it was all along said that the print was too old. At about 4 P.M. Moolchandani himself delivered the print at the TV Centre. The preview was limited to the technical quality of film as there was no time for anything else except to edit it for a smooth run, even if the print was faulty. It was thus, a miracle that 'BOBBY' could be telecast as announced.

The print of original film 'WAQT' was sent by our film section to Amritsar. As per chain of telecast, it was to be put out from there next Sunday. However, under Directorate's instructions the same was substituted and print sent back to us. Since then it is lying here.

After two or three days Shiv Sharma (CP-TV) at the Directorate spoke to me that in a meeting at the Ministry, ADG has been advised that a note on the subject may be prepared by me justifying the change in telecast of Sunday Feature Film on February 6, 1977. It was also suggested that a plea like the print being found defective a day earlier could be convincing enough. It could also be mentioned that SA to MIB's advice was sought in the matter and 'BOBBY' was put out as a substitute.

I thought this was not fair. I pleaded that since it was a political decision, it should be dealt with purely on that score and we, who were acting on specific orders from the authorities should not be expected to be party to the decision. Secondly the suggestion would imply that the print of 'WAQT' should be damaged to justify the stand, if taken. I thought it was a terribly immoral and cowardly act to do, even if one is to do so under duress. I, therefore, requested Shiv Sharma to impress upon the Directorate and the Ministry to reconsider the stand on the subject. Shiv Sharma fully agreed with me and assured me that he would do his best to convince the superior authorities to give up the line as above.

Although DG was ill, I visited his place the same night to apprise him of the developments and to seek his guidance. DG advised me that I should be guided by Truth alone. In the meanwhile Shailendra Shankar, DTC (Delhi) resumed duties after a brief illness. In one of the meetings he met SA to MIB, who told him that it was his impression that certain people at Delhi TV Centre are non-cooperative. He referred to the earlier advice, which he said was passed on to me through Chawla, ADG. Shankar conveyed to me this incident. I told him about what had happened and advised that he need not involve himself into this matter, since the telecast pertained to a period, when he was on sick leave. I had also not mentioned anything to the lower staff about the later developments, nor asked them to do anything, SA to MIB had desired.

Again sometime in the middle of March, soon after a news item appeared in the 'Indian Express' entitled "Now it can be told" Shiv Sharma spoke to me that he has been told that the Ministry has not taken kindly to our stand, and in case we don't toe the line there could be repurcussions. He, however, shared my feelings since there was no question of any going back on my part. I was thus prepared for the fait-accompli, which was averted in time due to the grace of God, I should say.

Mrs. G. Mookerjee	: *I was told along with the other officers that we were being taken to an office at Teen Murti for some translation work.*
Justice Shah	: *There you did get to know that it was the Congress Manifesto.*
Mrs. Mookerjee	: *In government . . . you know we have to do things. . .that we don't want to do . . .*
Justice Shah	: *Mr. Bhaskar Rao . . . I see you hold a doctorate and are a Professor of Mass Communication at the Institute in Delhi. Where did you obtain this doctorate ?*
Dr. Bhaskar Rao	: *From the University of Iowa in the VS.*
Justice Shah	: *You are a public servant . . . did you not realise the impropriety of preparing a paper on "Media-wise activities for the campaign". They contained some useful suggestions in regard to the methodology to be adopted . . .*
Dr. Bhaskar Rao **Principal Information Officer to the Government of India** **Dr. A. R. Baji**	: *I thought I would oblige them . . . Sir . . . I was only at the receiving end of the orders . . . made by non-professionals . . . It was the style of functioning of the government.*
Justice Shah	: *You have a Ph.d. in what subject ?*
Dr. A. R. Baji	: *In Indian History from Madras.*
Justice Shah	: *And . . .you were willing to omit the distinction between the State and the party !*
Secretary to the Government of India, S.M.H. Burney	: *Sir. . . Mr V. C. Shukla and the PM used to say to me. . . You are not managing the press well . .*
Justice Shah	: *What did it mean . . .?*
S.M.H. Burney	: *He would only repeat . . . The Chief Ministers are able to manage the news better.*
Justice Shah	: *They have DMs . .*
S.M.H. Burney	: *I thought they should abide by the Code of Ethics . . . Perhaps they were not observing this code . . .*
Justice Shah	: *In what manner. . . you have been in the ICS for 29 years,. . where does it say that if instructions are given by govern-*

ment . . .*I must carry them out unless I break a statute or law. . . Where does it say . . . if an order comes from the Prime Minister it must be followed . . .*

S.M.H. Burney : *My Lord . . . for me unhappiness is displeasure.*

Justice Shah : *Mr. Prasad. . . you were the Additional Secretary to the government. . . and yet you slept over this . . . a serious matter . . . .don't you think so ?*

Additional Secretary : *. . .I put my foot into it . . . I have* **to the Government of** *nothing to say.* **India, K. N. Prasad**

Justice Shah : *Mr. Shukla what is the meaning of loyalty. . . or is it that one's reliability is suspect ?*

(V. C. Shukla is trying to think of an answer)

Belonging is a matter of fact and suspicion is a view.

Former Minister of : *We presumed it to be the same . . .* **Information and Broad-** **casting V.C. Shukla**

Justice Shah : *Suspect by whom.? suspect by government . . . Had you been listening to AIR news . . . ?*

V. C. Shukla : *Very rarely . . .*

Justice Shah : *Why the double standard . . .?*

V. C. Shukla : *Because I regarded this as a serious matter.*

Justice Shah : *. . . What about the picture "Bobby". . .?*

V. C. Shukla : *If some people had raised an objection. . . the Heavens would not have fallen.*

Justice Shah : *How many irresponsible orders did you pass without applying your mind? . . . Was that expected of you as a public servant. . .?*

Editor HINDU : *Shukla phoned me and asked me if I* **G. Kasturi** *would head SAMACHAR . . .*

Justice Shah : *To carry out the law of the land however unpalatable is one thing and to choose to be independent is another. . . Why did*

		you regard yourself compelled to keep government advised. . . ?
G. Kasturi	:	*I did not want to run away from the problem . . . I wanted to face it.*
Counse	:	*They had time to check on how the birds in the Delhi Zoo felt . . .*
V. C. Shukla	:	*Strong arm method . . .this is the usual feature of the working of government. . . not just during the period of the emergency. . .Nothing that we did was illegal.*
Romesh Thapar	:	*General Habibullah was good enough to convey me a message from Mohd. Yunus in chaste Urdu which went something like . . .Tell the bastard we will seize his property.*
Cho Ramaswamy	:	*He says, "I am going to capture the fort . . . ", and then wants me to tell him who he is. All I said was to tell me his mother's name and the Censors banned it.*
Ramchander Rao	:	*It was fear that prevented me from saying it . . . During those days it was understood that if you did a mistake . . . you could go home and not come the next day. . . . as time went on you were not even sure if you could go home. . .Reason had taken a back seat in those days.*
Counsel	:	*You received some money for your translation work.*
Ramchander Rao	:	*Yes . . but I never counted it . . . After the elections were over I visited Badrinath and gave it away. . .*
Counsel **Khandalawala**	:	*Your conscience is clear now . . .*
Ramchander Rao	:	*I do not think my conscience can ever be clear . . .but atleast my sins are washed.*
Assistant Editor for Marathi	:	*There was a simple formula . . . I would wait for 5 minutes . . . and then do what everyone else was doing.*
AIR Translator D. Dholakia	:	*I had decided that if I am asked to sign anything. . . I will not use my brain.*
Counsel	:	*You were a heart patient in 1973? from*

	1973 to 1977 . . . you have been alright . . ?
AIR (Assamese unit)	: *No . . . I am having palpitations*
N. Rehman	*right now.*
Counsel	: *But you are smiling . . .*
N. Rehman	: *After all I am an artist.*
Counsel	: *If you lost your job today you would still have the same problems.*
S. S. Sarna	: *I can now go to Court.*
Counsel	: *You know how long it takes . . .?*
S. S. Sarna	: *I don't know . . . I have no experience. This is the first experience. . . Translation is an art and once I took at least 4 hours on a translation.*
Counsel	: *You said just a little while back that you could do 2 pages in an hour.*
S. S. Sarna	: *I can even do 5 pages in an hour but generally I don't do more than 2 pages. The translation was for the sentence :* *Forget the Government . . Do it yourself.* *I translated it as :* *Sarkar ko ram ram.* *Khud sambhalo apna kam.*
Counsel	: *You are not following that slogan today . . . ?*
S. S. Sarna	: *I never followed any slogan. . . I am just telling the truth.*

5 Demolition and Debris—
The Dream of Building
up...Sanjay

*A GOOD DREAM. . . .and his mother may have lived on it
for years. DOLLS—the Gutta-Percha in fancy and frilly
costumes of silk, the baby doll that squeaked when turned
over, the one which squealed when put on her back and the
third that cried "boo" when patted on the back. Even the
idea of a VANAR SENA—the army of the indestructibles
taken from the Ramayana may be a good effort. . . .but
there is a time for everything including fantasy—dolls,
princesses, Cinderella, Joan of Arc, Florence Nightingale
and even being the Rani of Jhansi.*

*The Indians, poor as they may be are not dolls. Unfortu-
nately dolls are dolls and they stay with you only as long
as you want them to stay. Thereafter, you must know what
you want and that he did! Did he know that the fantasy
trip has to change, even though he may have been able to
provide himself with "Human Dolls" instead of all those
unearthly looking creatures of his mother's dream?*

*He did and he did not. . . but his mother says, "he was
born prematurely while I was feeling faint and not fit
enough for an outing on that wintery evening, busy helping
Lady Stafford Cripps buy a Kashmiri Shawl". Incidentally
where was father Feroze? Who. . .Oh yes, "he was put up
in a tent outside".*

*It is a macabre situation, and so it was for those in
Kapashera, Sambhalka, Jahangirpur, Sarai Peepalthala,
Bhulswa, Jhandewalan, Gaffar Market, Arya Samaj
temple, Jama Masjid, Turkman Gate et al.*

XXX—KAPASHERA AND MARUTI AGAIN

A number of residential structures including some factories workshops etc. were demolished in village Kapashera in September/December, 1975 without giving any prior notice to the residents/owners of factories.

The residents who have formed an Emergency Sufferers Association in the village have alleged that in September, 1975 Ranbir Singh, Executive Officer of the DDA, Vij, Deputy Municipal Engineer, the S.D.M. of the area and other officers, accompanied by a large contingent of police and labour had surrounded the village and demolished their pucca residential houses. According to them, this was perhaps done at the instance of Sanjay Gandhi, who used to pass by the village on his way to Maruti Factory, and because of their houses on the eastern side of the road, his speed was hampered. The Association claimed that the houses demolished were as old as 25 years.

Nu Foam Rubber Industries, who were manufacturing latex foam rubber goods, have alleged that their factory situated on a plot measuring about 1224 sq. yds. in the 'Lal Dora' area of village Kapashera was demolished on September 17 and 18, 1975 without any prior notice or warning. As a result, they had suffered a loss of Rs. 4.39 lakhs. The DDA officers had told them confidentially that the action had been taken at the instance of Sanjay Gandhi, who was known for his anxiety to develop small scale industries in the Industrial Estate within the Maruti Complex.

Sanjay Gandhi was reportedly unhappy that while the industries had come up in this small village, no such growth had taken place in the Maruti Complex, only about 3 Kms. away. They had obtained a stay order against demolition of their factory from the court of S.L. Khanna, sub-judge on

September 18, and had shown the same to the officer super-
vising the demolition but he had paid no attention to it. When
their case against the DDA had come up for hearing on
November 11, 1975 they were threatened with arrest under
MISA if they did not withdraw their case from the court.

Delhi Paper Products Company, who had set up a paper
conversion unit under the Rural Employment Scheme of the
Government have also alleged that on Sept. 17, the DDA
and MCD officials accompanied by police force had cordoned
off their factory building and started demolishing it.
Machines, raw material and other stocks were buried under
the debris.

They had filed a writ petition on September 18, which was
fixed for hearing on September 22. On that day, the Land Sales
Officer (I) of the DDA had appeared before the court and
denied the demolition. The same day, he threatened them with
arrest under MISA if they did not withdraw the case. Accordingly, they withdrew the case on September 23.

Rati Ram, a resident of village Kapashera, who had a lathe
workshop in the village, alleged that his workshop was demolished on September 18 by the DDA and MCD staff. He had
suffered considerable loss as a result of this action which had
been taken without giving him any prior notice.

Similar allegations were also made by Duggal Engineering
Co. and International Industries.

The DDA have claimed that they had only assisted the
Municipal Corporation in removal of squatters in this area,
but admitted that there was no written requisition by the MCD,
for their demolition squad. According to them, in all 24
khokhas of recent origin and one unauthorised factory (Delhi
Paper Products) were demolished on September 17. However, the DDA do not appear to be sure of the number of
structures demolished and have in their various communications given varying numbers.

In their letter No. DDA/FFC/196/77 dated August 30
1977, 24 khokhas, 25 jhuggies. 49 boundary walls and 15 semi-
pucca structures have been stated as demolished in this village
on Sept 17, 1975. In another letter No. DDA/FFC/20/77 dated
October 5, 1977 the number of demolished structures had been

given as 24 khokhas and 4 factories. According to them, the factory of Nu Foam Rubber Industries and the lathe workshop of Rati Ram, had been demolished by the M.C.D., while some other factory owners had dismantled their unauthorised structures voluntarily in order to obtain allotment of alternative industrial plots.

S.S. Mann, who was posted as Zonal Asstt. Commissioner in the Rural Zone of the MCD with effect from December 1, 1975 stated that he was called by B.R. Tamta, Commissioner, MCD in his office along with V.P. Gupta his Zonal Engineer. On reaching the Commissioner's office they had found H.U. Bijlani, Municipal Engineer, B. Dayal, Superintendent Engineer and the Executive Engineer (Rural) also present there.

The Commissioner had taken them to Palam-Gurgaon Road and he was asked to note the constructions towards the left side of the road. Tamta had told him that these constructions from village Samalkha onwards upto Haryana border had to be demolished by December 31, 1975. He and his Zonal Engineer had pointed out that only a few of these constructions were booked as unauthorised, but Tamta had insisted on demolition of all the structures, irrespective of whether these were registered or not. Mann had no choice and fixed the operation for December 31, 1975. He contacted the police authorities for law and order arrangements and the other Zonal Assistant Commissioners for mobilising as many labourers and other staff as possible for its success. The Delhi Electric Supply Undertaking were asked to disconnect the power supply to the houses to be demolished. His Zonal Engineer (Bldg.) had under verbal orders of the Commissioner engaged a bull-dozer. Thus, on the December 31, 1975 the houses on the left side of the Delhi-Gurgaon Road from village Samalkha upto Kapashera were demolished.

Mann further stated that no file about this operation had been prepared by the Zonal Engineer (Building) although separate files are required to be prepared for removal of unauthorised constructions. According to him, his predecessor O. P. Gupta, had also been asked by the Commissioner to carry out the above mentioned demolition. He had not agreed to violate the prescribed legal procedure and was, therefore, asked to proceed on leave. Gupta was later reverted to a junior post. Mann explained that he was conscious of the treatment meted out to his predecessor who was senior to him, for his refusal to carry out the directions of the Commissioner. Therefore, he could not resist the patently illegal orders given to him by Tamta.

B. R. Tamta stated that the DDA had carried out certain demolitions in the MCD area at Palam-Gurgaon Road. After going half-way through the demolitions, the DDA had complained to Sanjay Gandhi that the Corporation staff was not cooperating with them. Sanjay Gandhi was annoyed and had insisted that he (Tamta) should depute his staff to the DDA. Sanjay Gandhi had also asked him to complete the demolition, as the DDA had left the buildings half demolished.

Tamta had tried to prevail upon Sanjay Gandhi that the DDA which had started these demolitions might be allowed to complete the operation, but he had insisted that MCD should complete it. According to Tamta, Sanjay Gandhi was annoyed when the house of Col. Yadav could not be demolished by the MCD staff. He (Tamta) had told him that this was an old building and could not be demolished, but Sanjay Gandhi had insisted that the building must be demolished at once. Later he was told to demolish whatever portion of Col. Yadav's house was unauthorised.

The land fell outside the urbanisable limits of 1981 and was 'agricultural green' as per its Master Plan land use. Subsequently, it was indicated by the DDA that it had been decided to locate cattle dairies shifted from the urban area on this land. However, in April, 1977 the proposal was shelved and the acquisition proceedings were dropped. It would therefore, appear that the land in question was and continued to remain a private property.

Strangely enough the DDA claimed that the demolitions were carried out by the MCD or at the instance of the MCD, and the MCD contended that except a few unauthorised structures, which were demolished by them, the other structures were demolished by the DDA. It was not a 'development area', declared as such under section 12 of the Delhi Development Act, 1957.

The DDA, therefore, had no legal authority to enter the area either to remove the unauthorised structures or to develop it. There is also no provision in the Delhi Development Act 1957 under which DDA could undertake demolition operation on behalf of the MCD or utilise its funds in rendering material assistance to the MCD in demolition operation outside a 'development area'.

The MCD failed to comply with the provisions of Section 343/344 of the DMC Act in most of the cases. In some isolated cases, such as the house of Col. Ram Singh Yadav, the Municipal Officers who had tried to go through the codal formalities appeared to have come to grief. For example, O. P. Gupta, ZAC was sent on leave and subsequently reverted to a junior post and P. N. Vinayak, Zonal Engineer was placed under suspension.

Since no survey of the structures to be demolished was carried out, DDA and MCD could not go into the legitimacy of the constructions or the status of their occupants.

According to B. R. Tamta, the then Commissioner, MCD, the clearance operations on Palam-Gurgaon Road also were undertaken at the behest of Sanjay Gandhi. Tamta claimed that he and his staff were terrorised by Sanjay Gandhi into submission. Tamta feared his own suspension if he failed to carry out Sanjay Gandhi's orders. The exact motive behind these demolitions is not clear. It has been alleged that the demolition of the house of Col. Yadav was desired on political considerations, but in respect of the other demolitions the version of the affected persons is that Sanjay Gandhi wanted to have these eyesores/traffic obstructions on the National Highway No. 8 removed as he used to go on this road enroute to his factory at Gurgaon. The owners of the factories demolished in village Kapashera also expressed the view that Sanjay Gandhi, who was anxious to develop the Industrial Estate within the Maruti Complex could not countenance their factories flourishing in this village so near the Maruti estate.

Ram Kishan of Village Kapashera has stated :

I am a resident of the village Kapashera. In this village I had sixteen concrete houses which were being made since 1953. After 1966 I did not build any house. Around my 7000 yds (7 Bighas) property, other residential houses were built by various people.

On September 4, 1975 about 1.30 in the afternoon all of
a sudden an officer Ranbir Singh of DDA who is a
resident of the neighbouring village Sankol (Haryana)
and who I know, came to our village with a police
force and with 100-150 members of the house demolishing squad. The labourers attacked the houses with
big steel rods. We did not get any prior notice. I
begged Shri Ranbir Singh not to do that and reminded him that he has been walking on this road to his
village for the last 20-25 years. What crime have we
committed ? Why are you demolishing our houses ?
But he said,

I am blind from my eyes and deaf from my ears.

He further added assuringly, thank your lucky stars
that the bulldozer is stuck in the Pasangirpur village
and that is why only a few houses are being demolished. Otherwise all the houses would have been
demolished. They did not give us even time to take
out our household effects including my agricultural
implements and utensils, 50 maunds of cattle fodder,
20 maunds of wheat, etc. were destroyed and mixed
with the remains of the demolished house. While
the houses were being demolished we were surrounded
by the police and were unable to do anything.

Children and women were left crying and no body
even took pity on them.

After the demolition of the houses, I and a few other
villagers which included Shri Bihari Lal, Sh. Ganga-
dutt, Sh. Pyare Lal, Sh. Raghubir, Sh. Mahendra
Singh and Sh. Hardwari Lal, went to meet Sh. Dalip
Singh, M. P. at his Meena Bagh residence. Sh. Dalip
Singhji said. "I can be of no help to you in this matter
and the demolition is taking place on the instructions
of Shri Sanjay Gandhi". He also requested that this
secret should not be divulged to anyone.

His words were :

*Ki is me main kuchh maded nehi kar sakta aur yeh ma-
kan girane ka karya Shri Sanjay Gandhi ke Ishare Per
ho raha heh.*

After this, on December 31, 1975 all of a sudden at 11 o'clock a bulldozer and 200-300 policemen etc. came to the village and they destroyed Shri Bihari Lal Yadav's and his sons' houses, their gardens and tube-well. This destruction passed on from the neighbouring houses to ours. An Officer with a flag was directing the bulldozer and was saying "bring it here, bring it here" (*Edhar lao, edhar lao*). There was a lot of commotion. No one was allowed to take out their household effects. The police had surrounded every-one. The demolition of the houses was carried out throughout the day. Till 5 in the evening about 7 bighas of residential area, on which existed houses and tubewell etc. were destroyed. My belongings and all my savings of generations were mixed with dirt. I suffered a loss of approximately 2½ lakhs of rupees.

After this, the remnants were removed by the Cor-poration trucks so that no evidence was left of the demolished houses. Our village is on the road going to Maruti Factory. Maruti Factory is at a distance of 2-2½ miles from our village. People on the road would stop to look at what had happened. I could not even tell the passers-by what had transpired. We have been living here for 20-25 years and have not had an occasion to see this kind of *Hatyachar*. They did not give us notice nor the time to take out our personal effects. Emergency was on and we were not even allowed to sit in our already demolished houses. The Corporation men were on guard. On asking them they used to say that Sanjay Gandhi passes from here and does not like the sight.

Puchene par ve hume kehte ki yaha se Sanjay Gandhi aate jate rahete aur ve aitraz karte hain.

He did not want these houses to remain and no human being or animal should be allowed to exist. My two dogs were forcibly killed and I do not know what crime we or the dogs have committed. From 9 A.M. to 1 P.M. the Corporation men were on duty on both sides of the road and no one was permitted to cross. Sanjay Gandhi used to go to Maruti at this time. The animals were not allowed to go towards the fields nor were we. On January 10-11, 1976 about 100-150 village men went to meet Sanjay Gandhi at his Maruti Factory. He brusquely told us "This is nothing, we have to demolish 500 more houses. Kapashera village is full of Badmashas."

Ye makan kya gire hain? Abhi to 500 makan aur giraye jayenge. Kapashera gaun bare badmashon ka hai.

On hearing these words we returned. After the declaration of elections in January 1977, we went to Indiraji in the month of February at her residence, 1 Safdarjang Road, New Delhi.

An Officer took our application. Someone said that he is Dhawan Sahab, Dhawan Sahab said, "You give me the application but bring 200-300 men and not 5-7 men, in trucks and flags and chanting slogans "Indira Gandhi Zindabad".

After this we returned and we are still homeless and oppressed. We cannot understand what is to be done.

Jagmohan	: *Sir, Tamta also joined the birthday celebrations of Sanjay Gandhi. . .*
Counsel	: *You asked him to also take files to Sanjay Gandhi.*
Jagmohan	: *Sir, Sanjay will not require Jagmohan's shoulders to ask Tamta to bring his files to him.*
Justice Shah	: *If it is according to law. . .it matters little if so and so came.*
Jagmohan	: *Sir, everything we did was according to the Act.*
Justice Shah	: *You are saying everything was done according to law. In my opinion there is hardly anything that was done according to law. . .*
Jagmohan	: *We gave them Notice. . .*
Justice Shah	: *All this may have been very generous of you, but as far as human considerations are concerned they are not a part of the DDA Act.*
Jagmohan	: *But Sir I gave you the background. . .*
Justice Shah	: *(cutting in) I have heard the word "background" so many times that it shocks me. . .*
Ganga Dar	: *I am also a Brahmin. . . Justice can only be done if the bulldozer is put on Indira Gandhi's farm.*
Khul Bhusan Gulati	: *I am an ex-soldier having served my country for 15 of my best years. . .They treated me as if I was not a citizen of India. As a result, today I am a father of 5 grown-up daughters and unable to provide them with even two square meals, leave alone their education.*
Jagmohan	: *Sir, we gave them land. . .*
Justice Shah	: *You demolish their factories and their homes and then give them land. . . This is not the law in this country fortunately. . .*
P.N. Vinayak	: *Jagmohan suggested to us to even backdate the Notices, and we were suspended. I asked him why he was suspending me. . .*
Jagmohan	: *If I had not suspended him I would have been suspended.*
Kanwar Lal	*While they were demolishing I fainted. . .I said leave at least the kitchen for my pregnant daughter-in-law. Later I went to see Jagjivan*

Ram, Malhotra. . .they all expressed sorrow but never **did** anything.

K.B. Gulati : *It is a National Loss. . .The government servants are supposed to serve us instead of oppressing us. . .*

S.K. Bhutani : *While I was taking pictures of the demolishing of my U-foam factory. . .my camera was snatched but I begged them to take the reel but return the camera. . .*

XXXI—THE FARM HOUSE OF COL. YADAV

The house of Col. R.S. Yadav was also one of the targets for demolition. However, this house could not be demolished as Col. Yadav had threatened to open fire if anyone touched his building. After two or three days, Tamta had called him (Gupta) to his office and expressed his displeasure over the non-demolition of Col. Yadav's house. He had persuaded Tamta to agree to the issue of a notice as per the prescribed legal procedure. Accordingly, the Zonal Engineer had issued a notice under section 343 of the DMC Act. Col. Yadav had sent his reply and was also heard in person by the Zonal Engineer.

Thereafter, the Zonal Engineer had issued a demolition notice under section 343/344 of the DMC Act against which Col. Yadav obtained a stay order from the court. Tamta felt annoyed at this course of events and suspended the Zonal Engineer (Building) after obtaining a note from him in which he was compelled to write that unauthorised constructions were going on in the zone and the Zonal Engineer (Building) had failed to control them.

Subsequently, Col. Yadav obtained a stay order from the High Court but the Corporation succeeded in getting it vacated. As they were preparing to domolish the house of Col. Yadav, a word came from the Commissioner to suspend the operation as a compromise had been reached. The operation was finally given up and Zonal Engineer (Building) was also reinstated. Although, O.P. Gupta had no personal information, he had heard that Sanjay Gandhi and Col. Yadav had developed some personal differences over the state politics of Haryana.

Col. Ram Singh Yadav, Education Minister, Haryana, has stated :

I took my premature retirement from the Army in November 1968, after serving for 24 years in the Army. I shifted to my farm house which is in the name my wife Sharda Yadav some time in 1975. I also own a petrol pump which is located immmediately in front of my farm house on the Palam—Gurgaon Road.

Sometimes in the middle of 1972 Wg. Cdr. Chaudhuri, then Manager of Maruti rang me up and asked me to see Mr. Gandhi at the factory. I went and saw Mr. Gandhi some time in the forenoon. Mr. Gandhi told me that he would like to take his petrol, oil and lubricant requirements from my Pump. Although having heard of his reputation I was not very keen to have him as one of my customers, nevertheless I agreed to provide him with whatever his requirements may be from my Pump. He immediately asked as to what commission I would be able to give. I pointed out that there was not much of a scope for any commision, but he insisted that I give him some commission. Thereupon I agreed to give him a commission of one paisa per litre. He insisted on 2 paise per litre to which I regretted my inability.

He said that one of the neighbouring Pumps was prepared to give him two paise per litre and I asked him that it would be best for him to take his requirements from that Pump and there the matter closed.

Having recently retired from the Army and being new to the business of running a Pump I had taken two partners for the running of the Pump namely Shri Balbir Singh and Shri Bir Singh. They were daily visitors to Mr. Sanjay Gandhi's factory near the Gurgaon border. Soon after my partners created an atmosphere of crisis and tension. One thing led to another and on December 30, 1972 they beat up some of the staff of the petrol pump for not acceding to their wishes. Thereupon I rang up and called the Flying Squad from Delhi. Soon after seven or eight people, one of them armed with a pistol, attacked my pump while members of the Flying Squad were at the pump. My 82 years old father was shot dead. I was hit by a bullet in the stomach and these ruffians terrorised the whole area.

Although these people were arrested they were soon released on bail, and although a murder had been committed

in broad daylight on a public thoroughfare in the presence
of at least five to six hundred people, they were let off scot
free and acquitted.

When this happened I met the then Lt. Governor who
replied in Hindi :

> Salon ne paise le liya honge . . . Kya Kar sakte hain
> (They must have been bribed. . . What can we do).

I then met the then IG who gave me a "blank no."

On September 20. 1975, some staff from the Municipal Corporation Delhi and the Delhi Development Authority visited
my house and served Notice No. 6071 and 1075/D/UC/RZ/75
dated September 20, 1975 in which I was asked to show cause
why the house should not be demolished.

I replied to the show cause notice on September 23, 1975
stating that the house had been constructed prior to the
coming into force of the Municipal laws. The Municipal Act
came into being in March 1958, while its existing record
showed the house to be in existence in 1953. Further I had
taken due permission from the Municipal authorities vide
their orders dated 15.2.73 for carrying out renovation and
repairs to the house. This permission had been granted and
no objection had been raised about the existence of the house
at that time.

Thereafter I also obtained a stay order from the Court of
Senior Sub-Judge at Delhi. The Municipal officers, however,
kept on harassing me and my wife. I was told in clear terms
that the orders for demolition had directly emanated from
Mr. Sanjay Gandhi and no power on earth could save the
house.

In the first week of October, 1975 I requested for an interview
with Mr. Sanjay Gandhi and he asked me to come see him at
No. 1 Safdarjung Road. I went and saw him at approximately 4.30 in the evening. He told me that it was a mistake
on my part to have got the stay order and I should have come
and seen him before obtaining the stay order. He advised me
in a sarcastic tone that the best course for me now was to
obtain a stay order from the High Court. I pointed out that

it would cost me a considerable amount of money which I could ill-afford at this time. He then told me "You are a Member of the Delhi Gymkhana Club. Go there in the evening and offer two Scotch Whiskeys to any High Court Judge and the stay order would be readily granted to you". I was amazed to hear such contemptuous words from a member of the Prime Minister's household. I realised that further conversation with him was a waste of time and effort.

At this particular time I happened to be the Vice-President of the Indian Ex-Services League which is an All-India body looking after the interests of ex-servicemen in the country. I took a delegation of senior retired Army officers comprising of Maj. Gen. Tara Singh Bal, Col. Kadam Singh, Col. Suri, and a few others to call upon the than Prime Minister. It was pointed out to Smt. Indira Gandhi the then Prime Minister, that such treatment towards retired Army officers would have a very demoralising effect on the Army Forces and the ex-servicemen in the country. Mrs. Indira Gandhi ordered Mr. Dhawan to see that my house was not touched. I thanked her and the delegation left the Prime Minister's House. After a period of approximatly 3 to 4 days in about the 2nd week of October, 1975 I got a call from Mr. Gandhi asking me to come and see him at No. 1 Safdarjang road.

I went to see him at approximately 8' o clock in the morning. I saw the Lt. Governor Mr. Krishan Chand, the Vice President of the DDA, Mr. Jagmohan and the Commissioner, Municipal Corporation Mr. Tamta lined up outside No. 1 Safdarjang Road. Mr. Sanjay Gandhi came out at about 8.15 A.M. and issued rapid fire orders to all these three men. All orders were pertaining to demolitions in the various parts of the city, the details of which I would not remember at this distance of time. Mr. Sanjay Gandhi then took me inside the room. He asked me that I should demolish the front portion of the house voluntarily.

I pointed out that the then Prime Minister had agreed that there was no need to demolish my house. Mr. Gandhi said that the choice was mine. I could either demolish half the house myself or the Corporation would demolish the complete house. Seeing that he was quite serious about it, I agreed that I would demolish half the house myself. I went back and called the workmen and asked them to demolish the front portion of the house comprising of one Verandah, one large room and one toilet. At this stage I might point out that I had sunk my entire life's savings in the purchase of this farm house and the renovation and repair of this house.

Apart from the financial loss, what hit me most was that after 24 years of exemplary service in the Armed Forces in the defence of the Motherland, this was the reward I was getting by being made to feel like a criminal. Throughout my service I hardly had any occasion to be posted in a station with my family and children and the opportunity that 1 got to stay peacefully with my family after my retirement was now being snatched away from me.

After the front portion of the house was demolished. I rang up Mr. Gandhi who was closely following the progress of the demolition by his daily visits to Maruti. I asked Mr. Gandhi whether the requirements of the Corporation were now met with. He said that I must further demolish the barsati and the water tanks located on the top of the house. Thereafter I demolished the barsati and I then went and saw Mr. Tamta, Commissioner Municipal Corporation of Delhi, who asked me further to give him a letter. . . . After taking this letter from me he issued me a letter . . . .

Sir, these are some of the instances that formed the background that led to my house being made the prime target for demolition during the days of the Emergency in that area. What pains me most is that to justify the demolition of my house a number of other houses and structures belonging to poor people were also demolished in this area. The demolition squad used to move like a military force and comprised of members from DDA (Delhi Development Authority), the Corporation and a strong police contingent. Normally no notice for demolitions was given and the whole operation was carried out with military precision.

Justice Shah : *Is this Statement correct?*

Col. Yadav : *Yes Your Honour.*

Justice Shah : *Would you like to add anything more?*

Col. Yadav : *(with a distraught look on his face) Yes. . .I have no other house. It was 1000 metres from the main road and on Diwali day in 1975 I asked my wife to clear the house as bulldozers were lined up near Dhaula Kuan. (breaks down). . . I was forced to tear down my own house while my wife and my child stood outside praying. . . OH GOD LET US SPEND THE NEXT DIWALI IN THE HOUSE. . . (breaks down again) Court Clerk offers him a glass of water and he sips it and breaks down again.*

Justice Shah : *(Visibly moved) Why don't you compose yourself and come back after 10 minutes.*

Col. Yadav : *(returning) Sir I have been receiving threatening calls not to appear before you. . .(then staring at Jagmohan sitting comfortably at the head of the Press desk in the first row, barely 6 feet from him)*

Mr. Jagmohan was too big a shot to deal with small fries like us in those days. And if I could not meet him, how could the poor people of Kapashera get an audience from him. . .

(Jagmohan stoically watches the revelation)

What pains me is that while a soldier is prepared to lay down his life for the defence of his country for a paltry sum of 150 to 200 rupees. . . these officers (pointing at him) were gutless. . .Why couldn't they defy him. . .? A transfer or a warning would have been a small price for them to pay. . .But these chaps were drunk with lust for power. . .

XXXII—MORE DEMOLITIONS

The D.D.A. demolished 1790 unauthorised semi-pucca structures on land falling under villages Sarai eepalthala, Bhulswa and Jahangirpur on different dates in May, June and November, 1976 and February, 1977. The area where the demolition was undertaken had already been declared as 'development area' under section 12 of the Delhi Development Act vide notification No. 42 (7)/66-LIB dated April 6, 1967.

The D.D.A. has contended that no prior notice to the occupants of unauthorised structures before actual demolition was necessary as the occupants/owners had voluntarily vacated the site and accepted the alternative accommodation offered to them. This does not appear to be correct in view of the writ filed by the residents in the Delhi High Court, receipt of a large number of complaints from the residents, and deployment of heavy police force at the time of demolition.

The unauthorised colonies in Sarai Peepalthala extension and Mahindra Park had come up during the period from September 1, 1962 to February 1, 1967 and are shown at SI. No. 41 and 97 of annexure IV of the report of the Committee set up by the Government of India vide notification No. J. 13037 (113)/74-UDI dated August 26, 1974. Regularisation of such colonies was being contemplated by the Government subject to fulfilment of certain conditions. In this context, demolition of these colonies by the DDA appear to be against the declared policy of the Government.

The DDA had taken over possession of these lands even without acquisition and built a resettlement colony on them.

The DDA had no legal right to take possession of the lands and build upon them.

Jhandewalan

The DDA had shifted about 108 cycle dealers from Esplanade Road to Jhandewalan cycle market on August 25, 1975.

In 1973, the affected cycle dealers of Esplanade Road had approached the Delhi High Court for a writ against their proposed shifting by the DDA on the plea that the action was discriminatory in nature, in as much as some other cycle dealers having their trade in the neighbouring Lajpat Rai Market were not being shifted.

The Delhi High Court in its judgement of May 31, 1974 accepted the case of the petitioners but allowed time to the DDA to issue notices to other cycle dealers also. The DDA informed the Court that such notices had been issued. The writ petitions were, therefore, dismissed. Dissatisfied with the judgement, the petitioners went to the Supreme Court, where again the DDA gave a commitment that all the 250 and odd cycle dealers carrying on their business at Esplanade Road and Lajpat Rai Market would be treated at par and would not be discriminated against. The appeal was, therefore, dismissed.

The DDA have pleaded that the affected cycle dealers had vacated their shops at Esplanade Road and handed over their possession of the shops to the DDA voluntarily. It has, however, been found that Jagmohan, Vice-Chairman, DDA, had recorded a note on August 14, 1975 in file No. F. 4(26)/76-IMP (Vol. 10) that the cycle dealers of Esplanade Road were called by him on the same day and that it was made clear to them that they should shift by August 18, 1975. The representatives of the cycle dealers had asked for time to consult the other members of their association and had also asked for some other reliefs. Jagmohan, however, wrote on the file that the DDA would deal with the cycle dealers firmly.

On August 23, 1975 Jagmohan sent the following note to the Superintending Engineer Jindal and Executive Engineer S. K. Lal of DDA :

The cycle dealers from Esplanade Road are being

shifted to the New Jhandewalan Cycle Market w.e.f. 25th morning. The Executive Engineer and other officers concerned should remain at the site and give possession of the shops in the New Cycle Market to the cycle dealers who would come to them after obtaining allotment order from the DC (Implementation), DDA.

On the same day, Jagmohan also wrote d. o. letters No. PA/VC/75-390 dated August 23, 1975 to the General Manager, Delhi Telephones, and No. PA/VC/ 75-391 dated August 23, 1975 to the General Manager, DESU, requesting them to withdraw telephone and electricity connections to the cycle dealers from Monday onwards.

It has also come to notice that on the day the cycle dealers were shifted, the DDA officials were accompanied by considerable police force comprising 1 DSP, 2 Inspectors, 8 Sub-Inspectors, 14 Head Constables and 44 constables. If the shifting was voluntary as contended by the DDA, no such heavy deployment of police was necessary.

The DDA had no jurisdiction as the area had not been declared as 'development area' under Sec. 12 of the Delhi Development Act.

The undertaking given by the DDA in the Delhi High court and later in the Supreme Court that all cycle dealers whether on Esplanade Road or Lajpat Rai Market would be treated at par, does not appear to have been given after proper examination of all aspects of the matter. The Cycle dealers of the Lajpat Rai Market were tenants of the directorate of Estates and, therefore, the DDA could not have shifted them. It was a commercial area as per Zonal Master Plan and cycle trade is covered under the category of commercial business, which is permissible in such areas.

XXXIII—ARYA SAMAJ TEMPLE, GREEN PARK

On September 25, 1975 a demolition squad of the D.D.A. accompanied by a large police contingent, demolished an Arya Samaj temple in Block No. W, Green Park, New Delhi which was constructed and owned by the Arya Samaj, Green Park, a registered society. The building was a pucca R.C.C. structure, comprising a hall, fitted with 10 ceiling fans, a built-in marble *yagyashala*, rooms for a charitable dispensary, reading room, rooms for residence, toilets etc. According to the society, the construction of the building was completed in 1974 and throughout the period of its construction no objection was raised by any authority. The corporation had on the other hand, sanctioned electricity and water connections for the building.

According to the D.D.A. records, the demolished Arya Samaj temple in Green Park was unauthorised construction detected by the Authority's field staff on February 18, 1975. The area in which the building was situated had already been declared as 'development area' under Section 12 (1) of the Delhi Development Act, vide notification No. F. 2-192/5LSG dated November 29, 1958. The D.D.A. had issued a notice in respect of the building u/s 30 (1) of the Delhi Development Act on February 24, 1975 addressed to the builders/owners/residents of eastern side of Arjun Nagar, New Delhi, to show cause why an order of demolition should not be passed in respect of this unauthorised construction. The process server who took the notice reported that he had found the construction work in progress but no one at the site was prepared to receive the notice. Another attempt was made to serve notice on Feburary 26, 1975 with the same result.

S. M. Dua, Executive Officer (Development Area) DDA,

then ordered the service of notice by affixation which was done on March 3, 1975 in the presence of a Section Officer of the D.D.A. The date by which the addressees were to make their representation against the proposed demolition action was fixed as March 14, 1975. Since no one appeared by that date, nor was any representation received, it was decided to proceed ex-parte.

However, the case was not decided on that day but was adjourned to March 21, 1975. On that day, statements of V. N. Verma, Section Officer, and Chandra Bhan, Process Server, were recorded and an order u/s 30 of the DD Act 1957 was made. This order was again addressed in the same manner as in the notice issued earlier and builders/owners were required to demolish the building within 5 days, failing which the DDA would demolish it at the cost and expense of the owner.

This order also remained unserved as the process server reported on April 2, 1975 that he had gone to the site, but the service of notice was refused. Another attempt was made on April 4, 1975 but the service was again refused. The service of the order was thereupon made by affixation which was done on April 8, 1975. The building was eventually demolished on September 25, 1975.

Although a period of six months had lapsed between the alleged detection of an unauthorised construction in the 'development area' and its demolition, no attempt seems to have been made to ascertain as to who the owner was or at whose instance the construction was being undertaken. The building bore an insignia on its facade that it was an Arya Samaj temple but the DDA officers concerned did not send their notices to the Arya Samaj Society through its office bearers as prescribed under Section 43(c) of the D.D. Act 1957. It was mandatory under this section to send the notices either by registered post or have them delivered at the Society's Office.

The proceedings conducted by the DDA officers with regard the demolition of the building also appear to be defective because no independent witness was examined to establish that the service of notices was refused, or that it was made by affixation. The notice addressed to 'builder/owners/residents of eastern side of Arjun Nagar' was also defective as it did not clearly describe the construction or the plot on which the construction was being made.

The standing instructions of the Lt. Governor (L. G.) Delhi that no religious place should be demolished without his prior specific approval and that while proposing demolition of such premises, the district magistrate should invariably be consulted do not seem to have been complied with in this case. These instructions were reiterated by the LG's Secretariat in their letter No. F. 75(373)/73-LGS/9420-27 dated August 31, 1973. Krishan Chand, L G has admitted that no orders were taken from him before undertaking this demolition. He also added that he was annoyed by this demolition and had ticked off Jagmohan for his indiscretion. Subsequently, an alternative site measuring about 1200 sq. yds. including a part of the land earlier occupied by the demolished building, was allotted to the Arya Samaj Society at a concessional rate of Rs. 5,000 per acre. The DDA also sanctioned the building plan of the proposed temple.

XXXIV—THE WALLED CITY, JAMA MASJID
AND TURKMAN GATE

Siraj Piracha, a Social Worker of that area, has stated:

Shri Sanjay Gandhi and Smt. Indira Gandhi were confirmed in their views that so long as the majority of of a particular community in the Jama Masjid area was not finished, the area would continue to cause headache to them.

Subhadra Joshi has also referred to a conversation she had with B.R. Tamta, Commissioner, Municipal Corporation of Delhi, which goes to show that the demolitions in the walled city had been undertaken on considerations other than merit. According to her, Tamta once mentioned to her "of feeling among the people that while shifting was being done in other areas, Jama Masjid area had been spared because it was inhabited by Muslims. I told him that there need be no question of Hindus or Muslims in these programmes, provided the people affected were given appropriate places before being shifted".

The Jama Masjid clearance operations in November, 1975, have been vividly described by A.K. Paitandy, Sub-Divisional Magistrate of that area, in the following words:

On November 22-23, 1975 about 300 shops around Jama Masjid were cleared by the Municipal Corporation with the help of the demolition squad of the DDA. The DDA officials had come to the spot to help the MCD to carry out this operation. In this operation we were not taken into confidence in advance and the notice was more or less sudden. We were told a day prior to the operation to reach Darya Ganj at 9.00 A.M. We were told that some clearance operation

will be undertaken in Jama Masjid area and that detailed briefing would be given in the S.P.'s office.

About 4 Zonal Assistant Commissioners including
Beant Singh and Ram Singh and a number of DDA's
officials, including P. Chakravarti and Satya Prakash
along with a number of trucks and demolition staff of
the Corporation and the DDA came to the S.P.'s
office. The meeting of officers was addressed by ADM
Central and S.P. Central. The police and the Magistracy
were told that their involvement in the matter was
limited only to maintenance of law and order. The
clearance operations were to be carried out by the
MCD with the help of the DDA. The meeting was
held at about 9.30 A.M. and we reached the spot at
about 10.00 A.M. I was not given any time to make any
assessment of the situation. The Police and the Magistracy did not get any time to talk to the local leaders
and take them into confidence about the operations.
The shops belonging to Cotton Market Association
and Commercial Market Association were pucca structures. Their number would be not less than 40 to 50.
The rest of the shops were wooden shacks and similar
other improvised structures. All these shop-keepers
were conducting business in eatables, motor-parts,
cotton cloth, radio and watch parts, etc. Many of the
shops were there for the last 30-40 years. While some
shop-keepers did seem to have some premonition of
clearance operation, the others were taken completely by
surprise. The Corporation authorities had given to the
shopkeepers about 45 minutes to 1 hour's time to clear
their stuff and vacate the shops. The police had arranged a heavy contingent of force and they were asked
to close the various exit routes in order to guard
against problems being created by the elements
outside.

A few of the shop-keepers agreed to vacate the shops
within the given time but most others were agitated
on this issue. Some shop-keepers had constructed
their pucca shops after the fire in the area in February,
1975 and they vehemently protested against the
demolition of their new structures. The members of

the Commercial Market Association were also in the same mood and staged a demonstration against the authorities. We had brought shopkeepers and officials together for talks but it did not produce any result. While this was going on some people started pelting of stones. We intervened and resorted to the use of tear-gas to disperse the miscreants. We had permitted the shop-keepers to bring their labour, members of their families and their transport to take away their goods and the Corporation officials had also offered help by providing their own labour for the purpose. As long as we were present during this clearance operation, we did not observe any loss of life or serious loss of property.

However, some people did complain later that they did not have sufficient time and resources to remove their goods. There was also a general complaint that alternative sites offered to the evictees were unsuitable mainly because of the long distance etc., but we advised them to negotiate this aspect with the DDA officials. We had asked the DDA officials to be as helpful to the evictees as possible. I had that feeling that but for the heavy development of police force and the suddenness of the operation, it would not have been an easy task to clear the area.

The Imam of Jama Masjid was hostile to this operation and some of the miscreants had thrown stones on the officials from the Jama Masjid. This incident could also get sorted primarily because of the heavy deployment of the police. We had arrested some people during this operation under DIR. Some of the arrests were not justified and this view was shared by the local SHO and SDPO. The case under DIR was subsequently withdrawn. The Corporation and the DDA had told us that these operations were being undertaken under proper authority of law and that a decision in this behalf had been taken at a very high level.

Whenever I asked my counterpart in the MCD and the DDA about the level of decision, they invariably told me that it was known to their respective Chiefs viz., the Commissioner, Municipal Corporation and the Vice-Chairman of the DDA and that they were not aware of full facts. The V.C. DDA had visited the site during this operation. The D.C. and the DIG (R) were also present. I think Shri Tamta had also come.

It may be mentioned that when the shops were being razed, a DDA bulldozer had damaged a part of the foundation of the mosque and and a water course. This had invited protest from the Imam. The Director General of Archaeology had to be consulted for rectifying the damage to the mosque.

The demolition operations in the Turkman Gate area were taken up by the DDA on April 13, 1976. It seems that 120 pucca houses and some semi-pucca/katcha structures were demolished between April 13 to 27, 1976. The residential structures of 764 families and commercial and industrial establishments of 199 were demolished. The demolition was done by manual labour and bulldozers. From the 13th to the 18th only one bulldozer was used for demolition. From 19th i.e. immediately after the firing upto the 27th April, the number of bulldozers/motor-graders used varied from 5 to 8. There was heavy deployment of police of the demolition Squad of the DDA, supplemented by the force of the District Police, Delhi Armed Police and CRPF.

According to Zahiruddin, resident of 3339, Turkman Gate, the house belonging to Zahira to whom he was paying a monthly rent of Rs. 15/- was demolished. Zahira had paid house tax of this house upto 1974. He had old records with him to establish his claim. According to Bashir Ahmed, the house No. 3299, Turkman Gate, since demolished on April 19, 1976, was owned by him and three other partners. The house had an area of 1470 sq. yards. It had beeen bought by them from Begum Shafikulnasha on May 21, 1973 through a registered sale deed which was available with him. They were paying Rs 300/- towards the House Tax to the MCD for this property. Except for a small portion, the entire house had been given on rent to the Standard Screw Factory, who were paying a monthly rent of Rs. 275/- to him.

The Manager of the Standard Screw Factory had informed him that the house had been bulldozed by the DDA and that goods worth Rs. 1 lakh had been buried under the debris. He had rushed to the spot with the Manager and told the DDA officers that it was a private property and should not be demolished. When they asked for evidence to this effect, he had shown them the papers. They had not paid any heed and had demolished the house. He had preferred a claim with the DDA about this property.

According to Anaro, House No. 3387 in Turkman Gate was owned by her. There were nine tenants in this house who were paying her Rs. 275/- P.M. as rent. This house was demolished. Ramzan Ahmed has stated that his nephew Nasir Ahmed was the owner of the house Nos. 3327 to 3332 in Turkman Gate, and that he had power of attorney to collect the rent from the tenants of this house. The building had an area of 503 sq. ft. and it was a three-storeyed constru-ction. The rental income from the building was Rs. 90/- per month and the annual house tax, which he was paying, was Rs. 162/-. He has not been given any tenement or plot in lieu of this building.

The matter was checked up with the House Tax records of the Municipal Corporation and it has been confirmed that the DDA was not the owner of any of the 29 properties and their actual owners were paying House Tax from year to year. The DDA have since received claims for compensation for some of the private properties demolished and a decision to pay compensation has been taken.

The file No. 402/NT(L) on which Jagmohan has claimed to have taken a decision regarding the demolition in the Turkman Gate area has some suspicious features. The file contains no despatch numbers although Kashmiri Lal had sent it on March 20, 1976 to A.C. (HQrs) and D.C. (slums), and D.C. (slums) forwarded it to the Vice Chairman on March 28, 1976. It also contains a note recorded by H.K. Lal on April, 19-20, 1976 regarding resettlement operation which had begun "with the consent of the people on the 13th instant and allotments were made and accepted by the parties on the above basis." Accor-ding to the file this note was seen by Jagmohan on April 20, 1976 who recorded a note, "This has been discussed with the Lt.

Governor at length. The police has already apprised him of
the position. Ministry of Works & Housing may be informed.
Issue letter dictated." Surprisingly, the letter issued to the
Ministry of Works & Housing does not contain any reference
to the voluntary nature of the operation, thus omitting a vital
fact.

The file was sent to the Forensic Science Laboratory for
examination. It has been found that the typed matter of the
note dated March 28, 1976 of H.K. Lal did not tally with the
typed matter from the typewriters available in the office of the
Slum wing of the DDA. On the other hand, it agreed with the
matter typed on the typewriter of the offices of the Vice-
Chairman, DDA. It may be mentioned that the offices of the
DDA and the Slum Wing are situated at a distance of about
3/4 miles. It was also observed that the endorsement of
Jagmohan on the note of H.K. Lal dated April 19/20, 1976
suffered from over-writing. The figure '76' in the date under-
neath Jagmohan's signature was written over the figure '77'
by writting the figure '6' over the original '7' in the unit place.
The subsequent figure '6' was written with ink of bule shade
whereas the original figure of '7' was written with ink of a
dark shade. Normally a person does not give the date of next
year and, therefore, there is a reasonable suspicion that the
endorsement of Jagmohan was written sometime in 1977 but
later made to show as if it was written on April 20, 1976.

Enquiries in the Slum Wing of the DDA have also shown
that no file bearing No. 402/NT (L) was opened in the year
1976 as is claimed in this file.

XXXV—TURKMAN GATE CONTINUED

The tension generated by the demolition in the area was compounded by the dissatisfaction in respect of forced sterlization being carried out in the nearby Jama Masjid area. A sterlization camp had been set up near Jama Masjid on April 15, 1976 under the overall supervision of Ruksana Sultana, a social worker deriving her strength from Sanjay Gandhi and enjoying the patronage of the High-ups in the Delhi Administration.

Early in the morning of April 19, 1976 it was found that a large crowd of mostly women had surrounded the family planning camp near Jama Masjid and they were raising anti-family planning and anti-establishment slogans. At the intervention of the district authorities the activities in the camp were suspended and an ugly situation which had the potential of developing into a serious law and order problem involving the Imam of Jama Masjid was averted.

In the meanwhile, near the site of demolition in the Turkman Gate area a large crowd consisting of men, women and children with some people wearing arm bands, were staging a 'Dharna'. The D.D.A. officials on the spot suspended further demolition operations. It seems that the assembled crowd wanted a firm assurance that no further demolition in the area would be carried out. The D.D.A. and district officers on the spot, however, found themselves in no position to give any firm commitment about the withdrawal of the demolition operations. In the meanwhile the crowd continued to swell.

The situation seems to have deteriorated around 1 P.M. The SDM warned the crowd to disperse or else arrests would be effected. Stone throwing appears to have been started. Efforts were made by the police to disperse the crowd by use of tear gas and cane charge. Although the crowd dispersed from the ground many persons climbed the top of the buildings and continued stone pelting from a vantage position. A ding-dong battle between the police and the crowd ensued and there was brick-batting by the crowd and tear gassing by the police. Around 2 P.M. it appears that some rounds were fired by a pistol near police post Turkman Gate. Senior officers including the Deputy Commissioner and the DIG (Range) arrived on the spot around 2.30 P.M. Heavy re-enforcements of the CRPF and DAP also arrived.

Thereafter firing was resorted to by the police at least in four sectors—behind the Godrej building, in the built up area at a little distance from the Asaf Ali Road, deep inside the built up area, and in the areas around police post Turkman Gate. According to the police version 14 rounds were fired and 6 persons died as a result of the police firing. One other person sustained a bullet injury. According to the district authorities curfew was imposed prior to the firing. Earlier there was an incident at the Fazli-ilahi Mosque in the area where three members of the police were alleged to have been attacked by a crowd, seriously injuring two of them.

A large number of persons and some members of the police and the district officers were reported to have been injured. Large scale arrests were made. Several complaints of beating of people, looting of houses and molestation of women had also been made. The situation continued to be tense for several days and the curfew was in force in the area upto May 13, 1976. An attempt was made to give a communal colour to the incident and no enquiry even of an administrative nature, was made into the incident.

The version of the police firings that has been recorded in the various records is grossly inadequate. The First Information Report (FIR) of the incident and the entries in the daily diaries of PS Jama Masjid and PP Turkman Gate do not give details of the incidents. For example, they do not give any information regarding the number of occasions on which firing was resorted to, the number of rounds fired, the number of persons killed/injured, the description of the places where the firings took place and the number of persons arrested etc.

K. C. Pandeya, Joint Secretary in the Ministry of Home Affairs, had recorded a note at about 5.30 P.M. on April 19 about these incidents. This note was based on the telephonic information obtained by him from the Chief Secretary, IGP and G. S. Mandar, DIG. In this note, he recorded that "firing had to be resorted to twice in which 2 persons have been killed." Later at 9.30 P.M. a meeting was convened by the Union Home Secretary which has attended, among others, by the IGP and D.C. Delhi.

At this meeting, the D.C. had stated that "In order to control the situation, curfew was also imposed at about 4 P.M. and firing was resorted to control the situation, resulting in the death of 2 persons on the spot and some further deaths later on". Neither the number of occasions on which the firing was resorted to and the rounds fired, nor a firm figure of casualties was mentioned.

Ashok Pradhan, ADM and R. K. Ohri SP had drafted for the Central Government a report on the incidents at about midnight, April 19/20. In this report also a very vague reference had been made to the number of rounds fired. It had been stated that 'few rounds were ordered to be fired, which led to the retreat of the rioters'. No details regarding the number of occasions on which firing was resorted to or the places where it took place had been given. The names of the police officers and magistrates who had authorised the firing had also not been mentioned in any of these reports, although R. K. Ohri has stated that he had come to know of the firings ordered by P. S. Bhinder, A. K. Singh and R. K. Sharma on the evening of April 19. According to J. K. Saksena, SDPO, on the evening of April 19, he had come to know from R. K. Ohri that 14 rounds had been fired.

In the reports sent to their senior officers, the CRPF officers who were on duty in the Turkman Gate area on April 19, have stated that the CRPF had fired 12 rounds. In their report to the Ministry of Home Affairs on April 26, 1976 the Delhi Police had reported that 8 rounds were fired by the DAP and 6 rounds by the CRPF. This information given to the Ministry of Home Affairs was used by the Ministry in preparing a statement that was given by the Deputy Home Minister about these incidents on April 27, in Parliament. The Delhi Police have now taken the position that 12 rounds had been fired by the CRPF and 2 by the DAP.

The CRPF had initially reported that 6 rounds had been fired by them under the orders of P. S. Bhinder and 6 under those of R. K. Sharma. Later in May 1976 they reported that they had fired 3 rounds under the orders of Bhinder, 2 under the orders of K. D. Nayyar, SP (New Delhi), one under the orders of Ashok Pradhan, ADM and six under the orders of R.K. Sharma, SDPO. Ultimately, according to the records available, it is found that the firings ascribed to Bhinder and Nayar were authorised by N. C. Ray, SDM. N. C. Ray has alleged that he was pressurised to give this authorisation. This was received by the CRPF only on June 12, 1976.

It seems that the position regarding the number of occasions on which the firings were resorted to, the number of rounds fired, and the weapons used for firing was different from what has been given out officially.

R.K. Ohri has confirmed that some rounds had been fired from a revolver by R.K. Sharma at about 2 P.M. near PP Turkman gate. This firing did not find mention in any of the reports given by the Delhi Police earlier. This firing finds confirmation in the entries in some of the wireless log books of Delhi Police. P.S. Bhinder, G.S. Mander and A.K. Singh have also confirmed that the message relating to this firing had come to their notice on April 19. It seems an effort had been made to tamper with the wireless log books with a view to hiding this firing incident. Some of the wireless log books were sent to the Central Forensic Science Laboratory for examination and it has been confirmed by them that there was tampering of entries relating to this incident in these books. The word 'revolver' was sought to be substituted by words 'tear-gas'.

According to S.K. Kain, AIG, Delhi Police he had seen A.K. Singh and R.K. Sharma firing from their pistols near Turkman Gate on the 19th afternoon. All the CRPF officers and men examined have alleged in their written as well as oral statements that the Delhi Police had also fired at or near about

places where they (the CRPF) had fired. Naik Ram Bhawan
Sharma and Constables Baikunt Pande and Nagendra Kumar
have stated that they had seen a Sikh Inspector/Sub-Inspector
of Delhi firing from his revolver.

The CRPF men have stated that they did not see any injuries sustained by any person as a result of their firings. A.K.
Singh, is the only officer who has admitted that at least one
person had died as a result of the 2 rounds that had been fired
under his orders by Attar Singh, a DAP Constable. A.K.
Singh himself had earlier written off the two rounds from the
Government property register as having been fired in the air.

Constable Attar Singh has asserted that he had fired in the
air and there were no casualties as a result of his firing. Thus
neither the fatal casualties nor the bullet injuries inflicted have
been explained. The officers of the DAP while despatching
police contingents to the riot affected area on the April 19,
did not make any mention in the daily diary, of the arms and
ammunition issued to the force. There was also no mention
of the arms and ammunition returned to the Armoury/Maga-
zine after the contingents had returned from this duty.
According to B.K. Mishra, Commandant, DAP, this was a
serious omission.

It is interesting that two blank firing orders, one signed by
R.K. Sharma, SDPO and the other by R.K. Ohri, SP on
April 19, 1976 have been made available by the Commandant,
21 CRPF. These were given to Sub-Inspector, B.D. Joshi
of 21 Bn and Ram Chander Dy. S.P. of 22 Bn. CRPF, respectively on April 19, 1976. These show that there was complete
lack of leadership and direction on the part of the senior
police officers and magistrates on the spot.

The version of the police firings as given by the public witnesses is substantially different from the official version. According to Siraj Piracha, Zahiruddin, Jamaluddin, Abdul
Hakim, Mohd. Idris, H. H. M. Yunus and Abdul Matini, the
police firing had started sometime between 2 and 2.30 P..M.
and had continued till about 5.00 P.M. According to
Zahiruddin, Jamaluddin and H. H. M. Yunus the firing had
been done by the police from the roof tops and that people
standing on the roofs were killed, has been alleged by Mohd.
Rafi, Akhlaq Khan, Mohd. Idris and Jamaluddin. According

to Mohd. Rafi, the firing party which had shot Mohd. Shahid from a roof was led by an officer of the Delhi Police. The fact that two dead bodies were found on the roof of a house has been confirmed by Constable, Ravibhan Singh of PP Turkman Gate.

The death of Zahuruddin due to firing and the bullet injury to Abdul Razak have not been reported at all by the District authorities. That the deceased Mohd. Shahid and Zahuruddin were not indulging in any violent activity at the time they were shot at, has been categorically mentioned by the witnesses. In fact, in the case of Mohd. Shahid, the postmortem report as analysed by Dr. Bishnu Kumar, Professor of Forensic Science, Maulana Azad Medical College, clearly shows that he was shot in his back.

The authorities seem to have decided to take the casualties to the police stations instead of sending them to the mortuary/ hospital direct from the scene. Some dead bodies remained lying at the police stations for almost the whole night before being shifted to the mortuary for autopsy. Similarly, the injured persons had also to wait in the police stations before being provided with medical aid. Dr. Bishnu Kumar, Head of the Department of Forensic Medicine, Maulana Azad Medical College, stated that during his long experience, he had never come across instances of such gross delays in the conveyance of dead bodies to the mortuary. This has led to considerable suspicion in the public mind.

As per decision of the Lt. Governor, the news of the incident was censored and the press could not report it immediately. A press note was later issued on April 21, giving the official version of the incidents.

A statement was issued by Mir Mushtaq Ahmad, Chairman, Metropolitan Council, about these incidents in which he blamed communal elements like the Muslim League and the JEI for violence in this area. The draft of this statement is available on a file of the Lt. Governor's Secretariat. This draft was corrected by Navin Chawla, Secretary to the Lt. Governor, who added the words 'Muslim League and the JEI' in it in his own handwriting. Navin Chawla has admitted having done this. Apparently, a communal colour was sought to be given to this incident.

The police action on April 19, had admittedly led to 6 fatal casualties and widespread harassment. No inquiry, administrative, magisterial or judicial was, however, ordered into these incidents. Krishan Chand, Lt. Governor does not remember to have ever suggested holding of a magisterial or judicial inquiry. There is nothing on the records made available by the Ministry of Home Affairs, to suggest that any kind of inquiry was ever contemplated into these incidents.

Om Mehta, Minister in the Ministry of Home Affairs has stated that he was abroad when the incident took place. He had convened a meeting of the concerned Ministers and officials on May 8, 1976 to discuss the need, for coordination in the implementation of demolition programmes etc., in Delhi. Although he claimed that he was shocked at the incidents he does not appear to have suggested holding of any inquiry into the incidents of firing. According to him "I had come to Delhi after about 2 weeks of the Turkman Gate incidents. It was for the Ministers already present at the time of the incident to consider whether it called for a detailed inquiry."

The police registered a case vide FIR No. 189 dated April 19, 1976 under Sections 147/148/149/353/332/186/188/307/430 IPC and 69 DIR at PS Jama Masjid in connection with the incidents in the Turkman Gate area on that day. The First Information Report (FIR) was recorded by Inspector Garib Ram of PS Patel Nagar and the case was investigated by ASI Govind Ram Bhatia of PP Turkman Gate. According to Inspector Garib Ram, R. Tiwari and Avinash Chander SDPOs had asked him to write the FIR, although his personal view was that it should have been written by an officer concerned with PS Jama Masjid. He admitted that before writing the FIR, he had made no efforts to ascertain the details of firings by the police. He also disclosed that the investigating officer had not recorded his statement although this was one of the first things to be done during the investigation.

ASI Govind Ram Bhatia, the Investigating Officer, feels that this case should not have been entrusted to him for investigation as he was himself an eye witness. He claimed, that he had written the case diaries as per directions of his superio officers. He neither examined the DDA officers who were on

the spot, nor the accused persons. J. K. Saksena, SDPO and
R. K. Ohri, SP (Central), agreed that the case had not been
properly investigated and that it should have been entrusted
to a more senior officer for a thorough investigation.

Ohri has said that he had made a suggestion to P. S. Bhinder DIG (R) to that effect but the latter felt that the case was
unlikely to be put in the court and, therefore, it should remain under investigation with the local police for some time
to act as 'levers of pressure on the accused people'. Bhinder has denied having said so. The case has not so far been
charge-sheeted in the court.

The entire area falling under the jurisdiction of PS Jama
Masjid (which included the riot affected Turkman Gate area)
was under curfew from April 19 to May 13, 1976. The authorities did not relax curfew on April 23 and 30 (Fridays) and
insisted that the people wishing to offer their Friday prayers in
the mosques, obtain curfew passes. Very few people took the
passes. R. K. Ohri, SP has stated that the situation had come
under control on April 19, itself and the police were in favour
of withdrawal of curfew after a few days.

However, the curfew was continued, perhaps to facilitate
the demolition operations and also to 'penalise the residents'
for their resistance on April 19. He had understood that
the decision regarding continuance of curfew was being taken
by the Lt. Governor or at an even higher level. Continuance of
demolition operation during the period of curfew and denial
of opportunity to the local residents to freely offer their
prayers in the Jama Masjid led to considerable resentment and
misgivings among the people about the attitude of the
authorities.

In addition to the 6 deaths due to police firing admitted by
the authorities, evidence indicating some more deaths has
also been received.

Nasiruddin r/o Phatak Ramkishan has alleged that his son
Zahuruddin aged about 13 years, had been shot while in the
house of his sister in Phatak Telian area. He was informed
that the deceased was standing on the first floor of the house
at about 3.30 P.M. when he was hit by a bullet in his chest. He
had died within 10/11 minutes of being shot. His son-in-law,

Jamaluddin, and some others had brought the dead body to his house and it was buried in the Delhi Gate graveyard the next day.   He produced the certificate in respect of the burial of the 'deceased, according to which also Zahuruddin was buried on April 20, 1976. Jamaluddin, brother-in-law of the deceased stated that the deceased was standing on a 3 ft. high parapet wall of his house on the first floor looking at the happenings outside when he was suddenly shot. He had avoided the police while carrying the dead body to the house of the deceased's father, Nasiruddin.   He had asked the family members not to weep aloud lest the police should come to know of the death and arrest them.   No immediate information of the death was given to the police or the magistracy.

There is an entry in the Daily Diary dated April 20, 1976 of PS Jama Masjid (Report No. 4-B recorded at 02.40 hours) regarding an information received from Const.   No. 3473 Sahib Singh at Irwin Hospital that Alauddin, s/o Imamuddin r/o 111, Moh. Rakab Ganj, Jama Masjid, who was injured during the course of disturbances in the Turkman Gate area on April 19, had succumbed to his injuries.   Another entry has been made at 8.55 P.M. (Report No. 47-B) the same day by Sub.Inspector Rishi Prakhash, in which he stated that he had made enquiries into the death in the Irwin Hospital of Salaudin, s/o Mohd. Yamin, r/o 1942 Kucha Chelan as had come to notice vide Report No. 4-B ibid.   The name, parentage, as well as the address of the deceased in the two reports are totally different. Absence of any reference to the death of Alauddin in the subsequent reports in the Daily Diary raises suspicions.

Bundo Devi has alleged that her grandfather (baba) Chandu Lal and her two minor daughters had been buried alive in their jhuggi, when a neighbouring pucca house was demolished in the Turkman Gata area on April 19, 1976. Shambhu, a Municipal Corporation employee has confirmed the alleged death of Chandu Lal in this manner. Bishan Chand, an employee of the G.B. Pant Hospital stated that he had attended the funeral of Chandu Lal. There is considerable difference among the witnesses about the date on which the funeral had taken place.   According to the death certificate issued on October 1, 1977 the date of death has been given as April 23, 1976 and was reported to the Municipal authorities on May 18, 1976. No one has come forward to confirm the alleged deaths of the minor girls.

Anaro of Phatak Telian alleged that her granddaughter had been bured alive under the debris of her house which was bulldozed on the evening of April 11. The girl was aged about 11 months. She was taken out alive but succumbed to her injuries the next day. No corroboration of this allegation has been available.

Mohd. Deen, originally r/o 3354 Phatak Telian has alleged that his wife, Jannat Begum had suffered miscarriage on April 14, and her condition had deteriorated on April 18. He was taking her to the hospital on April 19, but had to stay at Fazli-Ilahi mosque on account of disturbances in the area. Later, the police fired tear gas shells in the mosque as a result of which his wife felt suffocated and her condition worsened. His two sons were arrested and he himself got separated from his wife. Jannat Begum was put in a truck and left in Trilok-puri. He had joined her in Trilokpuri on the next day. Her condition continued to deteriorate and she ultimately died on April 26 or 27. She was buried in Trilokpuri.

Ibrahim, originally r/o 3354 Phatak Telian, confirmed the allegation of Mohd. Deen and testified that he had helped in carrying Jannat Begum from Mohammad Deen's house to the hospital but, she had to be kept at Fazli-Ilahi mosque on account of disturbances, arrests. etc. He agreed that the condition of Jannat Begum had deteriorated on account tear-gas.

Shahodan w/o Latif Ahmed, and Abdul Majid, Latif Ahmed's brother, have stated that Latif Ahmed who was arres-ted on the night between April 20/21, 1976, while sleep-ing outside his house, had died while in custody. They alleged that at the time Latif Ahmed was in police custody there were indications that he had been tortured. They were not allowed to meet him. The death certificate of Latif produced by Shahodan, however, indicated that Latif Ahmed had died of cholera on May 2, 1976 while in jail.

According to H.H.M. Yunus, one Mohd. Asghar, r/o Phatak Telian was so shocked by the demolition of his house and alleged beating and arrest of his family members, that he died on April 20, 1976.

According to the Delhi Police, 146 persons including 58 police personnel and 2 magistrates, had sustained injuries during the riots. Only one person namely Iftikhar Hussain had sustained a bullet injury. One Sub-Inspector and 2 Constables sustained stab injuries.

According to the reports received from the Medical Department 21 injured persons, came to the Willingdon Hospital all of whom (except Mohd. Arif who died) were discharged on April 20, 1976 after treatment. The police surgeon (Police Hospital, Rajpur Road) received 57 cases on April 19 and 20. In 11 cases X-ray examination was advised. In the Irwin hospital, 54 cases were received, out of which 17 were admitted as indoor patients, two (Salauddin and Om Prakash) were brought dead, and one (Abdul Malik) expired on April 24, 1976.

Among the members of the public admitted as indoor patients, Abdul Hamid had fractures on both left fore-arm bones. Both the bones of the right leg of Jahiruddin were fractured and Mohd. Yakub was found to have sustained cerebral concussion and fracture of the 6th rib. One Ahmed Sayeed was also admitted with fractured trapesium. In Hindu Rao Hospital, 19 injured persons were received, all of whom had simple injuries. This brings the total of the injured to 146 (excluding 4 dead).

Names of 36 persons including those of 22 police officials and one Magistrate, figuring in the list furnished by the police do not figure in the lists of injured furnished by the medical authorities. The lists given by medical authorities, however, include names of 35 persons who do not figure on the list of those injured on the police records.

These serious discrepancies between the medical and the police records in respect of the injured persons would seem to indicate that more persons were injured than shown by the police in their records. It is also well known that even seriously injured people avoid going to a hospital due to fear of getting involved in a criminal case of riot. The number of injured police officers and Magistrates appears exaggerated.

Some complaints of alleged beating etc. by the police have been received. The more serious among these are :

Mohd. Yusuf, r/o 1772 Turkman Gate has alleged that a police party had come to his house at about 3.30-4 P.M. on April 19, and had taken him to a 'piao' (Kiosk) near Turkman Gate where he was severely beaten. His left forearm was fractured at two places and one finger joint of his right hand was displaced. He had lost consciousness as a result of beating and had fallen in a drain. Because of serious fractures his left arm had become practically invalid. He claimed that the police had not arrested him due to his serious injury.

Chhanga r/o 2213 Gali Dakotan, Turkman Gate, alleged that he was picked up from his house by the police at about 2.30 P.M. on April 19, and taken to PP Turkman Gate. He was severely beaten on the way and while trying to shield his head with his hand, he was given a severe blow as a result of which it was fractured. He was arrested. He did not tell even the jail officials about his injury because of fear.

Abdul Razak, originally resident of 3380 Turkman Gate, alleged that at about 4.30 P.M. when he came out of his house, he suddenly felt that he had been hit by some object and he had started bleeding. He became unconscious and fell down. On regaining consciousness, he found himself in the Anjuman mosque, Pahari Bhojla. Somebody had bandaged his abdomen and arm. He did not report his injury to any Government doctor/hospital due to fear. Marks apparently of bullet injury were still present on the body of Abdul Razak.

Dr. Bishnu Kumar, Head of the Department of Forensic Science, Maulana Azad Medical College, was consulted to ascertain whether it was possible for a person to survive a bullet injury in the abdomen. He opined that the injury on right side above the waist region could be caused by a bullet entering and exiting out after passing through the abdominal wall tissue only and not entering the abdominal cavity in its track. He said that if this happened, the injured would survive and would not need rigorous medical care. Dr. Bishnu Kumar added that injuries in the right arm could have been caused either by the same bullet or by grazing of another bullet.

Abdul Jabbar, r/o 2452 Gali Kue Wali Chitlikabar stated that at about 2.30-3 P.M. on April 19, 1976 a police party had come to his house and started beating him. He was dragged to Asaf Ali Road and arrested there. His two fingers had been fractured as a result of beating by the Police.

Allah Rakhi, r/o House No. 1796 Phatak Telian, Turkman Gate, stated that at about 4 P.M. on April 19, 1976, 6 to 7 police-men had broken into her house and started beating her family members. She had tried to come between the police party and her husband and son in order to save them but was given a blow by a rifle butt on her forehead, causing her a serious injury. Somebody had informed the Irwin Hospital from where an ambulance van had come and taken her there. She also alleged that the policemen had manhandled the women-folk in her house.

Mohd. Yusuf, Chhanga and Abdul Razak do not figure in the lists of injured persons, furnished by the medical and police authorities. Allaha Rakhi, however, figures in the list of injured furnished by the medical authorities.

Several complaints containing allegations of looting of property, dishonouring of women etc. against the police and others were received.

Mohd. Sultan r/o 2243, Gali Dakotan, Turkman Gate alleged that on the April 19, 1976 some CRPF personnel broke into the house (2171, Turkman Gate) of his daughter Nazima Begum and took away Rs. 1600/- in cash and jewel-lery worth about Rs. 15,000/-. The policemen had left their cane shields behind which he had handed over to the author-ities along with his complaint. Sultan also complained that the police took cognizance of his complaint only on April 22, 1976, and he got has had no relief so far.

Enquiries from the Delhi Police revealed that they had registered a case vide FIR No. 192 under section 380 IPC at PS Jama Masjid. The case was investigated by ASI Govind Ram Bhatia of PP Turkman Gate who had filed it as untraced on June 26, 1976. The Investigating Officer had observed that the husband and father-in-law of Nazima Begum, having been arrested in the case FIR No. 197 under section 147/148/ 149/156/158/332/353/186/188/307 IPC and 69 DIR (regarding

alleged dragging of policemen in Fazli Ilahi mosque) of PS
Kamla Market, her allegations against the police did not
inspire confidence. He does not, however, seem to have taken
into consideration the fact that the complainant had produced
cane shields which proved the visit of the policemen to her
house and their leaving them there in a hurry.

A.K. Paitandy, SDM, Punjabi Bagh, was also asked by
Ashok Pradhan, ADM to enquire into the complaint of Sultan.
Paitandy closed the enquiry on the plea that the police were
already investigating the criminal case registered in this
connection.

A complaint that some policemen had tried to misbehave
with some girls had come to the notice of Ashok Pradhan,
ADM, shortly after April 19. Under his orders, A.K.
Paitandy, SDM had conducted an enquiry on April 24 and
25, 1976. Constable Ravibhan Singh of PP Turkman Gate
had told the SDM that he had himself rescued 2 girls from
being molested by the CRPF personnel. Constable Ravibhan
Singh has confirmed this in his statement before the Committee and claimed that he had brought this incident to the
notice of ASI Govind Ram Bhatia. Bhatia agreed that the
Constable had told him about the incident but he did not take
any action on it as it lacked sufficient details.

Paitandy submitted his report to the ADM on the May 14,
1976, stating that some CRPF personnel did molest two girls.
His report was discussed with Sushil Kumar, DC, on
May 21, 1976. Curiously, the report remained pending without any action. It was not even brought to the notice of
the senior police authorities for follow-up action. On June
29, 1976, Pradhan made a note on the file that the matter be
kept pending.

R. K. Ohri, SP (Central) District has stated :

> On the evening of April 20, 1976, DIG (R) Shri Bhinder
> had sent me a wireless message conveying that he along
> with Sanjay Gandhi was reaching Turkman Gate and
> that I should receive them at the PP. Sanjay Gandhi
> was travelling in Bhinder's official car. I had received
> them as ordered. Bhinder had asked me to occupy
> the front seat, making his wireless operator to get down.

This had been done as Shri Bhinder was not quite familiar with the area and could not give to Sanjay Gandhi the details of the incidents that had taken place on the previous day.

I had taken them (Sanjay Gandhi and Bhinder) to the streets and the area where trouble had taken place and explained to them what had happened. Sanjay Gandhi had stayed in the area for hardly 10 minutes and then went back to his residence. Shortly after, I received another message from Shri Bhinder conveying that Sanjay Gandhi had decided to visit the Irwin Hospital to see the injured police personnel and that I should receive him there. Accordingly I went to the hospital, later IGP also arrived. Sanjay Gandhi was accompanied by the DIG (R).

He was received by the IGP, myself and some officials of the hospital and had gone to the ward where the policemen were being treated. He encouraged the injured policemen. Later DIG (R) had told the L. G. that Sanjay Gandhi desired them to be rewarded. As far as I remember, some of the seriously injured policemen had been rewarded. Sanjay Gandhi did not visit any members of the public, who were injured during the riot and were admitted in the Irwin Hospital.

The firing orders given to the CRPF by magistrates and Delhi Police officers are as follows :

Ashok Pradhan ADM	1 round to Sub-Inspector Bhanwar Singh
R. K. Sharma Dy. SP	6 rounds to Constable Matadeen
N. C. Ray, SDM	2 rounds to Naik Ram Bhanwar Sharma
	2 rounds to Constable Nagendra Kumar
	1 round to Constable Baikunth Pande

This does not include the 2 rounds fired by Constable Attar Singh under the orders of A. K. Singh, Commandant DAP.

According to the CRPF, the orders of firing behind the Godrej Building had not been received by them till June 12, 1976. S. K. Kapoor, Dy. SP CRPF, had repeatedly visited the office of P. S. Bhinder, DIG (R) to obtain written orders for 5 rounds fired in this area by the CRPF. The contention of the CRPF is supported by entries in the monthly diaries submitted by Kapoor to his senior officers. Extracts of these monthly diaries have been given to this Committee.

The circumstances under which N. C. Ray had to sign the firing orders have been narrated by Sushil Kumar, DC, Ashok Pradhan, ADM A. K. Paitandy, SDM and N. C. Ray himself. According to Sushil Kumar :

> After a few days of the firing incidents, ADM (Central) had informed me that the police had asked SDM N. C. Ray to sign the firing orders of which Shri Ray said that he had not issued them. I told ADM that whoever had ordered firing should own it up. I also informed the Lt. Governor about this development and he said that we need not raise any controversy over the issue and that whoever had ordered firing should own it up. Towards the end of May or beginning of June, I received a message from the Prime Minister's house calling me there.

> On reaching I was ushered in a room in which Shri Sanjay Gandhi and Shri P. S. Bhinder, DIG(R) were present. Shri Sanjay Gandhi told me that according to DIG, Bhinder, firing orders were given by the magistrate present on the spot and he was not prepared to own it up now. I told him that since I was not present on the spot where the firing had taken place, and have been informed by the magistrate that he had not ordered the firing, it is not possible for me to ask him to own up something which had not been reportedly done by him.

> I further mentioned that it is quite permissible for the police in situations like these to also order firing and, therefore, there need be no controversy or any effort to pass the responsibility. Shri Sanjay Gandhi wanted to talk to the other magistrates present in the

Turkman Gate area on April 19, to ascertain facts.
DIG(R) had kept on maintaining that the magistrate
had ordered firing and be should own it up.

Next day, I along with Ashok Pradhan, A. K.
Paitandy and N. C. Ray went to the Prime Minister's
house, as was desired by Sanjay Gandhi and found P. S.
Bhinder present there. In this meeting also he maintained that since the magistrate was present at the
spot and firing had been ordered at his instance, he
should sign the firing order. Ashok Pradhan, A. K.
Paitandy N. C. Ray gave an account of the incident
they had witnessed to Shri Gandhi.

I again mentioned to him that since I was not present
on the spot it is for the magistrate to explain the
position. Ultimately N. C. Ray signed the firing
order. I informed the Lt. Governor about these developments. Lt. Governor remarked that Bhinder had a
personal equation at the Prime Minister's house and
there is hardly anything which can be done about it.

Ashok Pradhan confirmed that in the first week of
June, the DC had told him about the magistracy not signing
the firing order. At the instance of the DC, he asked A. K.
Paitandy and N. C. Ray to come to him the next morning
with a view to taking them to the Prime Minister's house.
On reaching there, they had found the DC, but DIG(R)'s arrival was being awaited. A wireless message was flashed to him
(Bhinder) to report to Prime Minister's house. He arrived
within a few minutes.

Pradhan gave details of all that had transpired in the presence of Sanjay Gandhi. According to him Bhinder had
said that instructions to give the magistracy its due weight in
important law and order situations already existed, "but it was
just not possible to run to a magistrate and obtain his orders
if a situation was handled by the police officers at a short
distance". Sanjay Gandhi also said that since the SDM was
around when the firing took place near the Godrej building
"he should give protection to the police and own it up".

After a few days, when draft firing orders were brought to
Pradhan, he had rung up the DC. The DC had told him

that "since a decision had already been taken that N.C. Ray should sign the firing orders, the papers should be sent to him." Pradhan maintained that he had never asked N.C. Ray to sign these firing orders. He also mentioned that after the April 19 incident, he had, on the authority of DC told N.C. Ray and A.K. Paitandy that they should not sign any firing orders if they had not actually ordered it.

A.K. Paitandy gave details of what had transpired at the Prime Minister's house on June 3, 1976 regarding signing of firing orders and stated "We left Prime Minister's house with the impression that Sanjay Gandhi wanted N.C. Ray to sign the orders authorising firing near Godrej building. Subsequently I came to know that Ray had signed the orders. He had told me that he did not want to enter into any controversy and that DC and the ADM had asked him to put his signatures on the orders."

N.C. Ray corroborated the details of talks held at Prime Minister's house on June 3, and stated : "I told Sanjay Gandhi that no doubt I was following the party but I had neither seen firing, nor had ordered it and, therefore, the question of my signing the firing order should not arise. Sanjay Gandhi said that the magistrate who was following the party must sign it. Myself and Paitandy were asked to leave while the DC, D.I.G (R) and ADM (Central) stayed behind in Sanjay Gandhi's room. On June 4, 1976, I was called by ADM (Central) who gave me some papers regarding the firing order. I took these papers, signed them and handed them back over to the ADM. If a meeting of this type had taken place in the Lt. Governor's office or in the DC office and not in the Prime Minister's house, I might not have agreed to sign the order, but since the decision was taken in the Prime Minister's house, I signed the order of firing."

The contention of Bhinder that he had not ordered firing near the Godrej Building has been controverted by the Magistrates and the CRPF. The Delhi Police officers present on the spot have also testified that Bhinder ordered this firing. According to R.K. Ohri, "I had come to know that in the first two deaths, i.e. Sagir Ahmed and Om Prakash the firing was made by the police party led by Shri P.S. Bhinder, DIG (R) and accompanied by Shri N.C. Ray, SDM Kamla Market."

Ohri added that he had been told by J. K. Saksena, SDPO, Darya Ganj that "the firing order relating to this was not being signed by any police officer or by Magistrate. I had mentioned this to Pradhan, ADM and Bhinder DIG(R). Both had promised to resolve this issue. I had come to know that N. C. Ray had signed the firing order. I have no personal knowledge how this controversy was resolved. Pradhan had told me that Sanjay Gandhi had intervened".

According to Avinash Chander, SDPO, Bhinder had led a party towards the Godrej building where earlier R. Tiwari, SDPO was on duty. He added that "As the parties went inside, we heard the sounds of firing from the side of the Godrej building. We also heard the noise 'Goli Chal Gai, Goli Chal Gai." He had also heard on the same day about a controversy regarding firing orders in respect of firing near the Godrej building. A view-point had been expressed that if the DIR (R) had ordered firing, he should sign the firing orders.

Bhinder has completely denied that he was ever summoned by Sanjay Gandhi about the firing in the Turkman Gate area. When he was shown an entry in his wireless log book which indicated receipt of a message at 0900 hours on June 3, 1976 to the effect that Sanjay Gandhi wanted him, he explained "I cannot explain why I was called and what is the background of this message. I cannot recollect any discussions between myself, DC, other Magistrates and Sanjay Gandhi regarding any controversy over signatures of firing orders. No such discussion had ever taken place. I have a feeling that I must have been called at the instance of somebody else who wanted me. It is also pertinent to note, if there was any such discussion, I would have been accompanied by my own officers who were present on the spot."

Former NDMC	:	*I was in Om Mehta's room when on the*
President S.C. Chabra		*Prime Minister's orders I was removed*
		from the office of President of NDMC. . .
		I then thought that the mother in her was
		more important then being the PM. . .
		CBI was known to plant cases and haras-
		sed me for not supporting her directions
		that "Sanjay should emerge as a big
		power."
Former Minister of	:	*There was utter confusion in Delhi in*
Works and Housing		*those days.*
K. Raghuramaiah		
Justice Shah	:	*You were a lawyer of some standing. . .and*
		you did not know that the demolitions were
		taking place on a such a large scale . . ?
K. Raghuramaiah	:	*I have now got to know . . . The right*
		hand did not know what the left hand was
		doing . . .
Justice Shah	:	*You were the Minister for Housing . . .*
K. Raghuramaiah	:	*The PM was herself incharge . . . What*
		can a poor Minister do . . . ? The Presi-
		dent of India called me to convey his un-
		happiness about events in the Turkman
		Gate area . . . I said . . . You better talk
		to the PM.
Justice Shah	:	*Why was it being tolerated . . .?*
Former Deputy	:	*I did not tolerate it . . . I made a note in*
Minister of Home		*the file.*
Affairs F. H. Mohsin		
Justice Shah	:	*Why did you not go to the Prime Mini-*
		ster ?
F. H. Mohsin	:	*I told my minister I have done my duty. . .*
Commissioner MCD:		*Sir . . . Sanjay Gandhi was the de facto*
B. R. Tamta		*Administrator of the Delhi Administra-*
		tion.
Justice Shah	:	*Closeness is a relative term . . .*
Secretary to Lt.	:	*I have known both since 1969.*
Governor of Delhi		
Navin Chawla		
Justice Shah	:	*Did you discuss the demolitions with*
		Sanjay Gandhi or Dhawan ?
Navin Chawla	:	*No.*

Justice Shah	:	*. . . You had a compartmentalised rela-tionship . . . Why was it that you closed your eyes . . . ?*
DIG of Police R. K. Ohri	:	*. . . In those days Sanjay Gandhi was the SAIN . . . the Great Man.*
Justice Shah	:	*In the maintenance of law and order one would assume that this would include lawful orders . . .*
		In those days opposite faith was considered a taboo in our society . . .
Vice Chairman DDA Jagmohan	:	*Even Minister Raghuramaiah phoned me up one day and said . . . I can't sleep because there is slum . . .*
Justice Shah	:	*In my view there is a difference between Hell and Heaven . . .*
Jagmohan	:	*Everything I have done has been appro-ved by the Indian Cabinet.*
Justice Shah	:	*There cannot be a policy other than the Act . . . Is there any power vested in you specially*
Jagmohan	:	*Sir . . . I will give you the background . .*
Justice Shah	:	*You ought to be more precise . . . you have been making submissions for the last 3 hours. We are only concerned with your statutory authority. . . I have a very bad habit of concentrating on one point at a time . . .*
Jagmohan	:	*But Sir we gave them alternative accomo-dation.*
Justice Shah	:	*You were so magnanimous . . . All this may have been very generous of you . . . but did you know that 27 of them had been paying taxes and yet their houses were demolished . . . I feel shocked.*
Jagmohan	:	*Sir. . .I will give you the background . . .*
Justice Shah	:	*I have heard the word "background" so many times that it shocks me . . . Yes I know they were not keen to go but they were anxious to go . . . On the one side you are pulling down their houses . . . on the other police is firing . . . What were people to do ? . . . I must compliment you*

		. . . *that you were very persuasive.*
Jagmohan	:	*Sir . .*
Justice Shah	:	*. . . It is the extremely simplistic solutions to complex human problems that raise these cries of anguish. . .*
B.R. Tamta	:	*Sanjay Gandhi wanted me to even remove the dogs when he was driving to his in-law's house in Defence Colony. I asked my ZAC ensure this . . .*
Subhadra Joshi	:	*Sir the President told me that "PM does not listen to me. . . Sanjay Gandhi will lock up the Mother if need be" . . . Indira Gandhi once said to me, "Punjabis have less brains and have no political sense. . .".*
Justice Shah	:	*In this country there is no minority or majority . . . they are Indians . . .*

XXXVI—IMAGE BUILDING—SANJAY

On May 2, 1976 Sanjay Gandhi, accompanied by the then Chief Minister, N.D. Tewari, visited Agra. He travelled to Agra from Delhi by car. Some senior Central Government and UP Government officials accompanied the party from Delhi. B.S. Gidwani, the then Additional Director General of Tourism, Government of India, has stated that he had to cut short his visit to Honolulu where he was leading the Indian delegation to the PATA conference and return to India in time to attend Sanjay Gandhi's meeting at Agra on May 2, 1976. When Gidwani received the message at Honolulu to cut short his visit, he tried to explain that this would result in absenting from the last session of the Conference but he was told that "the Minister's orders were definite on the subject and that it was essential for him to attend the meeting in Agra."

Enroute the party stopped at the ITDC restaurant at Kosi. The Kosi restaurant had been losing money and various proposals and schemes were under consideration for improving the economics of the restaurant. It had been suggested by the ITDC to the State Government that the land between Kosi restaurant and Delhi Agra road be either landscaped by them or handed over to the ITDC for this purpose. The matter had been pending with the State Government and no action had been taken in this matter for several months. During this particular visit of Sanjay Gandhi as per the minutes of the meeting recorded by the officials of the Department of Tourism, "Shri Sanjay Gandhi agreed and the Chief Minister ordered that the land adjacent to the Kosi restaurant should be handed over with immediate effect to the ITDC for landscaping."

In fact, the Chief Minister told the ITDC officers that they "should take it for granted from that moment onwards that the land belonged to ITDC who should immediately take up the landscaping work. Vibha Pandhi, Deputy Director General, ITDC, has stated that the Minister for Tourism and Civil Aviation was kept informed and he took a personal interest in this subject and gave verbal orders to ITDC to proceed with the work even while the formalities were being completed. However, when the scheme was discussed at the time of the consideration of the Tourism Annual Plan in 1977-78, the Planning Secretary did not agree to its inclusion. But in the meantime the work had progressed as per instructions and plans approved by the Minister personally.

At Agra a meeting of senior officers of the State and Central Government was arranged at Circuit House. The points for consideration were certain schemes drawn by Government of UP/Central Government for development of facilities for tourists required in Agra city. As stated by K. Kishore, the then Commissioner, Agra Division, UP, Sanjay Gandhi came into the room and occupied the main chair while the Chief Minister "kept hovering around, occasionally sitting down." S.N.P. Agarwal, the then Executive Engineer in the Development Authority, Agra, who was also present there, has stated that "the meeting was practically conducted by Sanjay Gandhi and the Chief Minister was assisting him by calling out the officers and giving instructions after a point had been discussed and decision taken." A very large number of items were discussed at this meeting and detailed minutes of those items were recorded by a Secretary of the UP Goverment. According to the Summary record of discussion maintained by UP Govt., "Sanjay Gandhi also participated in the deliberations and gave the benefit of his advice in arriving at appropriate decision for immediate implementation."

One of the items discussed concerned the development of Transport Nagar, Agra. According to S.N.P. Agarwal, the scheme for shifting transport agencies and truck operators from Jamuna Kinara road to Transport Nagar to be developed on Mathura Road was explained to Sanjay Gandhi who desired the work should be completed by June 30, 1976. Agarwal explained that since there were very deep and large pits on the proposed site, it would not be possible to complete the work within the stipulated period even if they put their maximum effort. Sanjay Gandhi did not like this explanation and looking at N.D.

Tewari said "If this engineer cannot do the work, he may be shifted". "Shri Sanjay Gandhi further announced that the scheme will be completed by June 30 and Shri Tewari will inaugurate it on 1st of July 1976 positively". Agarwal has stated that the work relating to the development of Transport Nagar was of a stupendous nature and could not have been completed but for the help obtained from the Indian Army. Heavy earth moving machinery belonging to the Indian Army was put into operation for levelling work. A Lt. Col. was put in as in-charge of the operation, so that the work could be completed by June 30.

According to K. Kishore, at the instance of Sanjay Gandhi several decisions were taken during the meeting. He desired that sites for Five Star Hotels should be selected in the cantonment area. He also desired that Mahatma Gandhi Road was extremely shabby and should be improved. He further directed that Agra Development Corporation should impose an entry fee Rs. 2/- per head on each of the major monuments.

At 7 P.M. on the same day a public meeting was addressed by the Chief Minister and Sanjay Gandhi. According to K. Kishore the Chief Minister proclaimed that a new star has arisen on the political firmament. The Chief Minister stated that Sanjay Gandhi has solved many long standing problems of Agra and further promised that he and his Government should work according to the instructions given by Sanjay Gandhi from time to time.

XXXVII—NORTHERN RAILWAY

On August 13, 1975 the CBI received a complaint from one Gopal Das a loco shed man, Railways, Delhi to the effect that one Sudarshan Kumar Verma, a clerk in the Northern Railways New Delhi, had demanded a sum of Rs. 200/- as illegal gratification from him in consideration of fixing his scale of pay favourably. On the basis of this complaint a case was registered under the Corruption Act and a trap was arranged by the CBI, Delhi Branch. As a result of the trap S.K. Verma was caught red-handed after he demanded and accepted the aforesaid illegal gratification from the complainant.

On completion of the investigation of the case, the Delhi Branch of CBI sent the SP's report incorporating the result of the investigation and recommending that Verma should be prosecuted under Section 161-IR and Section 5R r/w. Section (5)d of the P.C. Act. The SP's report in duplicate was received by the Vigilance Officer Northern Railway on January 1, 1976 and one copy was forwarded to the Divisional Superintendent's office on February 3, 1976 for necessary action in connection with the issue of sanction order for prosecution of Verma.

It appears that the action of CBI Delhi Branch recommending prosecution of Verma was not liked by the Director CBI, D. Sen, who apparently was keen to favour Verma due to certain pressure. Normally in CBI the cases involving non-gazetted officers are dealt with at the Branch level and Director or even Jt. Director are not concerned with the finalisation of such cases. But in this particular case, shortly after the recommendation regarding the prosecution of Verma had been sent to the Railways, Director CBI, called A.P. Mukherjee, DIG, CBI, Delhi Branch and told him that the case should have been put up to the Director before finalisation. The Director then desired that the case should be examined once again. After this interview with the Director, DIG Delhi came to his branch and discussed with his officers the possibility of getting back the SP's report from the department.

Though such a step was unprecedented since the SP's report recommending prosecution against Verma had already been sent to the Railways, the DIG asked the Superintendent of Police, R.K. Gupta to retrieve the SP's report through his personal contacts. Gupta made an attempt to get the SP's report back from the Railway authorities. This attempt to retrieve the report could not succeed. The Railway authorities in the meantime kept on writing to the CBI Delhi Branch requesting them to detail an officer to show the original documents to the disciplinary authority so that the sanction for prosecution could be issued; but apparently the CBI was no longer interested in receiving such a sanction order. Many reminders were sent to the SP, Delhi Branch by the Vigilance authorities of the Railways, but no action was taken by the CBI.

On receipt of a representation from Verma in September 1976 i.e., 7 months after recommendation for prosecution had been sent to the Railways, D. Sen desired that Delhi Branch should send the comments on the petition and these comments should be sent to him through Joint Director A.B. Choudhary. A.P. Mukherjee of Delhi Branch sent his parawise comments on the representation submitted by Verma on September 6, 1976. The points raised by Verma in his petition were adequately commented upon by DIG Delhi who found that the allegations made by Verma had no substance in them. A.B. Choudhary was apparently not satisfied with the comments put up by the Delhi Branch and on September 9, 1976 he called the DIG to come and see him with case records which was accordingly done by A.P. Mukherjee. The case was discussed and it was desired by Choudhary that a public prosecutor should examine the representation and give his views. After 7 months of inaction on the part of the CBI, on September 9, 1976 A.B. Choudhary found the matter to be very urgent and asked the Public Prosecutor Jamuar to treat this case against a junior official as a priority case.

The CBI machinery swung into action, and on the same day the Public Prosecutor Jamuar gave his comments, first finding no substance in the points raised by the petitioner, but at the end suggesting a circumstance which could justify reconsideration of the case. Jamuar mentioned that at the time of the trap the independent witness who had seen the acceptance of bribe and had overheard the conversation was with the CBI Inspector and therefore the accused could take a plea in the court of law that the independent witness was under pressure of the police officers. This plea was not taken by the accused himself in his repres entation. Another argument advanced by Jamuar to justify the reconsideration of the case was that at the time of search of the accused a pronote worth Rs. 300 was recovered from his person and that the accused may take a plea that the loanee had returned a part amount through the decoy. Jamuar was careful to mention that although no such plea was taken by the accused till now, it will be worthwhile to get the evidence evaluated through a departmental enquiry, for being on the safe side to know all the probable explanations of the accused before the case is sent for trial.

A.B. Choudhary agreed with the comments of Jamuar and endorsed the recommendation that the case should be sent for departmental action first, to be on the safe side to know all the probable explanations of the accused. The Director, D. Sen on September 9, 1976 itself agreed with Choudhary's suggestions and accordingly orders were issued to the Delhi Branch for taking further necessary action. The SP Delhi Branch Jacob Jackson made a fresh attempt, this time in writing, to take back the SP's reports which had been sent to the Railway authorities earlier. The Railway authorities on receipt of request in writing agreed to part with the SP's report. Moreover the Railways were asked to return both the copies of the SP's reports along with the enclosures.

On receipt of the SP's report from Railways in which CBI had recommended prosecution of Verma, a fresh report was prepared recommending departmental action against him and sent to the Railway authorities again.

Justice Shah	: *He was a clerk who had been caught taking a bribe . . . Why was it necessary for you to intercede . . .?*
CBI Director **D. Sen**	: *I received a representation at the Prime Minister's house . . .*
Justice Shah	: *Were you under pressure . . .*
D. Sen	: *No. . .*
Complainant	: *Even the 200 Rupees that I gave to Verma have not been returned to me.*
Counsel **Khandalawala**	: *Have you ever heard of an accused who says the evidence against him is false . . .*
D. Sen	: *It is a simple case . . . and it is being made complicated.*
Justice Shah	: *It seems so. . . Did you receive reminders . . .?*
D. Sen	: *. . . From where?*
Justice Shah	: *From the PM's house . . .*
Counsel **Khandalawala**	: *You see Mr. Sen. . . Did you try to apply your mind . . .? All this was utter rubbish.*
Justice Shah	: *In your opinion the Government Officers' Corruption Act should be repealed . . . It is a traversty of justice if someone has been corrupt and is let off because he has the sympathy of someone in the PM's office.*
Counsel **Khandalawala**	: *You see . . . Mr. Sen delay could only harm the prosecution.*
D. Sen	: *We weve only trying to investigate . . .*
Justice Shah	: *How you must stop the case . . . Thereafter everyone went to sleep.*
Counsel	: *Who in the PM's house asked you to look into this matter?*
D. Sen	: *Sir, I used to go to the Prime Minister's morning Durbar and there someone mentioned this case to me.*
Counsel **Khandalawala**	: *Was this one of your Command Performances?*

XXXVIII—MARUTI AND "THE EXTRA INCOME TAX ACT"

Sharda Devi of 29, Mukta Ram Babu Street, Calcutta and and Shanta Devi of 149 Cotton Street, Calcutta were shown as shareholders in Maruti Ltd., having shares of the face value of Rs. 30,000/- and Rs. 25,000/- respectively. In his letter dated July 1, 1975 to the then Commissioner of Income Tax, Kanpur, K. Srinivasan, the then Commissioner of Income Tax, West Bengal I, had written that enquiries made at his end, had failed to reveal the identities of two ladies as there were no such persons at those addresses.

Srinivasan had, therefore, requested in his letter to Commissioner, Kanpur, that the Income Tax Officer dealing with the case of Maruti Ltd., might be asked to obtain particulars as to the mode of payment of the subscription moneys for the said shares, that is, whether they were paid for by cheques or in cash, the dates of the payment and if the payments were made by cheques, the name of the bank on which cheques were drawn. These enquiries were considered necessary by the then Commissioner of Income Tax, West Bengal "Since it is probable that the names of these ladies have been utilized by somebody who has invested his funds in various assumed names", thus evading tax.

The Commissioner of Income Tax, Kanpur, passed on the D.O. letter from Commissioner, West Bengal, to N.S. Raghavan, Director, Special Cell, New Delhi, for necessary action as the case of Maruti Ltd., was not assessed in Kanpur charge. Raghavan, Director, Special Cell, in his turn, passed on the letter received by him from the Commissioner, Kanpur, together with its enclosure to Harihar Lal, Director of Inspection (Investigation) for necessary action because the case of

Maruti Ltd., was not being investigated by the officers of the Special Cell.

The above correspondence was put up to Harihar Lal by the Deputy Director, on July 19, 1975 with a note as under :

> If approved, we may send C.I.T. W.B's letter dated 1st July, to the Board requesting for instructions whether in view of what has been stated in their letter dated February 13, 1975 (SI. No. 140) C.I.T., Patiala may be asked to get the required information collected and sent to the C.I.T., West Bengal.
>
> Sd/- K. Singh
> Dt. 19.7.75

"Serial No. 144" referred to above is a letter dated February 13, 1975 from the Central Board of Direct Taxes to the Director of Inspection (Investigation) regarding collection of information in respect of a Lok Sabha question regarding arrears of tax of shareholders of Maruti Ltd. The Board directed, inter-alia, in this letter as under :

> It may please be noted that the information should be collected through official agencies only and neither the Company nor the shareholders should be approached for furnishing the information.

Harihar Lal, the Director of Investigation, recorded as under on the order sheet :

> Discussed, no action for the present.
>
> Sd/- H. Lal.
> 24.7.75

Simultaneously, Harihar Lal also recorded the following note at the top of the letter dated July 8, 1975 from N.S. Raghavan to M.D. Verma, copy of which was endorsed to him:

> Chairman has desired that no enquiries should be made regarding this case till further instructions from him.
>
> Sd/- H. Lal
> 24.7.75

In this connection, Harihar Lal in his statement dated November 12, 1977 has stated as under :

The file containing the above correspondence was put up to me, by the DDI (North Zone) with a note dated July 19, 1975 suggesting that the C.I.T., Patiala (in whose charge Maruti Ltd. appeared to be assessed) might be asked to obtain the required information about the shares in Maruti Ltd., in the names of two ladies aforesaid. However, as the previous notings in the file indicated that my predecessor had received instructions that enquiries relating to Maruti Ltd. should be undertaken only after prior permission from the Board, I mentioned the matter personally in the then Chairman, C.B.D.T., S.R Mehta, on or about July 24, 1975 and showed him the relevant correspondence. I told him that I proposed to make a reference to C.I.T., Patiala in order to have the required enquiries made at his end. S.R. Mehta, however, told me verbally that no enquiries should be made regarding this case till further instructions from him. I recorded these instructions of S.R. Mehta in a note dated July 24, 1975 at the top of the letter dated July 8, 1975 from N.S. Raghavan to M.D. Verma.

Shri Eradi has enquired from me whether the facts stated in K. Srinivasan's letter dated July 1, 1975 to Shri M.D. Verma did not prima-facie indicate that the shares of the face value of Rs, 30,000/- and Rs. 25,000/- in Maruti Ltd. in the respective names of Sharda Devi and Shanti Devi were *benami* share holdings and, if so in what circumstances no further enquiries as to the real identity of the shareholders and the source of the investment were pursued.

Regarding the above query, I informed Eradi that the information contained in Srinivasan's letter did prima-facie indicate that the two ladies aforesaid were either non-existent or *benamidars* of some other persons and, therefore, it was proposed to have enquiries made by the C.I.T., Patiala as to the mode and dates of payments of the subscription moneys for the said shares to Maruti Ltd. Ordinarily, I would have written about this to the C.I.T. Patiala in the normal course without seeking any instructions from the Chairman C.B.D.T. However, in view of the notings in the file which clearly indicated that Board's prior permission had to be obtained before enquiries could be made in relation to the affairs of Maruti Ltd., I brought the matter to the notice of the then Chairman, C.B.D.T. personally. In view of his directions that no enquiries should be made regarding this case till further instructions from him, I had to keep the matter pending.

The Board's direction referred to in paragraph 3 above was issued pursuant to the order recorded by S. R. Mehta, the then Chairman, Central Board of Direct Taxes, on page 6 of the note side of the Board's file No. 294/218/74-II (Inv), dealing with unstarred question number 4355 relating to Arrears of Taxes against shareholders of Maruti Ltd., which was answered on December 13, 1974 by furnishing an assurance that the information is being collected and that it would be laid on the Table of the House. The Chairman's minute referred to above is as under :

Information should be collected through official agencies only. Neither the Company, nor the shareholders should be approached for furnishing the information. This should be made clear in the draft letter to DI (Investigation).

It would appear that there were un-written instructions requiring that the draft replies to Parliament Question connected with Maruti Ltd., etc. should be approved by the Prime Minister. This is clear from one instance of these instructions being followed as under :

There was an unstarred question (No. 4269) due to be answered in the Lok Sabha on 22.3.74 regarding "evasion of taxes by companies under the director of Maruti Ltd."

It is evident from the Ministry of Finance, Department of Revenue & Insurance File No. 162/12/74—Tech. Cood. that the draft reply by way of furnishing an assurance that the information will be collected and laid on the Table of the House was seen by the then Prime Minister because it has on the face of it the following remark in pencil :

P.M. has seen.

This was apparently written by M.M.N. Sharma who was one of the Personal Assistants attached to the Prime Minister's Office.

It is further seen that the draft reply in fulfilment of the assurance was submitted for approval by M.G. Abrol, the then Addl. Secretary (Cood) to P.K. Mukherjee, the then Minister for Revenue & Banking, on February 18, 1976. The Minister desired that the Addl. Secretary should discuss the matter with him. It would appear from the file that Abrol discussed the matter with the Minister on February 28, 1976 and that on the same day the file was "submitted" by the Department of Revenue informally to the Joint Secretary to the Prime Minister.

It is further seen from the file that because of the delay in the return of the file from the office of the Prime Minister, the Department of Revenue was not able to fulfil the assurance given to the Parliament within the specified period and that, therefore, they had to seek extension of time more than once. The reason given by the Department of Revenue for delay in fulfilling the assurance, referred to above was that, "the information received in fulfilment of the assurance is being compiled and its compilation will take some more time", whereas the compilation was by then already complete and the draft was merely awaiting the approval of the persons concerned in the then Prime Minister's Secretariat. It is further seen from the file that M.A. Rangaswamy, the then Addl. Secretary (Cood) had spoken to J.K. Kohli, the then Joint Secretary to the then Prime Minister on more than one occasion in November/December and that thereafter the file was collected from the Prime Minister's Secretariat and the assurance was fulfilled on December 8, 1976.

Similarly, it is seen that in the case of Lok Sabha Unstarred Question No. 4355 relating to arrears of taxes against shareholders of Maruti Ltd. referred to in paragraph 6 above, file No. 30/4/75-ST of the Sales Tax Section of the Ministry of Finance, Department of Revenue, which dealt with collection of some information relating thereto was sent for by the office of the then Minister for Revenue & Expenditure (P.K. Mukherjee) "for the perusal of M.R.E.". It is seen that the file was thereafter sent to R.K. Dhawan, the then Addl. Private Secretary to the then Prime Minister. File No. 162/64/

74-PC of the Tech. Coordination Section of the Ministry of Finance, Department of Revenue, which too dealt with this Parliament Question, was also forwarded by the office of the then Minister for Revenue and Expenditure to R.K. Dhawan, with the following note :

> As desired the relevant file (No. 162/64/74-Tech. Cord) regarding Unstarred Question No. 4355-arrears of tax against shareholders of M/S Maruti Ltd., is sent herewith.

M.G. Abrol, Chairman, Central Board of Excise and Customs :

> I have been shown file No. 162/12/74-TC and another file bearing the same number but marked Part I. On going through the files I find that I had put up a draft statement for fulfilment of an assurance given in respect of a Parliament Question. The then Minister for Revenue and Banking had minuted on 25/2 that I should discuss it with him. When the matter was discussed the Minister had said that the draft statement appears all right but it may be shown to Prime Minister's Secretariat also. Accordingly, the file was sent to Joint Secretary to Prime Minister. My recollection is that in a couple of other cases concerning Maruti also the draft replies were sent to the Prime Minister's Secretariat.

Sd/-

(M.G. Abrol)

Chairman

Dt. 15.11.1977   Central Board of Excise and Customs

Justice Shah	:	*Why did you pass such orders . . .?*
Chairman CBDT	:	*It was always required by Parliament . . . and*
S.R. Mehta		*I wanted it to be authentic . . .*
Justice Shah	:	*Why was the company not to be approached . . .?*
S.R. Mehta	:	*The Income Tax office could always obtain the information . . . but this was a sensitive company . . .*
Justice Shah	:	*Two wrongs do not make a right.*
S.R. Mehta	:	*But Sir . . .*
Justice Shah	:	*Don't try to be impertinent . . . You are suggesting some explanation and I am trying to see if there is any substance in what you are saying . . . It is a frivolous argument.*
Counsel Khandalawala	:	*What do you mean by the sensitivity of the case?*
S.R. Mehta	:	*Because questions were being asked in Parliament.*
Khandalawala	:	*Not because the PM's son was a owner . . .?*
S.R. Mehta	:	*No.*
Khandalawala	:	*What was the authority under the Income Tax Act which enabled you to pass this order . . .?*
Justice Shah	:	*The Extra Income Tax Act!*
Harihar Lal	:	*He told me . . . nothing should be done till further instructions from him.*
S.R.Mehta	:	*What trouble did you expect . . .?*
Justice Shah	:	*A lot of people did in those unfortunate days . . .*

6 The Yoga Revolution

What if the Guru is a fake. What if your Guru does not even look like one. Silken kurtas, well-oiled hair with hundreds of foreign admirers following, hardly make one a Guru, or a politician for that matter. Potbellied, spotless white dhoti (six yarder) complete with shirt from the drycleaners can only make you pass for one, if Brahamchari is the only one we wish to know.

Karma Yoga, Raja Yoga, Jnana Yoga, Hatha Yoga all help you, so the Brahamchari says, in seeing Reality. Reality can mean different things to different people. His evidently was seeking favours from Cabinet Ministers and Government officers like getting temporary telephones of "friends" converted to OYT and transfer orders of petty officials cancelled. All this became a dull drab ritual and instead he embarked on comfort, fun and frolic—not a bad combination and which you will soon get to know.

This is far from the suffering of incarceration of Virendra Kapoor, for telling off Ambika Soni a junior Foreign Service officer's wife, but then she was also the secretary of the Youth Congress. Pravir Purkayastha of JNU, Kuldip Nayar, Kundan Lal Jaggi, 82 year-old writer Guru Dutt and Karunesh Shukla—their crime too was being in the right place at the wrong time! Sometimes, you can be in the wrong place at the right time— then you get demolished—Joshi, Shashi Bhushan, Andheria Mor, Bhagat Singh Market and Arjun Nagar. What if you are related to the right person at the wrong time like the Haksars. Then you are finished—except one wished that for once Government would continue to function that efficaciously. But then you have to be a Dhirendra Brahamchari !

XXXIX—DHIRENDRA BRAHAMCHARI AND THE APARNA ASHRAM

Dhirendra Brahamchari floated a company named Aparna Agro Private Ltd., with its Registered Office at A/50, Friends Colony, New Delhi. The main objects of the company appear to be to undertake and carry out aerial spray of fields, plant protection and other activities. As per the Articles of Association, the first Directors were shown as Dhirendra Brahamchari, Sanjay Gandhi and S.C. Kishore.

In April, 1973, he called for brochures, price lists and other information for aircrafts manufactured by Maule Aircraft Corporation. On April 24, 1973, he wrote a letter to B.D. Maule, President of Maule Aircraft Corporation. The relevant portion of this letter reads as under :

It would be highly appreciated if you could kindly let us have the following information about your Maule M-4 Strata Rocket at the earliest possible :

How much discount would you give us on the aircraft? Is spraying equipment available with you?

Is it possible for you to give us dealership in the name of Messrs Aparna Pvt Ltd., A/50 Friends Colony, New Delhi-110014? If possible, could you kindly send immediately necessary proforma for making an application for it and also send us necessary terms and conditions for the same.

Maule Aircraft Corporation agreed to give a dealership in the name of Messrs Aparna Pvt. Ltd., A/50 Friends Colony, New Delhi-110014.

On March 29, 1976, Brahamchari addressed a letter to the Chief Minister of J&K asking for permission to accept the gift of an aircraft for his Mantalai ashram.

The application was cleared in two days' time and the Secretary to the Chief Minister of J&K Government addressed a letter to the Secretary, Foreign Trade, Govt. of India stating that the State Government will have no objection to the import of the spraying aircraft. This letter in original, it appears, was handed over to Brahamchari himself as it has been found attached with the form for getting Customs Clearance Permit from the Office of the Chief Controller of Imports & Exports (CCI&E).

On March 29, 1976, Brahamchari also sent a letter to V.N. Kapur, Director of Aeronautical Inspection, asking for permission to have an "Agricultural spraying aircraft".... Later Brahamchari addressed a letter on April 21, 1976 to the Director General of Civil Aviation stating that he was proposing to import one Maule (M-5) aircraft "for my personal use for the purpose of furthering the activities of Aparna Ashram" and desired that the request be recommended to the Ministry the same afternoon.

On the same day Kapur discussed the case with the DGCA and recorded a note as below :

... the applicant has made it clear in his letter dated 2.4.76 that he wants to use the aircraft for his personal affairs (not for agricultural purposes) we may permit the import of a/c. No foreign exchange is involved.

On April 2, 1976 itself, Kapur recorded a forwarding note for the consideration of the Ministry of Tourism and Civil Aviation, wherein he recommended that the proposal had been examined and that import of the aircraft may be permitted.

The Joint Secretary of the Ministry of Tourism & Civil Aviation discussed the case with the Minister on April 2, 1976 itself and then it was decided that from the Civil Aviation point of view, there should be objection to the Ashram importing aircraft subject to clearance from the Ministry of External Affairs and Ministry of Finance (Department of Economic Affairs), if the Ministry of Commerce considers it necessary. That very day the Ministry of Tourism and Civil Aviation marked the file to N.K. Singh who was Special Assistant to the then Minister of Commerce—who marked the file to the Chief Controller of Imports & Exports on April 3, 1976. The CCI&E on the same day marked the file to the Ministry of Finance (Department of Economic Affairs) who recorded a note on April 5, 1976 stating that they have no comments to offer since no out go of foreign exchange was involved, as the aircraft was to come as a gift. The file was received back on the same day and the CCI&E on the same day again marked it to Home Ministry. C.V. Narasimhan, Joint Secretary in the Ministry of Home Affairs (Internal Security) recorded a note stating that acceptance of a gift from a foreign source is not per-se prohibited by any existing law and therefore there is no objection from the security angle to this proposal, though he raised a point that the letter of Brahamchari does not clarify the motivation behind the offer of this gift by Maule Aircraft Corporation. He, however, felt that this matter can be got clarified by Chief Controller of Imports & Exports. This note was recorded by Narasimhan on April 14, 1976 and on the next day the CCI&E, P.K. Kaul, marked the file to the Ministry of External Affairs for their concurrence. The matter was examined in the External Affairs Ministry on the same day and it was felt by the Joint Secretary that from the political angle, there may be no objection if the gift is "otherwise permissible under the law". The Foreign Secretary considered this gift to be of "an unusual kind" but stated that in view of the advice of the interested Ministries there may be no objection. He thereafter marked the file on April 15, 1976 itself to Foreign Minister (Y.B. Chavan) who accorded his approval to the proposal.

On April 21, 1976, the then Commerce Minister, D.P. Chattopadhyay approved the issue of CCP and the same was handed over to Brahamchari on April 22, 1976.

The value of the aircraft with spares was shown as Rs. 3 lakhs in the application for CCP. However, before CCP was issued, on April 21, 1976 a request was made that the value should be raised to Rs. 4 lakhs. The CCP was issued for a value of Rs. 4 lakhs. Between April 21, 1976 and July 19, 1976 the figure of Rs. 3 lakhs was raised in four stages to Rs. 6.14 lakhs purely on Brahamchari's repeated requests.

Brahamchari left Delhi for London on April 27, 1976 and arrived there the next day. He left London for the USA on

April 30, 1976 and reached the USA the same day. He
returned to London on May 21, 1976 and reached Delhi on
May 24, 1976.

V.R. Lakshminarayanan, Joint Director, CBI & Spl. IGP/
SPE, New Delhi has stated :

> In the course of certain enquiries, we received infor-
> mation that Shri Dhirendra Brahamchari had imported
> into India one M-5 Maule aircraft during 1976 falsely
> declaring it as a gift.

Along with this letter the following photostat copies have
been sent by Lakshminarayanan of a letter head Memorandum
captioned "Dhirendra Brahamchari," dated October 25, 1977,
Georgia, maintained in the file at FBI Headquarters, Washing-
ton. The Memorandum reads as under :

> Maule was specially asked whether or not he had
> donated the aircraft as indicated by the letter dated
> May 6, 1976, and replied, "No, but that's the way he
> wanted it".

> On October 14, 1977, Mr. Billy Fallon was interviewed
> at his law-office, Moultrie, Georgia. During the
> interview, Mr. Fallon also stated that the aircraft had
> in fact been sold for a cash sum, stating that the
> purchaser had approximately $ 20,000 in cash with
> him and prior to delivery of the aircraft he made a
> trip to New York City, returning with the balance of
> the cash needed to complete the total payment.

It is interesting to note here that the Director of Aeronautical Inspection in the DGCA V.N. Kapur continued to treat
this aircraft as a gift and was willing to allow its certification
without taking cognizance of a cable sent by the manufacturers stating that the aircraft had been paid for.

About the time Brahamchari was planning his visit abroad,
an informant gave some specific information to the Enforcement Officer—R.S. Seth of Delhi Office of the Enforcement
Directorate. He appeared before Seth on April 28, 1976
and recorded a statement in Hindi, giving his name and
address. A free translation of his statement in Hindi is
reproduced below :

...On 26th, Shri V.K. Jain who resides at ... has given to Shri Direndra Brahamchari, whose Yoga Ashram is near Gol Dakkhana, dollars worth Rs. 3.50 lakhs, after purchasing these from the shops. These dollars have been purchased by Virendra Jain at the rate of Rs. 9.60 from... and....Swamiji is leaving for London within two or three days and is carrying along with him dollars whose value is approximately Rs. 3.50 lakhs. Swamiji is carrying a delegation with him. On behalf of Swami, Shri V.K. Jain has also arranged at Bombay for remittance of Rs. 10 lakhs. The party through whom transactions have been finalized at Bombay is... and his telephone number is....It implies that Virendra Jain will take Rs. 10 lakhs in India and will arrange to get Swamiji pounds worth Rs. 10 lakhs at London.

(Address 28-4-1976)   Sd/-

(Details intentionally omitted)

Thereafter, the file was given to A.M. Sinha, the then Deputy Director in the Enforcement Directorate. Sinha discussed the matter with the Enforcement Director, S.B. Jain on April 28, 1976. On May 12, 1976 Sinha recorded a note accordingly in the file saying: No action.

On instructions from Sinha, however, A.P. Nanday, Chief Enforcement Officer received a confirmation from the Reserve Bank that in fact Dhirendra Brahamchari's 'P' form had been approved on April 14, 1976 and that he was to travel by AIR INDIA for New York. The matter was not pursued further.

Central Board of Excise and Customs

On July 1, 1976 Brahamchari addressed a letter to the Secretary, Central Board of Excise and Customs (CBEC) for exemption from customs duty for the import of a Maule aircraft. He also addressed letters on July 12, 1976 to Pranab Mukherjee, the then Minister for Revenue and Banking (MRB) and R.K. Dhawan, Additional P.S. to the then Prime Minister forwarding copies of his letters to the Secretary CBEC and to the MRB for doing the needful in the matter. On July

12 itself, Dhawan sent copies of these letters addressed to CBEC & MRB received by him to Pranab Mukherjee with a 'personal' note which reads as under :

Kindly see the attached letter of Swami Dhirendra Brahamchari—Sd. R.K. Dhawan 12.7.76.

On receipt of the application for exemption from customs duty the concerned section of the CBEC recorded a note analysing the policy adopted in such cases. The note inter alia, reads as under :

...In view of the above policy, the Ashram does not qualify for either of above mentioned two categories. The party has not mentioned the purpose for which the aircraft is required. Moreover, we do not seem to have granted exemption for the import of aircraft with accessories in the past by any technical/educational institution. In view of this, the request is not covered by our policy, we may perhaps regret.

The Under Secretary concerned, A.K. Sarkar, also agreed with the above view and made the following note :

We may perhaps regret.

These notings were made on July 23, 1976 when the file was sent to V.K. Gupta Secretary, he made a note 'pl. speak' and marked the file to the Under Secretary. Later, on July 26, 1976 Gupta recorded that on reconsideration he had decided to examine the case in depth. Before giving his recommendation, he referred the case to the Education Ministry on July 26, 1976 for comments.

On the same day, the Ministry of Education and Social Welfare recorded a note as under :

The Ministry of Education & Social Welfare (Deptt. of Education) has no information about the *locus-standi* and/or activities of the Aparna Ashram, Mantalai P.O. Suddha Mahadeva Dist. Udhampur. For the same reason the question of this Ministry agreeing to sanction a suitable grant to Aparna Ashram authorities to cover amount of the Customs duty does not arise.

After receipt of the file from the Education Ministry there was a discussion between the then Finance Secretary H.N. Ray, Members (Tariff) K. Narasimhan and M.A. Rangaswami Member (Custom) of the Central Board of Excise and Customs about the application of Brahamchari addressed to the Central Board of Excise and Customs and Pranab Mukherjee, Minister for Revenue and Banking.   V.K. Gupta, the Deputy Secretary was also present during the course of this discussion.   After the meeting, he recorded a note on July 28, 1976 recommending grant of exemption.

When the file was sent to Member (Tariff), K. Narasimhan, he also referred to the discussion that had taken place with the Finance Secretary and Member (Customs) and, inter alia, recommended grant of exemption on the following grounds :

> According to what Shri Dhirendra Brahamchari spoke to him on the telephone, the Ashram was engaged in the training and research of high altitude Yoga Abhyasas which is possible only on mountain peaks. . .

The file was seen by the Finance Secretary and he approved grant of exemption on July 29, 1976 with the following observations :

> The duty exempted is stated at 'A' prepage to be Rs. 36,000, while the max. extent of duty is said to be Rs. 2,02,500 on another interpretation. In either case, for the reasons stated by M (T) it may be appropriate to grant an exemption to the Ashram on the importation of the plane which appears to have been *donated* to the Ashram by a foreign donor. May be shown to MRB for post-facto approval.

The file was received back by the F.S. on July 29, 1976 and an ad-hoc exemption order was issued on the same day. A communication was also sent to the Collector of Customs on July 29, 1976 itself by telex and a letter. This file was marked to MRB on August 9, 1976. His personal staff has made a noting on August 10, 1976 that MRB has seen the file and approved.

K. Narasimhan, the then Member (Tariff) has indicated the urgency in taking this action by stating :

Shri R.K. Dhawan, Additional Private Secretary to the former Prime Minister, spoke to me and enquired whether Shri Pranab Mukherjee (former Minister of Revenue and Banking) had given any directions to me with regard to the representation made by Shri Dhirendra Brahamchari for the grant of exemption on the aircraft which has been imported by him as a free gift. I told him that the Minister had not given any directions to me but to my colleague, Shri M.A. Rangaswamy. Thereupon, he impressed on me the urgency of deciding the case as Shri Dhirendra Brahamchari was wanting to see the Prime Minister in this connection.

D.C. Duggal, Aerodrome Officer, submitted a report regarding the airport on August 27, 1976. From this report it is obvious that the work of construction of an airstrip at Mantalai by Aparna Ashram was already in progress and levelling, dressing, cutting and filling up of earth was already complete on a portion measuring about 150 metres when the Aerodrome Officer visited the place. After perusal of the report, it was decided that a copy of the same could be sent to the applicant and the Air Headquarters could be addressed for clearance for construction of the airfield. This was done on September 18, 1976.

The request was examined at the Headquarters and it was found that the proposal could not be acceded to. The following noting was made in the office of Air Headquarters :

Since the proposal envisages carrying Indian as well as foreign nationals from Delhi to Mantalai and back, we cannot agree to the construction of a private airstrip in the vicinity of . . . being a sensitive area.

On November 24, 1976, Brahamchari made a request to DGCA for pursuing the matter once again with the Air Headquarters, emphasizing :

We are sure they may accede to our request for construction of a private airstrip at Mantalai as it will prove

to be a national asset to help promote and develop
scientific researches in the field of Yoga . . . .

This letter was considered in the Civil Aviation Department and they reluctantly agreed to recommend a review of
the case to Air Headquarters.

On December 23, 1976 Brahamchari addressed a letter to
Bansi Lal, the then Minister of Defence in the Government
of India, enclosing a copy of the letter dated December 20,
1976 from S.K. Bose, Deputy Director (P) of the Office of the
DGCA addressed to the Air Headquarters asking the Air
Headquarters to review the case. How Brahamchari got a copy
of this official letter of S.K. Bose is not known. In this letter
Brahamchari requested Bansi Lal that he may look into the
matter personally and have the approval of the Air Headquarters expedited for landing of aircraft on the airstrip at
Mantalai, However, on December 29, 1976, the Air Headquarters wrote to DGCA (S.K. Bose) that their decision on the
subject again remained unchanged.

Subsequently, P.P. Singh, Air Cdre., Director of Intelligence examined the case again. He recorded a note on December 30, 1976, and marked it to Joint Secretary (Air) in the
Ministry of Defence stating that the proposal to grant permission was undesirable from the security angle.

After this note a separate communication dated December
31, 1976, was prepared by P.P. Singh and this was also marked
to JS (A) in the Defence Ministry. The two reasons given in
this note for considering the proposal undesirable from security angle were *proximity and interference in day operations.*

Markings on the papers show that both the communications dated December 30 and 31, 1976, were received in the
office of the JS (Air) on December 30, 1976 and January 3,
1977 respectively. However, these seem to have been returned
to P.P. Singh and were cancelled in the Directorate of Intelligence (Security)'s office. P.P. Singh recorded another note
dated December 30, 1976, wherein he recommended that
"permission can be given in view of larger interests and subject
to imposition of certain conditions to ensure the safety both to

the aircraft going to Mantalai and the Fighter Aircraft flying in this area". He spelt out six conditions in this note.

This was conveyed to Brahamchari by a D.O. letter from JS (A) Vinay Vyas; A copy of the letter by Vinay Vyas was 'unofficially' received in the DGCA's office by Bhardwaj on February 9, 1977. Till then they had not received any communication from Air Headquarters regarding Brahamchari's request.

On May 12, 1977, the Air Headquarters cancelled the approval accorded by them for the construction of the airstrip at Mantalai, which was earlier given by them in the month of December, 1976.

Use of the Aircraft

From the log book maintained for the aircraft, it has been noticed that both Sanjay Gandhi and Rajiv Gandhi have been using this plane for going to various places.

Out of the 213 flights recorded during the 9 month period (August 12, 1976 to April 28, 1977) 123 were local flights including 56 categorised as instructional/practice flights. Airdashing to Delhi, Jammu, Nainital, Amritsar, Karnal, Sultanur, Lucknow, Rae Bareilly and other places was made frequently. It is significant that 18 flights were made to Rae Bareilly mostly in March 1977.

The use of the aircraft by Sanjay Gandhi has been admitted by Brahamchari in his statement dated April 29, 1977 before B.R. Bhatia, Superintendent, Directorate of Revenue Intelligence, New Delhi.

The aircraft imported by Brahamchari is registered under category 'A' of Rule 30 of Aircraft Rules 1937 and was issued with a certificate of airworthiness in the category 'Private'. The owner of this aircraft has not been granted a non-schedule operator's permit which is an essential requirement for operation of aircraft to carry passengers for hire and reward.

Brahamchari, founder of the Aparna Ashram has allowed the use of the aircraft to Sanjay Gandhi solely for his own purposes for which he has been billed and recoveries are being made from him.

Director of Aeronautical Inspection V.N. Kapur	:	*He phoned me and said "I am Dhirendra Brahamchari. . .You have seen me on TV. I am interested in the import of a aircraft. . ."*
Justice Shah	:	*Were you afraid. . .*
V.N. Kapur	:	*Why should I be afraid. . .I was only doing my duty.*
Justice Shah	:	*A lot of people were in those days.*
Former Joint Chief Controller Imports & Exports N.C. Rastogi	:	*I noticed the encouraging pace of the file. . .I would not say that it was not worth recording. . .But I knew the consequences of recording as Mr. N.K. Singh's writ ran through the entire Ministry. . . I did not want to do something which would throw me into disfavour.*
Additional Secretary P.K. Kaul	:	*I did look into all this. . .*
Justice Shah	:	*You did not care what happened. . .What were you gentlemen afraid of. . .Did you not have the backbone ?*
Deputy Director Enforcement Directorate A.M. Sinha	:	*I was hoping the complainant would come.*
Justice Shah	:	*You never called for him. . .But you were praying that he comes. Apart from the RBI enquiry what discreet or indiscreet enquiry did you make ?* *(Someone in the audience quips "All I want to know is was the informant arrested"?)*
Director Enforcement S.B. Jain	:	*The information was vague. . .*
Justice Shah	:	*Who underlined the name VIRENDRA BRAHAMCHARI ? Once you noticed the name you lost all interest in the case.*
Deputy Secretary V.K. Gupta	:	*Sir it was an ashram high in the hills.*
Justice Shah	:	*Just because it was high in the hills does not give it an added sanctity . . . You gentlemen were anxious to help . . . or would the Heavens have fallen ?. . .*

Epilogue

It is fortunate at this moment when the book is going for its second printing that the first interim report of the Shah Commission has been submitted, though it only covers conclusively 21 of the 55 cases that have come before the Commission and exhaustively covered in this book. In 11 cases Indira Gandhi has been found to be guilty of "gross misuse of power". In the case of the questionable manner in which the emergency was imposed the Commission's findings describe her actions as unjustified and an "excess" in itself. Her vindictive actions in regard to the harassment of officials from the State Trading Corporation and the decision for putting 10 textile and customs inspectors behind bars receive equal condemnation. The favouritism shown in the appointments of the Chairman of the Reserve Bank of India and Punjab National Bank smacked of "irregularity" and "gross disregard of established practices", according to the Commission's findings. V. C. Shukla has received his share of strictures for his bullying of the mass media during the emergency and its blatant use for ulterior purposes.

Finally, the Commission took note of the grave injustice and harm done to innocent people by many senior public servants who acted in the most unconscionable and illegal manner during the emergency. Krishan Chand, D. Sen, R. K. Dhawan, Navin Chawla, Bhinder and some of Delhi's now infamous magistrates, are just a few who could be prosecuted, while Sanjay Gandhi and Yogi Brahamchari are still not willing to accept the Commission's summons to tell us what they are hesitating to say and we are eager to know. What they are unable to say now and why we continue to allow them this privileged status only the courts will tell in the not too distant future.

Meanwhile the Commission is making useful recommendations for well established government institutions like the
CBI, Income Tax, Police and the magistracy so that at least in
the future the chances of their deployment for needs other
then those in the interest of the people of India are minimized.
The most abiding part of the report is not the needless indict-
ment of Indira Gandhi or Sanjay Gandhi, but what the Government of India must do to make these multifarious institutions
work in a manner which is becoming of them, and inspire confidence in the Indian people.

The fabric of our society stands destroyed today and the
honourable Commission has done its part. It is now up to the
Government and the people of India to ensure if not for them
at least for their children, that this tearful tragedy never
happens again. Let us hope for once the maxim "You get
what you deserve" is not true!